❧ *Inventiones* ❧

D0916355

INVENTIONES

Fiction and Referentiality in

Twelfth-Century English Historical Writing

⤐ Monika Otter ⤏

The University of North Carolina Press

Chapel Hill and London

© 1996 The University of North Carolina Press

All rights reserved

Manufactured in the United States of America

The paper in this book meets the guidelines for permanence and durability of the
Committee on Production Guidelines for Book Longevity of the Council on
Library Resources.

Set in Minion type by Tseng Information System

Printed by Thomson-Shore, Inc.

Design by April Leidig-Higgins

Library of Congress Cataloging-in-Publication Data

Otter, Monika. Inventiones : fiction and referentiality in twelfth-century
English historical writing / by Monika Otter.

p. cm.   Includes bibliographical references and index.

ISBN 0-8078-2293-0 (cloth : alk. paper) — ISBN 0-8078-4600-7 (pbk. : alk. paper)

1. Great Britain — History — To 1485 — Historiography. 2. Geoffrey, of Monmouth, Bishop of St.
Asaph, 1100?-1154. Historia regum Britanniae. 3. William, of Malmesbury, ca. 1090-1143. De
antiquitate Glastoniensis ecclesie. 4. William of Newburgh, 1136-1198? Historia rerum anglicarum
Wilhelmi Parvi. 5. Giraldus, Cambrensis, 1146?-1223? Itinerarium Cambriae. 6. Map, Walter, fl.
1200. De nugis curialium. 7. Reference (Philosophy) 8. Invention (Rhetoric) 9. Rhetoric,
Medieval. 10. Fiction — Technique.   I. Title.

DA129.5.088   1996   96-6232

941'.0072 — dc20   CIP

Portions of this work appeared earlier, in somewhat different form, as "New Werke:
St. Erkenwald, St. Albans, and the Medieval Sense of the Past," *Journal of Medieval
and Renaissance Studies* 24 (Fall 1994), copyright 1994 by Duke University Press,
and "*Gaainable Tere*: Symbolic Appropriation of Space and Time in Geoffrey of
Monmouth and Vernacular Historical Writing," in *Discovering New Worlds: Essays
on Medieval Exploration and Imagination*, ed. Scott D. Westrem, copyright 1991
by Garland Publishing, Inc., and are reprinted here with the permission of the
publishers.

00 99 98 97 96   5 4 3 2 1

[Für alle Otters, Friedrichshafen und Wangen]

⤚ Contents ⟞

Acknowledgments ix

Introduction 1

[1]

Inventiones 21

[2]

Gaainable Tere

Foundations, Conquests, and Symbolic
Appropriations of Space and Time 59

[3]

Underground Treasures

The "Other Worlds" of William of Malmesbury,
William of Newburgh, and Walter Map 93

[4]

Quicksands

Gerald of Wales on Reading 129

Conclusion 157

Notes 163

Works Cited 201

Index 223

⤏{ Acknowledgments }⤎

It is a pleasure to thank the many people who have helped me shape, refine, and revise my thinking while I worked on this book. First, I want to thank my colleagues here at Dartmouth College, Alan Gaylord and Peter Travis, whose friendship, advice, and encouragement have been invaluable, and who have read and commented on various parts of this project in various stages (Peter Travis, in particular, has read the whole thing not once but twice!); Charles T. Wood for his friendly comments and suggestions on the Gerald of Wales section; all members of the Medieval Faculty Seminar for many stimulating discussions in general and for their suggestions on my Walter Map paper in particular. Special thanks are due to David Rollo, who generously shared with me the manuscript of his forthcoming book, *Specious Histories and Politic Fictions: Ethnicity, Counterfeit and Romance in Twelfth-Century England*. We read each other's work at too late a stage in our work schedules to incorporate each other's perspectives fully, but even as they stand, we think our discussions complement each other beautifully. Farther back in the history of the book, I owe special thanks and affection to Robert W. Hanning and Caroline Walker Bynum, who supervised it when it was a Columbia dissertation. Also at Columbia, I received valuable input from Joan Ferrante, Howard Schless, and John Magee, as well as the graduate student members of the Columbia Medieval Guild, especially my friends Angela Jane Weisl and Elizabeth Patton Miller. Brian Stock and Jane Rosenthal may or may not be aware of their contributions to this book: their seminars, at Toronto and Columbia, respectively, provided two very different but equally crucial initial sparks. I want to thank Barbara Hanrahan at the University of North Carolina Press, the staff members with whom I've had the pleasure of working, and the readers for the Press, Nancy F. Partner and especially Robert Stein, whose careful reading and challenging, incisive comments made this a much better book than it would have been otherwise. (Of course, the responsibility for any errors and inaccuracies is entirely my own.) Dartmouth College's generous research support policies were an enormous help. So was the wonderful staff at Dartmouth's Baker Library, especially the Interlibrary Loan Department, and staff at Columbia and Union Theological Seminary, at the British Library, the Bodleian Library, and the Parker Library of Corpus Christi College, Cambridge. I thank Duke University Press and Garland Publishing for permission to reprint previously published material and the Board of Trinity College, Dublin, the Master and Fellows of Corpus Christi College, Cambridge, and the Conway Library, Courtauld Institute of Art, for permission to reproduce illustrations from Matthew Paris's work. Finally, warmest thanks and much love to my family for their support and their patience. Although it is written in a language not all of them read fluently, this book is dedicated to them.

⇥ Introduction ⇤

his study is concerned with a recurrent and intriguing cluster of images in the historical writing of twelfth-century England: episodes of travels and conquests, of searching and finding, of digging, of what one might call archaeological discovery. "Historical writing" includes what we would readily recognize as histories, as well as hagiographical material that is closely tied to the history of a given location, and a set of narratives that are much harder to label, that in the classification of a modern bookstore would probably end up in the fiction rather than the nonfiction section. Within their historiographical context, the discovery episodes have usually been taken either as incidental factual comments or casual digressions that provide an entertaining respite from the history proper, treating the reader to "marvels" and touches of local color. I propose to show that they often have a much more central and interesting function in the text, organizing it and mirroring its intellectual operations. These episodes help define the historians' self-image and show their awareness of the complexity of their enterprise. By complicating the readers' notions of referentiality, by playing with narrator roles and truth claims, these images show a latent sense of fictionality. They can contribute to our understanding of the medieval sense of history and fiction, as well as the role of Latin writing in comparison to the vernacular, during a formative period of intellectual activity in England.

It has often been argued that fictionality, in the sense familiar to us, had its first flowering in twelfth-century narrative, as a by-product of widespread literacy and of a certain secularization of intellectual enterprise. This notion is fairly widely accepted, though not uncontested. But the argument is usually limited to vernacular, especially French, romance. In fact, some critics (especially Peter Haidu and Franz Bäuml) have argued that fictionality is a specific property of vernacular writing, that it is precisely the trait that marks the emancipation of vernacular writing from the Latin ecclesiastical tradition.[1] My reading of Latin historiography suggests that we need not exclude Latin writing from that argument, that, on the contrary, Latin chroniclers like William of Malmesbury and Geoffrey of Monmouth develop the narrative sophistication associated with vernacular fiction early, and perhaps even assist its development in vernacular romance. I am, for that reason, particularly interested in a group of texts that would now be considered on the borderline between historiography and fiction: Geoffrey of Monmouth's *Historia Regum Britanniae*, Gerald of Wales's *Itinerarium Kambriae*, and Walter Map's *De Nugis Curialium*. Apart from their similar literary personae, these writers also share certain biographical traits: they are school-trained clerics in administrative positions, moving between the church and the court. This helps us situate the rise of self-consciously fictional narrative within the development of a secular, half-courtly, half-clerical intellectual tradition. I propose to take these "borderline" texts seriously as complex, self-aware literary texts, and thereby help redefine the position of Latin writing in the intellectual landscape of high medieval England.

The common denominator of the images of travel and discovery, and the related episodes listed above, is that they all concern, in the first place, the literal, physical finding, the locating of places or material in space. One starting point of this study is the observation that topography, or the spatial setting, seems to be an unusually prominent concern in English history and historical hagiography.[2] This is true, first of all, in the simple factual sense pointed out by Sir Richard Southern, who has described English historiography as "anchored in the countryside": most English historiography of the period is local in content or focus, and much of it is quite literally concerned with real estate.[3] Twelfth-century England is neither the time nor the place to look for larger historical systematization. Contrary to what general statements about "medieval historiography" would lead one to expect, universal history is not a very prominent genre — much less so than in the thirteenth century.[4] Nor are the theoretical considerations of theology or general chronology of much concern. While all twelfth-century historians knew Bede's work intimately, and presumably regarded his division of historical eras in *De temporum ratione* as etched in stone, those considerations seem to be rather remote from their historiographical practice. There is no English equivalent to Otto of Freising, the writer modern scholars most often seem to have in mind when they generalize about medieval "Geschichtstheologie."[5] In twelfth-century England, the vast majority of all historiographic activity emerges from the monasteries, and the writers have the interests of their houses at heart, be it material interests or a more spiritual concern with the sanctity and prestige of the monastery. Even a "universal history" like that of Orderic Vitalis is ultimately very local in its concerns.[6] Most typical of the period is the monastic chronicle, which is either entirely concerned with the house that produces it, or has a strong predilection for local materials even in histories of national scope. Many chronicles are really cartularies, collections of local documents combined with portions of narrative history.[7] Many monasteries produce, or commission, hagiographical literature on their local saints in conjunction with such historical works, either as integral parts of them or as separate *libelli* or collections. Even histories that are not concerned with the real estate of individual monasteries are often intimately connected with geography and local lore. The monk William of Malmesbury organizes his *Gesta Pontificum*, a survey of English ecclesiastical history, geographically rather than chronologically. Gerald of Wales, not a monk but an archdeacon with both ecclesiastical and courtly ambitions, writes on local topics for a variety of monasteries, as well as topographies and itineraries, which are, if anything, even more "anchored in the countryside" than local monastic history. So is a famous work by another archdeacon, Geoffrey of Monmouth's *Historia Regum Britanniae*.[8]

The practical, local concerns that lie at the center of most historical writing of the period, the strong sense of an underlying mental map of the country, give the texts a particular matter-of-fact tone that has often been commented on. This is the second meaning implied in Southern's dictum that English history is "anchored in the countryside": apart from local interests, he is also referring (not without a certain degree of ethnic stereotyping) to a kind of realism, a "down-to-earth" quality. Antonia Gransden makes this point more explicitly throughout her overview of English historical writing, as well as in an essay entitled "Realistic Observation in Twelfth-Century England." In the twelfth century, she argues, historians show a new delight in detailed description, a new interest in places, artifacts, local "antiquities" for their own sake, that is best described as "antiquarianism." Yet the label of realism does not by any means cover all instances of spatial reference in historiography, let alone explain them. On the contrary: many are used to undermine realistic reference and to shake the text's truth claims.

The treatment of space, as well as time, is always a useful indicator of the way a narrative situates itself with respect to the reality it tries to represent. Auerbach discusses the geography of Arthurian romance as a clue to its mimesis: writers like Chrétien de Troyes often work with "absolute" rather than relational localization ("to the right" — of what?); this puts us on alert that the significance of the topographical details is "ethical" rather than realistic, which in turn colors our reading of the entire text.[9] Mikhail Bakhtin defines the "chronotope" of a literary text, the interaction between its temporal and spatial framework, as perhaps the most important genre marker:

> In the literary artistic chronotope, spatial and temporal indicators are fused into one carefully thought-out, concrete whole. Time, as it were, thickens, takes on flesh, becomes artistically visible; likewise, space becomes charged and responsive to the movements of time, plot and history. This intersection of axes and fusion of indicators characterizes the artistic chronotope.
>
> The chronotope in literature has an intrinsic *generic* significance. It can even be said that it is precisely the chronotope that defines genre and generic distinctions, for in literature the primary category in the chronotope is time.[10]

We can take Bakhtin's observation as an encouragement to take seriously the treatment of space in historiography, a narrative genre that is obviously primarily focused on time. Of the "three major circumstances of history" identified by Hugh of Saint Victor in the twelfth century—time, place, and persons—place seems indeed to be particularly important in pinning down the referentiality of historical texts, perhaps because it is the most durable of the three categories, therefore the easiest to relate to and verify over time: we still operate and orient ourselves in roughly the same space as that described by historians of earlier periods. Thus the treatment of the chronotope's spatial component is significant not only as an indication of the writers' geographical awareness, their powers of observation, or the importance they attach to realistic detail, but as a constitutive category of their poetics.

As one reads monastic histories and local hagiography, it soon becomes clear that, in addition to its obvious referential meaning, the narrative's spatial setting can function in metaphoric ways. When monasteries defend their land claims, describe the growth of their real estate, and document their building activities, they are also describing the growth of their communities. When they tell foundation stories that involve digging up a saint's relics, the dig—the search and the descent to a "deeper level," the "opening up" of what lay "hidden"—says as much about the intellectual process of projecting a past, a historical origin, as it does about the physical origin of the physical relics kept in the monastery.

Apart from such relatively straightforward metaphors, there are digging stories, special spaces, in some histories that are positively disquieting in their metaphorical implications. In the third chapter, I will discuss a number of episodes in narrative histories that concern a character's descent into an underground realm, either filled with treasures or inhabited by fairies, and the attempt—usually unsuccessful—to take away one of the treasures found there. It is hard not to read such stories emblematically, especially since in most, the protagonist is said to be personally known or to have a special connection to the historian: the underground explorer is clearly a stand-in for the historian himself. But read in this way, the episodes are not apt to inspire confidence in the historian's ability to retrieve material for us from the past. Either the attempt to bring up an object from the other world fails entirely, or the items thus obtained turn out to be useless, unreal, impermanent. Moreover, the association with magic or even stronger signals of a diabolical influence cast into doubt the morality of the whole enterprise. Such emblematic episodes cause problems—indeed, seem designed to cause problems—not only for a referential conception of truth but for most conceptions of historical truth one might think of. They certainly do not sit easily with the assumption that medieval authors and readers naively believed their history to be an unproblematically "lucid medium of transmission," transparent enough to allow us an unobstructed view of real events.[11] Nor do they easily lend themselves to a theological interpretation of historical truth, if only because of the diabolical and magical stage business that accompanies them. I read the episodes as "poetic emblems" or "mises-en-abyme": mirror episodes in which the narrative doubles and depicts itself.[12] Such devices suggest a degree of self-conscious textuality that is usually associated with a high degree of *litterarité*; they encourage us, even force us, to look at the texts as sophisticated literary narratives, not mere utilitarian collections of "facts."[13]

Far from being too naive to recognize that history is textual, medieval readers and writers, as Janet Coleman recently reminded us, took the textuality of history for granted; the ideal that historical study ought to circumvent that textuality and go directly to "the facts" is a relatively recent notion.[14] But evidently history's textuality, or the mediated nature of historical knowledge, was enough of an issue to be addressed at least indirectly, and often ironically. This textual self-consciousness, I believe, also moves away from the other kind of "truth" often looked for in medieval historiography: an allegorical truth that would link the narrative typologically to salvation history, and/or a moral truth that sees history as a collection of exempla for moral conduct. The more the text is emphasized as a self-contained structure, with "horizontal" connections, the less importance attaches to "vertical," allegorical connections, to extrinsic sources of meaning. My argument therefore pushes against (although it does not deny) two kinds of referential backing for the historical narrative: simple, literal reference, in which "facts" in the text are assumed to correspond directly to "facts" in outside reality, and allegorical reference, in which the narrative is seen as reproducing or "clothing" a higher truth.[15] A third mode of referring arises naturally from the writerly practices of the more sophisticated historians and in many texts comes to predominate over the first two. In the same shorthand in which I labeled the first two modes "literal" and "allegorical," I will call this third mode "metaphoric." It is the metaphoric mode that can produce, or at least flirt with, fictionality.

A discussion of fictionality in medieval historiography will inevitably encounter two kinds of objections, arising from each of the two terms, "medieval" and "historiography." One objection relates to genre: "fictionality" is by definition inapplicable to history, which is defined by its strict referential truth claim. The other objection is historical in nature. The term "fictionality," the argument goes, is inappropriate, or at any rate unhelpful, in considering the literature of the Christian Middle Ages. Not only is there no medieval terminology that corresponds in any precise way to our notion of fiction; the division between factually "true" and "invented" narrative was blurred, or simply rendered unimportant, by a view of reality that located all truth in God and saw all everyday reality, including fictions, as mere versions of that higher Truth. This description is, of course, accurate up to a point; yet if it is elevated to the level of dogma, it creates an artificially (often nostalgically) consensual, univocal view of the Middle Ages and desensitizes us to the often very lively polyvocality of much medieval writing. (The complaints by some twelfth-century writers, including Gerald of Wales and Walter Map, that univocity and consensus are lost in their time only underscore how multifarious and confusing their world appeared to them.) It is the contention of this book—paradoxical though it may seem—that twelfth-century Latin historiography and hagiography is not a bad place to look for and analyze such polyvocality. While it is not my intention to refute or explain away either the generic or the historical objections, I will use them to delimit and define the fluid, often tentative concepts of "fiction" that one encounters in twelfth-century historical narrative.

"Fictionality," as I am using it here, is defined by two different though not entirely separate approaches: a textual and a pragmatic one. A certain sense of textuality—that is, a self-aware notion of textual coherence by the text's own internal criteria, "absence" of the author, and fictionalization of the author role—must be given in order for fictionality to be possible; on the other hand, once these conditions are given, they will almost automatically produce fictionality.[16] This approach, though, makes the definition so broad as to be virtually useless: it would make any text that is consciously textual "fictional."[17]

If taken to its logical extreme, this threatens the very notion of historiography, the more so since, as many have observed, there is no reliable formal distinction between historical and fictional narrative.[18] The obvious corrective to the broadly textual definition is pragmatic: the understanding between authors and readers as to how this text should be taken, how it refers to outside reality, what its truth claim is. Fictionality is not a linguistic property or even a function of the truth of the assertions (it is, of course, perfectly possible to make true assertions in a fictional context); it is a contract between author and audience. In a brief, informal essay, "The Logical Status of Fictional Discourse," John Searle explains that fiction performs the same illocutionary act as a nonfictional assertion, but in a "nonserious" manner; it consists in the pretense to make an assertion: "The pretended illocutions which constitute a work of fiction are made possible by a set of conventions which suspend the normal operation of the rules relating to illocutionary acts and the world. In this sense, to use Wittgenstein's jargon, telling stories really is a separate language game . . . , and the language game is not on all fours with illocutionary language games, but is parasitic on them."[19] The rules of this language game regulate the "illocutionary stance that the author takes towards" the work,[20] as well as the reactions a competent audience can reasonably have. In Karlheinz Stierle's words, the rule for the audience is not that none of the assertions within the work will be true, but "that fictive statements are possible, and that in that case a better knowledge of the 'true facts' will be beside the point."[21] Another way of putting it is that fiction is assertion within a kind of role play: the author, as it were, impersonates someone making an assertion. (This is one way of explaining why the self-conscious narrator and therefore textuality is one of the crucial steps in the development of fictionality.)[22] However one chooses to describe the game, for fiction to be recognized as such, there must be a "contract" that suspends or "brackets" truth claims and therefore protects the speaker from the charge of lying, although in a strictly referential reading his or her assertions may not correspond with reality.[23]

Such bracketing of truth claims is intimately connected with the nature of reference in the text. An assertion about a fictional character, such as Sherlock Holmes or Lancelot, is meaningless—does not successfully refer and is therefore without truth value—unless it is understood that the speaker is referring to a fictional character and his truth claims obtain within that fiction only.[24] More interesting are references within a fiction to persons, places, times, or circumstances that we recognize as existing outside the fiction as well. In that case, there are a number of possibilities. If Arthur Conan Doyle can be shown to have made an error regarding London geography, we recognize this as an error.[25] But this is not necessarily true of all fictions: it depends on the precise nature of the fictional contract.[26] While a Sherlock Holmes novel may operate under the rule that its topography is homologous with real-life topography and may invite its readers to trace the homology, this is not true, for example, of Arthurian romance, where, as Auerbach has observed, and many have repeated after him, you can travel from Cornwall to Brittany without crossing the sea.[27] Clearly, "real" place names and geographical features are here subordinated to the narrative's own geography. If in a realistic novel any geographical data has a double reference, fitting both into the narrative's internal map and into the map of real life, the reference here is almost entirely internal, pulled inside the narrative, so to speak, with only the faintest trace of an outside reference to a real place.[28]

This, however, shows that there are degrees and shades possible here as well. Once it is recognized that the basic contract is "fiction," the chronotope is at the writer's disposal. While any spatial (and temporal) data must fit into a coherent internal system of reference (though, as Searle remarks, "what counts as coherence will be in part a function of the contract between the author and the reader"), the external reference can be actualized or left alone, or brought forward teasingly but not fulfilled.[29] Different options may even coexist within a single work, as in the *Lais* of Marie de France, where some of the narratives operate with recognizable place names and a spatial setting more or less close to real-life geography, whereas others are located in a decidedly metaphoric and psychological landscape; sometimes both types of localization occur in one and the same *lai*. In either case, though, geographical reference is entirely in the service of the narrative's internal logic. Outside reference can be activated or suspended at any time, but it is always subservient to an internal "map" that emphatically does not correspond to anything outside it.

The freedom to create such an autonomous spatial and temporal framework is one of the distinguishing features of fiction as opposed to historiography. At one extreme, as Marie-Louise Ollier says of Chrétien's romances, fictional space (as well as fictional time) refers to nothing outside it but coincides with itself; this creates an "immédiate plénitude," a "saturation des coordonnées spatio-temporelles." [30] In historiography, on the other hand, our "contract" with the author is that all place names will have outside reference, that the internal geography of the narrative will faithfully reproduce, or at least be consistent with, the real-life map of the area under discussion. Any disturbance of the homology, any discontinuity in the internal geography—even the conspicuous absence of localization of important events—will seriously shake our faith in the history. Spatial references are thus one of the most important guarantors of the referentiality of historical narrative. This, however, is also what makes space such an attractive category for disturbing referentiality. For a historical narrative to allow for the possibility that its chronotope could be anything else than the real-life map and the real-life *series temporum* is to flirt with fictionality. But if pragmatic categories—the understanding between author and readers as to how the text is to be taken—are all that really safeguards the referentiality of history, then surely any challenges to that contract are highly significant, even if they are not fully serious. As I have briefly hinted above, and will discuss more fully in the following chapters, some historical writers playfully undermine their own authority, their truth claim. Apart from illuminating the particular texts in which they happen, such challenges are also important as indicators that the categories of truth claim, of reference, and of author are close enough to the surface of the writers' awareness, and problematic enough, to be available for such play.

The insight that history is a text, and a text whose relation to reality is uncertain, is by no means foreign to medieval thinking.[31] History, for the longest part of its existence in Western culture, was understood as a branch of rhetoric rather than an empirical study of evidence. The standard medieval definition of history, derived from Isidore of Seville, "Historia est narratio rei gestae, per quam ea quae in praeterito facta sunt dinoscuntur," seems to recognize at least a very basic distinction between the *res gesta* and its representation. History is not reality, not a sequence of events, but a means of "recognizing" past facts.[32] In many medieval uses of *historia*, the semantic elements of cognition and of truth outweigh the semantic element of "pastness." To Walter Map, for instance, *historia* is contrasted not, as it is for us, with "present" or "future," but with "fabula" ("historia, que ueritate nititur, et fabula, que ficta contexit").[33] At the same time, Walter is very interested in the distinction of past, present, and future (even though he does not use the term "historia" in that context) or, more specifically, in the way they are known to us. That, to him, is the criterion that distinguishes "nostra tempora" or "modernitas" from all other epochs:

> Nostra dico tempora modernitatem hanc, horum scilicet centum annorum curriculum, cuius adhuc nunc ultime partes extant, cuius tocius in his que notabilia sunt satis est recens et manifesta memoria, cum adhuc aliqui supersint centennes, et infiniti filii qui ex patrum et suorum relacionibus certissime teneant que non uiderunt. Centum annos qui effluxerunt dico nostram modernitatem, et non qui ueniunt, cum eius-

dem tamen sint racionis secundum propinquitatem, quoniam ad nar-
racionem pertinent preterita, ad diuinacionem futura.

And by our times I mean this modern period, the course of these last
hundred years, at the end of which we now are, and of all of whose
notable events the memory is fresh and clear enough; for there are still
some centenarians alive, and there are very many sons who possess, by
the narration of their fathers and grandfathers, the certainty of things
which they did not see. The century which has passed I call modern
times — not that which is to come, though in respect of nearness to us
they are of like account — for the past belongs to history and the future
to divination.[34]

The very undertaking of lining up all historical time — past, present, and
future — with corresponding modes of cognition — *narracio, manifesta memoria,* and *divinacio* — suggests a primarily hermeneutic "take" on historiography, an inkling that, as Brian Stock puts it, "historical writing does not treat
reality; it treats the interpreter's relation to it."[35] At the same time, Walter's
division is an attempt to find a time where this does not obtain, where the *res
gestae* can be apprehended as directly as possible, where the intervening layer
of textuality can be eliminated. This desire is not, of course, unique to Walter; it is also implicit in Isidore's view that true history is always an eyewitness
account, an opinion that, despite its obvious inaccuracy and impracticality,
was frequently repeated in the Middle Ages.[36] This is an issue that invites self-
conscious theoretical speculation. We shall see in chapters 3 and 4 that many
historians dramatize, half ironically, both their desire for direct access and the
impossibility of that wish.

The point of such reflections, medieval or modern, is not to establish that
all history is fictional; indeed, treating "textuality" and "fictionality" as syn-
onymous is unhelpful, since, as we have seen, pragmatic expectations do obtain: historiographic narrative is read differently, and for different reasons,
than fictional narrative. But one need not espouse the extreme, "postmodern," skeptical formulation that history is nothing but discourse, that there is
no reality outside the text, in order to acknowledge that history is a linguistic
construct, a text.[37] Not only has this argument become commonplace in recent decades, it was also, as we have seen, thoroughly accessible in the twelfth
century. Reality does not come in narrative form; it is an unlimited, unstructured field of data with multiple connections. History, however, must translate it into narrative, a more or less orderly sequence, one or just a few causal
chains, a beginning, middle, and end. The process is marked, at the very least,

by selectivity and by some form of "emplotment," as Hayden White has called it.[38] Thus, whether fictional or not, narrative consists, first of all, of a selection from a potentially endless number of entities and events. It must provide not only a beginning and an end, but also closure; that is, the beginning and end must be related to each other in a way that is "relevant." Whether fictional or not, the text's "relevance criteria"—Karlheinz Stierle's term for both the selection criteria and the specific modes of connecting facts within the plot—are its internal poetic. The crucial difference is that fiction is beholden only to its own relevance criteria; history is doubly bound, both to its narrative structure, or relevance criteria, and to the external facts it represents.[39]

But Stierle's approach, while preserving the distinction, also shows that the categories are not nearly as impenetrable as one might think. On pragmatic grounds, history would indeed be neatly distinguished from fiction, in that its "contract" specifically includes a truth claim, a promise to the reader that its assertions are real, not "pretended" ones, therefore subject to real truth claims and verification or falsification by its recipients. Historiography is defined, in Hans-Ulrich Gumbrecht's words, by a reader expectation that "historiographic texts have reference to reality in all their particulars and at all their constitutive levels."[40] This means, presumably, that we expect historiography to be clearly referable to reality not only in its names, dates, places, "facts" (whatever that means), but also in each of its assertions as well as its larger form and conceptualizations. Yet this pragmatic distinction leaves open the question whether such a truth claim is possible, or what it would mean: the demanding reader's expectation can hardly be fulfilled, or, at any rate, it would be hard to ascertain whether or not it has been fulfilled. As Louis O. Mink points out, there are in nature no "events" that historically narrated events could be referring to: "event" already implies a narrative structure, a unit with a beginning and an end, a before and after; it is therefore an abstraction from narrative, not its "raw material."[41] Moreover, while we can establish reference for individual persons, objects, and places in the text and assess the truth value of individual sentences, that is not the kind of truth we really look for in historical narrative: we need to look at the truth of the entire account—but we lack mechanisms for describing either the reference or the truth value of that.[42] We cannot easily say what the narrative construct, the emplotment, of a historical text refers to, or whether it is true, any more than we can easily determine the reference or truth value of a fictional text.

Recognizing this difficulty might well stymie a serious historian; on the other hand, it can also suggest new possibilities for irony, playfulness, reflexivity, in short, literariness. It can open up the text to self-aware reflections about the nature of historiography and even—paradoxically—to fictionality. The suggestion cited before, that fictional discourse consists in role play, in "pretend" assertions, implies a binary choice: either you make "serious" assertions or you make "nonserious" assertions; either you are committed to your speech act or you are not. Given the games some writers of historical texts seem to play, we may need to consider the possibility of a middle ground—in fact, the possibility that there can be any number of positions between "serious" and "pretend" assertion, as well as the possibility that the position can shift even within one text. Richard M. Gale's formulation that fictional statements are "an act of illocutionary disengagement" is helpful because it allows for the possibility of gradations.[43] Our authors, while being mostly "engaged," can also temporarily, or partially, "disengage" themselves—with the result that, at least for a short time, referentiality is called into question, truth claims are suspended, and fictionality becomes a possibility.

To Paul Ricoeur, fictional discourse is closely related to metaphoric discourse; indeed, it is a special case of metaphor. His dynamic model of suspended primary reference is useful for my purposes, in part because it can accommodate my notion of a sliding scale from "more fictional" to "less fictional." Metaphor, according to Ricoeur, is a case of "split reference." We understand a primary reference and a secondary reference; the primary one, as he puts it, "perishes at the hands of semantic impertinence," that is, we see it does not fit; this automatically puts the secondary reference into effect, as it were.[44] This works even at the level of the single-image trope. When, for instance, William of Malmesbury begins his *Gesta Regum* by declaring his intention to "mend the interrupted sequence of time" (interruptam seriem temporum sarcire), he is alluding to a common metaphor for historiography: a textile, a fabric.[45] To understand his sentence properly, readers must first of all reject the common reference of "sarcire"—"the action of sewing together the edges of a torn fabric with a needle and thread"—as inapplicable in this context: it is "semantically impertinent," since there is no fabric involved, nor is the historian using needle and thread. This frees up space, as it were, for a secondary reference, which is suggested by the context: "the act of filling in the gap between the last major history and writers on current affairs; reestablishing continuity."[46]

But Ricoeur is more interested in metaphor as predication. Here it becomes important to look at the way metaphor predicates, more specifically at the copula, "is," whether stated or understood: in metaphor, the "is" includes an "is not," and it is important to keep both, the equivalence and the difference, in balance when trying to explain metaphor. In the above example, the metaphoric predication is merely understood; but one could reformulate it explicitly, something like "history is a fabric," or "our national history is a torn fabric." Obviously, while William is asserting that history is a fabric, he is at the same time implying, or presupposing, that it is not; he is establishing a resemblance, not an identity, but in such a way as to create a semantic tension.

Both these elements—the obliteration of primary reference and the equivocal copula, is and is not—combine to explain fiction as a kind of very large-scale metaphor: "The literary work through the structure proper to it displays a world only under the condition that the reference of descriptive discourse is suspended. Or to put it another way, discourse in the literary work sets out its denotation as a second-level denotation, by means of the suspension of the first-level denotation."[47] The equivocal copula is summed up in a phrase used by oral storytellers (borrowed from Roman Jakobson): "Aixo era y no era," thus it was and was not.[48]

It is extremely important to Ricoeur to show that fiction denotes, or refers, at this second level, that with the cutting of the primary reference, it does not turn in on itself completely and become entirely self-referential. Despite the presence of self-reference in most texts, and despite the limiting case of some poetic texts in which self-reference predominates, reference is rarely "abolished": "My contention is that discourse cannot fail to be about something. . . . In one manner or another, poetic texts speak about the world. But not in a descriptive way. . . . The reference here is not abolished, but divided or split. The effacement of the ostensive and descriptive reference liberates a power of reference to aspects of our being in the world that cannot be said in a direct descriptive way, but only alluded to, thanks to the referential values of metaphoric and, in general, symbolic expression."[49]

Ricoeur's theory, then, allows for varying degrees of suspended reference, and, once again, spatial reference is a good test case. In Ricoeur's terms, a fiction typically abandons the primary reference of its spatial framework, almost as a signal that the entire text placed within that framework is to be read as metaphorical discourse, thus making room for a "secondary reference," a fictional "redescription of reality." On the other hand, nonfictional texts—"letters, travel reports, geographical descriptions, diaries, historical monographs, and in general all descriptive accounts of reality"—may, by tacit agreement between writer and readers, simply retain everyday reference, of which they then "merely restructure . . . the conditions." In that case, the text's temporal and spatial framework is understood to coincide with that of the outside world: "The heres and theres of the text may be tacitly referred to the absolute here and there of the reader, thanks to the unique spatio-temporal network to which both writer and reader ultimately belong and which they both ac-knowledge."[50] Between these two cases, there must surely be any number of more or less referential positions.

The historiographical texts discussed here cut their primary reference only partially, for obvious reasons: historical writing cannot forgo primary refer-ence entirely without ceasing to be understood as historical. Instead, some historical texts truly operate with "split" reference, making room for a sec-ondary reference while still retaining the primary one, thus creating new levels of meaning and drawing attention to their own textuality. This also means that there are mechanisms other than "semantic impertinence" that alert the reader to a secondary reference; after all, the primary reference does not "perish" but still remains more or less in place. Some of these mechanisms are simply those that have long been recognized as the signals of a poetic text: overdetermination, repetition, the "ungrammaticalities" that, according to Riffaterre, help readers see past the referential illusion to the "intertext."[51] Many images are recognized as such simply because they are conventional. Sometimes, however, the signals that alert us to the second level are more ex-plicit. In some cases, they almost literally "cut," or undercut, the first level. In chapters 3 and 4, I will discuss images that portray the historian as a liar, a magician, or an unsuccessful explorer of underground worlds whose attempts to bring the subterranean treasures to light are frustrated. If one does not want to dismiss these episodes as mere irrelevant digressions, one is forced to look beyond the first-level reference the tales suggest; in so doing, one is almost inevitably led to regard them as images of the text itself—in which ca-pacity, as I have already hinted, they tend to be troublemakers, throwing into doubt the first-level reference of anything in the narrative. Nonetheless, these episodes are sufficiently contained to emphasize the text's self-reference with-out forcing it to abandon other forms of reference; they tease our sense of referentiality, or historical truth, without unsettling it altogether. There is no reason why self-reference and outside reference, both metaphoric and non-metaphoric, should not be able to coexist, and even to enhance each other, in the same text.[52]

I have dwelled on Ricoeur's model of fictional discourse at some length be-cause it is particularly efficient in accounting for the peculiarities of the works about to be discussed. It also chimes nicely with what literary historians have been saying about the twelfth-century emergence of vernacular fiction. A neat categorical distinction between fiction and other modes of discourse is not to be expected in twelfth-century thought. Indeed, the lack of a clear distinction has often been cited as one of the main signals of the "alterity" of the Middle Ages, and the ease with which the boundaries as we understand them were crossed in the Middle Ages—from romance to history, hagiography to romance, or vice versa—is well documented.[53] But scholars like Haidu, Bäuml, Zink, and others have described the distinctive qualities of twelfth-century romance in terms similar to Ricoeur's. Unlike earlier vernacular genres, which are still much closer to the poetics of oral narrative, romance is marked by the notion of absence, that is, the insight, stated or not, that a written text is independent of its producer's voice; by the concomitant development of that thoroughly "literary" institution, the self-conscious fictional narrator; and by an emphasis on the text's own "relevance criteria," to use Stierle's terms again. Above all, romance is self-consciously "fictional," and its fictionality has been described as the suspension, or "withdrawal," of referential function.

The passage from orality to literacy, and the birth of the "author" that it makes possible, is the place where many critics of vernacular narrative have sought to locate the new sense of fiction in the twelfth century.[54] Fictionality and the self-conscious "author" are interdependent: "The moment when literature recognizes that its material is fictional is also the moment when the author enters the scene. This is the moment of the *roman*."[55] In traditional narrative, orally transmitted, or, even when written down, dependent on performance (*chanson de geste*), the speaking subject, the "je," is that of the current reciter; in the *roman*, the first truly "written" vernacular genre, the "je" is that of the author, absent but dramatized as a fictional persona. As Marichal put it, "The birth of the *roman* therefore implies at the same time the birth of the author as well as that of his reader."[56]

The creation of this author role is a direct and necessary consequence of the writing down of the text.[57] Bäuml argues that the independence of the written, as opposed to the oral, text necessarily entails certain poetological features: "A further consequence both of the fixity and the independent existence of a fixed text is the fact that it does not necessarily require the commitment of its bearer to its content; the scribe, the reciter, or the reader of a written text can confront that text critically, even ironically. . . . The increased distance between author/scribe and text, and between text and reciting reader, leads to an increase in the distance between text and content: the content, no longer dependent on formulation by traditional themes and formulae, can now be subjected to alienating functions of a text."[58] Fiction in the narrower sense consists not only in textuality but also in the pretense "that the fiction is not a fiction," that is, in its treatment as an autonomous, "coherent pseudo-reality."⁵⁹ The development of this mode, and its growing acceptance "not as a lie, but as a third category beside 'truth' and 'falsehood,'" is the specific contribution of vernacular narrative in the twelfth century.

Therefore, the textuality of romance in itself necessitates and creates a new poetics, new specifically in that it discards and emancipates itself from religious modes of signification and modes of truth-telling. A famous locus for such arguments is Chrétien de Troyes's notoriously elusive critical vocabulary, "matière et san" and "conjointure." Walter Haug, among others, argues that these terms mark Chrétien's (and vernacular romance's) departure from the typological or allegorical methods of constituting literary meaning, from the *integumentum* argument that sees invented narrative as a disguise or "clothing" for an accepted moral or theological truth:

> Chrétien does make use of the exegetical imagery for interpretation in order to claim for his work a truth that is not identical with the literal sense; at the same time, however, he makes it clear that this is precisely not the truth of a second, allegorical level. Thus, *conjointure*, in one sense, is opposed to *conte*, insofar as it has to be derived from *conte*. But whereas the *conte* presents its material in a corrupt, fragmented fashion, the *conjointure* is the meaningfully ordered whole, and it is this structured whole that carries and communicates truth. The sense of the narrative, then, is not simply a hidden meaning that must be uncovered; rather, it is constituted in the act of literary fashioning. It is to be found, then, not behind a *narratio fabulosa*, as in an exemplum or in an allegorical construct, but in the fictional form itself; it is, therefore, to be understood neither as *sensus moralis* nor as *sensus allegoricus*. . . . This change of perspective signals the new literary genre of fictional romance and the representation and transmission of meaning proper to it: *conjointure*, in the final analysis, refers to the Arthurian plot model and implies an awareness of its meaning-constituting function.⁶⁰

In other words, vernacular narrative emancipates itself—not immediately, but gradually over the course of the twelfth century—from the truth-telling requirements that bind Latin writing; it frees itself from truth claims that rest in prior texts or in theologically revealed truth that is accessible through allegory. But since this autonomy, as Bäuml says, is achieved through "the fiction that the fiction is not a fiction," it is, not surprisingly, prone to breaches of the division between fiction and reality; therefore, fictionality, as well as the role of the narrator, is open to play, to ironic distortion, from its very inception. Fictional assertion is role-play assertion; therefore, a narrator figure that is sufficiently "fictional," textual, independent of the author and traditional *auctoritas* to be available for textual games is both a condition for and an open invitation to fictionality.[61]

Considerations of this sort lead Peter Haidu to propose that vernacular fiction (for him, fiction is by definition vernacular) is from its inception "parodic." It departs, consciously, from the "serious" purpose of language, namely to reveal God and his purpose for the world; fiction "empties" language. It is thus subversive of the authoritative modes of discourse, and where it is not condemned outright, it is tolerated only on the assumption that it is playful, inconsequential — yet another kind of "withdrawing" of serious function: "Where language was filled with the promise of salvation, it now loses that promise, the function of ascertaining the modalities of that promise, to fall into a disconnected mode of autotelic existence. . . . By withdrawal of its referential function, language becomes self-referential, and obtains its *litterarité*, not as an additional aesthetic complexity, but by the withdrawal of another function, the subtraction of divine purpose."[62] Whereas Ricoeur defines fiction generally as the withdrawal of outside reference, Haidu, Bäuml, and Haug see its historical inception in the withdrawal of allegorical reference, its emancipation from religious, Latin, ideologically prescribed means of literary production and literary interpretation.

Especially in its most agonistic formulation by Haidu, this argument excludes Latin writing, and all overtly Christian writing, by definition: fiction is a function of the emancipation of vernacular language from Latin, of secular language from religious language. For Bäuml, Latin writing can, in principle, participate in this new mode of writing (Geoffrey of Monmouth is one of his major examples), but it tends not to. Typically, Latin raises expectations "that it concerns itself with an elucidation of other texts," or that it "functions *per tropologiam*"; it is, in other words, too strongly associated with the church, with theological commentary or with religious allegory, to constitute an autonomous "pseudo-reality." But like most arguments that define a literary or historical movement in contrast to something before or alongside it, this argument tends to simplify the contrasting term, to paint it as unified and internally consistent.

In my experience of twelfth-century Latin writing, there is a good deal more flexibility, creative skepticism, and polyvocality than these critics are willing to recognize. We shall see that many of the authors about to be discussed — clerics all, though to various degrees semisecular in their professional lives and outlook — are perfectly capable of the textuality, the self-conscious voicing, the self-reference, the playfulness, the "parodic" quality that has been diagnosed so persuasively in their vernacular counterparts. Our readings will make a similar argument that in Latin narrative, too, the "horizontal" dimension of the text, as a self-consciously artistic structure, can be proposed as the main vehicle of meaning, and readers can be invited to decode the narrative itself, not an allegorical level behind or above the text. There are clear parallels between the auctorial bravado of Chrétien de Troyes, Marie de France, or Wolfram von Eschenbach and that of Geoffrey of Monmouth, Walter Map, or Gerald of Wales. All of them, in my view, make similar claims for their narrative and very largely bypass allegorical models of meaning.

The following chapters will examine the different modes of reference used in medieval histories, specifically those that have a strong spatial component. There will be constant attention to the ways in which these modes of reference coexist and overlap. The first two chapters discuss two types of historical foundation narratives that are intended to be strictly referential yet employ rhetorical and plot patterns that lend themselves to metaphorical complications. Chapter 1 introduces a little-known hagiographic genre, the *inventio* or finding of saints' relics. Focusing especially on texts related to St. Alban and the Abbey of St. Albans, and contrasting them and other English *inventiones* with the ancestor of the genre, the fifth-century *Revelatio Sancti Stephani*, it demonstrates that even such relatively mundane, utilitarian texts are capable of a number of metaphorical twists and self-aware textual maneuvers, while at the same time remaining tied to their immediate context in local historiography and monastic self-promotion. Chapter 2 begins by considering another basic narrative genre, the monastic foundation narrative. Like *inventiones*, these texts concern discoveries, "findings"; but while *inventiones* are typically archaeological, that is, they dig up relics from earlier periods, the emphasis here is on conquering and appropriating unclaimed spaces. The discussion then moves on to literary transformations of that motif in Walter Map, Geoffrey of Monmouth, and some vernacular texts inspired by Geoffrey: Denis Piramus's *Vie de Seint Edmund*, the Anglo-Norman romance *Fouke le Fitz Waryn*, and Laʒamon's *Brut*.

Chapters 3 and 4 form the core of the book. They examine highly self-conscious historical narratives that develop and bring to their logical conclusion the features and motifs discussed in the first two chapters. No rigid patterning is intended, but chapter 3 loosely corresponds to the first chapter in that it concerns "archaeological" motifs, and chapter 4 correlates with the second in that it is about conquests and travel. Chapter 3 discusses some rather astonishing and slightly unsettling episodes of "discovery": descents into underground worlds and treasure hunts that are, I argue, designed to shake our faith in historical representation. The principal works considered here are chronicles by William of Malmesbury and William of Newburgh as well as Walter Map's *De Nugis Curialium*. Chapter 4 concentrates on a close reading of Gerald of Wales's *Itinerarium Kambriae* (*Journey through Wales*), an underappreciated and highly entertaining text that combines many of the themes and concerns of the other works. Explicitly involving the reader in the "itinerarium," and often setting elaborate traps for the unwary, Gerald's *Itinerarium* perfectly illustrates the full literary potential of the *inventio* and discovery motifs in the hands of a master of ironical narrative.

The conclusion looks ahead in time to the fourteenth-century Middle English poem *St. Erkenwald*, which closely follows the *inventio* model but uses its metaphoric significance for purposes other than referential historical narrative. It is, among other things, a reflection on historical discovery and historical consciousness, thus addressing fully and overtly concerns that are implicit in the twelfth-century *inventiones* discussed in chapter 1. *St. Erkenwald* helps us isolate and understand the metahistorical significance of the earlier texts and also shows the enduring appeal of the *inventio* plot far past the time of its highest popularity as a hagiographic genre.

The arrangement of texts, it should be noted, is not chronological, nor is a chronological development implied. William of Malmesbury, whose "underground world story" I treat as an instance of highly developed *litterarité*, is relatively early (1120s). So is Geoffrey of Monmouth (1130s); in fact, many of the more interesting *inventiones* are aware of and work with Geoffrey's *Historia*. What I am showing is a continuum in historical writing from "most referential" to "least referential" (or "most fictional"): a range of possible positions a text can take from a truth claim that depends on outside time and space, to a complete lack of such a truth claim, or thorough subversion of such a truth claim. The extreme of the last position is not taken, of course: historical narratives cannot and do not relinquish their referentiality. But they do complicate and subvert it; and fictionality, while not embraced as it is in vernacular romance, becomes a playful (and sometimes alarming) possibility in Latin historical writing.

Inventiones

*nventiones* have long been recognized as a hagiographic genre, but they have rarely received the scholarly attention they deserve.[1] Most historians who comment on them at all more or less subsume them under *translationes*, narratives about the transfer of relics to a different location or to a different shrine within the same church.[2] *Inventiones* are indeed closely related to these narratives, but their purpose and their "built-in" imagery is sufficiently different to warrant treating them as a separate category.

Inventio as a liturgical term refers to the discovery of a saint's relics and to the feast commemorating that event. More important to my purpose here, *inventiones* are brief narratives about such findings of relics. The medieval English *inventiones* discussed here are almost all of monastic provenance, and they usually concern a particular monastery's patron saint or another important relic the house owns. Most are connected to the story of the house's foundation. The connection may be direct or oblique, but *inventiones* are told, by and large, to explain a monastery's origin.[3]

The genre of *inventio*, as a written form and sometimes even as a staged event, flourishes under outside pressure. Monasteries write or commission *inventiones* when their interests are under attack. On the Continent, *inventiones*, along with related hagiographical narratives and other local monastic historiography, are most popular in the tenth, eleventh, and early twelfth centuries, the time of the great monastic reforms; perhaps the competition of different observances played a role, although, on the Continent as in England, economic interests and privileges are the major immediate objective.[4] England, as has often been observed, lags behind the Continent in the production of such local historiography, and pre-Conquest *inventiones* are correspondingly rare.[5] The great time of English *inventiones* is from the late eleventh to the late twelfth century. This new vogue was aided, if not caused, by a number of

Continental hagiographers, such as Folcart and Goscelin of St. Bertin, who lent their services to several English houses.[6] The need for such texts was greatly stimulated by the need to reassert rights and privileges, and generally to reestablish historical continuity, after the disruption caused by the Norman Conquest; but there was also a more general desire to fill in the historiographical gaps, to consolidate in writing what was previously oral or sparsely documented local tradition.[7] Later in the twelfth century, it was chiefly quarrels over land, privileges, or status and sometimes conflicting traditions about the location of certain relics that prompted local historiography. A major shift in economics late in the century, which favored larger, administratively sophisticated landholders over smaller ones, was also an incentive for getting one's books in order, both the documentation and the narrative;[8] the result was composite works, narrative cartularies, that contain the house's most important documents with more or less narrative tissue between them.[9]

In the early twelfth century, historians in England were catching up on work that had been neglected, rallying the historiographical forces after the disruption of the Conquest. The standard image conjured up by modern historians is of Anglo-Saxon monks frantically defending their native traditions, and above all their saints, against the skeptical and arrogant Norman abbots and bishops forced upon them against their will. In an important recent essay, Susan Ridyard cautions against overly simplistic views of ethnic tensions in post-Conquest England: the Norman newcomers were by no means universally contemptuous of Anglo-Saxon traditions, but on the contrary often helped promote them.[10] A nice visual illustration of the collaboration and blending of the ethnic groups can be seen in one of the most important manuscripts of Goscelin's works, an early twelfth-century manuscript from St. Augustine's, Canterbury: it contains the lives of the abbey's local saints written in a pre-Conquest English hand, a hand of the typical Norman-influenced style that was being developed next door at Christ Church Cathedral, and a hand that combines both types; the hands alternate, often in mid-narrative, and give an impression of peaceful collaboration in a common cause.[11] It is also worth recalling that much English historiography at the time was written for Norman patrons. As Frank Barlow puts it, "the parvenu Normans were appropriating Old-English history."[12] But the much quoted instances of Norman hostility that Ridyard seeks to play down show, if nothing else, that there was a perception of such hostility; and, even if the spate of historiographic activity did not break down along ethnic lines, it is true that monasteries perceived the need to put their local traditions into writing for defensive reasons. Glastonbury commissioned William of Malmesbury — of mixed Norman and

Anglo-Saxon descent—to write up its local traditions, emphasizing particularly its antiquity and its impressive relic collection.[13] Eadmer—an Anglo-Saxon—did extensive work for Christ Church, Canterbury, aggressively defending its ownership of many important relics.[14] Goscelin of St. Bertin—a Fleming—acted as a kind of roving hagiographer for several monasteries, particularly for St. Augustine's, Canterbury, where he eventually settled.[15] On a larger scale, William of Malmesbury spent the 1120s and 30s systematically collecting information and traditions from churches and monasteries all over England for his "gazetteer of ecclesiastical England," the *Gesta Pontificum*.[16] He considered his own work both pioneering and urgently necessary: his secular history of England, the *Gesta Regum*, begins with the observation that with the exception of Eadmer, there had been no serious large-scale narrative history in England since Bede, and that this gap needed to be filled.[17]

Although in the latter part of the century there seems to be a sense that the ground-breaking work has been done, that the framework of English history has been established,[18] the need for defensive local historiography does not subside. On the contrary: the second part of the twelfth century is typically the "golden age" of local historiography in England. At Bury, around the year 1200, Jocelin of Brakelond is defending the "terra Sancti Edmundi" against encroachment from the local bishop, secular neighbors, and above all the Crown. Besides the obvious practical purposes of such work, the abbey's lands also seem to be of great emotional value to the monks. One recalls Jocelin's famous New Year's present to Abbot Samson: after careful consideration, the young Jocelin decides that the perfect gift for the abbot (whom at that time he still worships as a hero) would be to draw up a catalogue of all the monastery's lands.[19] Lands and possessions are the central concern of Bury historiography and hagiography over several centuries.[20] At neighboring Ely, the *Liber Eliensis* is compiled between 1131 and 1174, in part from earlier local sources. In the last third of the twelfth century, Abingdon, Ramsey, Waltham, Hexham, and others are all consolidating in writing their claims of land, prestige, privileges, and relics.[21]

St. Albans, a center of historiography, art, and book production in the twelfth and thirteenth centuries, allows us to observe the development of an *inventio* account and its place in local historiography over several generations. Although generally in very good shape both historiographically (the legend of its founding saint is told by no less an authority than Bede) and materially, in terms of its property claims, privileges, and exemptions,[22] St. Albans begins a major hagiographic initiative around 1178, probably in response to Ely's claim that it possesses the true relics of St. Alban, a claim Matthew Paris was still fighting two generations later.[23] At that time, the abbey added an additional patron saint to its roster: St. Amphibalus, the missionary, unnamed in the early sources, who converted St. Alban to Christianity. His relics and those of several other martyrs were "discovered" in 1178, and the event was, as Matthew Paris notes, commemorated in a *libellus* containing the life of the new saint and other materials pertaining to both him and St. Alban.[24] The life, by a monk named William, is extant (though the original *libellus* is not), and will be discussed at length later in this chapter. Almost simultaneously, William's life was rendered in elegiac verses by Ralph of Dunstable; both texts were copied several times, often together, and often augmented, in an arrangement typical of such *libelli*, by treatises on the *inventiones* of both saints and the miracles associated with them. In the thirteenth century, St. Albans' great historiographer and artist Matthew Paris further shaped and consolidated the Alban and Amphibalus legend. He reworked all the material on the two saints and their *inventiones* in the *Chronica Majora*, the important universal chronicle he took over from Roger Wendover in 1235; he also described both *inventiones* in the appropriate places of his house chronicle, the *Gesta Abbatum Sancti Albani*.[25] Moreover, he produced a separate manuscript on the saints. His autograph manuscript (Trinity College Dublin Ms. 177) contains William's and Ralph's lives and treatises from the earlier collections, as well as Matthew's own French verse translation of William's life. Matthew illustrated the French *Vie de Seint Auban* with a cycle of tinted outline drawings, in his customary strip-cartoon style, that continues past the end of the poem to narrate the *inventio* of St. Alban and the foundation of the abbey by King Offa of Mercia in 792.[26] There is thus a rich, unbroken, and evolving tradition of local hagiography at St. Albans in the eight decades from about 1178 to Matthew's death in 1259; this body of material is extraordinarily fruitful for the study of *inventiones*.

With his astonishing gift for creating vigorous, plausible new iconographies, Matthew provides a striking visual representation of what had clearly become firmly established as a mental image in the collective imagination of medieval western Europe.[27] In the illustrated *Vie de Seint Auban*, the sequence on Alban's *inventio* begins with King Offa's dream, in which an angel directs him to the site; it then shows him and several bishops riding there, guided by visions of a celestial ray descending on the martyr's grave. The dig is shown in a particularly vivid scene: Offa stands on the left, gesturing toward the ground and the diggers. Workmen, with realistically depicted tools and wicker crates, uncover a rectangular tomb containing something labeled "ossa martiris" (fig. 1). The public is represented by two clerics on the right,

Fig. 1. King Offa discovers the relics of St. Alban. From Matthew Paris's *Vie de Seint Auban*, Trinity College Dublin Ms. 177, fol. 59 r. Reproduced by permission of The Board of Trinity College Dublin.

both with "speech bubble" phrases: one is praying "Te deum laudamus"; the other, with his index finger to his nose, says "Redolet." The rhymed captions at this point become unusually expansive, covering more than the usual two couplets per picture:

Crosent de besches e picois;
Asaartent boisuns e bois
Enportent zuches e racines;
Ostent blestes, ostent espines;
En hotes portent cailloz e tere.
Ne finent de chercher e quere.
Querent aval, querent amund.
Li reis i est ki les sumunt,
Tant k'est truvez li tresors
E les reliques du seint cors
Envolupez k'erent de paille
Ki ne pert ne culur ne taille.

They dig with spades and picks; they tear out shrubs and trees, carry away stumps and roots; they take off brambles and thorns; they carry

Figs. 2–3. King Offa oversees construction of St. Albans Abbey. From Matthew Paris's *Vie de Seint Auban*, Trinity College Dublin Ms. 177, fols. 59 v and 60 r. Reproduced by permission of The Board of Trinity College Dublin.

pebbles and dirt in baskets. They do not cease to search. They search up and down — the King is there to supervise them — until the treasure is found, and the relics of the sacred body, which were wrapped in a pall that had lost neither color nor shape.[28]

This picture leads directly to a two-page representation of the building of the monastery (figs. 2 and 3). The connection, already strongly suggested by the general left-to-right orientation of the illustrations, is emphasized by one of Matthew's usual continuity devices: a worker walking out of the *inventio* picture at the right.[29] The remaining pictures show the appointment of the first abbot, the solemn *elevatio* of the relics, the institution of an annual procession to commemorate the *inventio*, and Offa's endowment of the abbey.[30] The sequence forms an invaluable visual record of what an *inventio* "looked like" in the minds of medieval Europeans; most *inventiones*, both on the Continent and in England, conform rather closely to the model illustrated by Matthew.

Heinzelmann reports that in the two major Continental manuscript libraries he surveyed (Paris and Brussels), the vast majority of *inventiones* are copies of two extremely popular texts: the *Inventio Crucis* (BHL 4163) and

the *Revelatio Sancti Stephani* (BHL 7850–56).[31] The influence of both is clearly felt in our *inventiones*. At least since Geoffrey of Monmouth, St. Helen was thought to be British, so allusions to her in English hagiographical literature are to be expected. Indeed, there are two monastic foundation stories in our period that involve the finding of a cross rather than a saint.[32]

Much more important, though, is the *Revelatio Sancti Stephani*, an early fifth-century text that rapidly spread throughout Europe and remained influential throughout the Middle Ages. The Greek original is a letter by the priest Lucianus, in which he recounts his discovery of the bones of Saints Stephen, Nicodemus, and Gamaliel and Gamaliel's son Abibas, at Caphar-Gamala near Jerusalem. The Latin translation was made very soon after, by another priest named Avitus. In his preface, Avitus explains the occasion for the translation: he has arranged for Paulus Orosius, in town for conciliar business, to take some of the relics to Braga. Avitus's letter, with the translation of Lucianus's account, is to accompany the gift of relics for authentication.[33] The bones, which were eventually distributed between Menorca and Uzalis in North Africa, were among early medieval Europe's most distinguished relics. Augustine took a lively interest in the cult of St. Stephen.[34] Bede mentions the relics' transfer to the Latin West by Orosius in his *De temporum ratione* as one of the key dates of postbiblical history.[35]

The text of the *Revelatio* is now extant in two rather different redactions, but the basic story is the same in both.[36] The priest Lucianus is visited in a dream by a man dressed in white, who identifies himself as "Gamaliel qui Paulum apostolum nutrivi et legem domini docui in Hierusalem [Gamaliel, who took care of Paul the apostle and instructed him in the law of the Lord at Jerusalem]."[37] He demands that Lucianus pass on an important message to his bishop: it is God's will that the bodies of Stephen, Nicodemus, Gamaliel himself, and his son Abibas be "revelati" at this time. He gives a circumstantial account of each saint's burial and reveals the location of the tombs. Lucianus is deeply impressed, but decides to wait for the dream to recur a second and third time before acting on it. The saint does reappear two more times; in each visit, he expands on his original message; the third time he rebukes and threatens Lucianus for hesitating so long. Lucianus then informs the bishop and obtains permission to begin the search in the field indicated by Gamaliel. As Lucianus, along with several helpers, is digging in the field, he is informed that Gamaliel has appeared to a monk named Migetus, to tell him that the party is digging in the wrong spot and to give meticulous directions to the true site. This time the search is successful. The diggers come upon a stone inscribed with four names: "Celiel, Nasoam, Gamaliel, Abibas, hebraica quidem verba, litteris autem grecis. Interpretatio vero nominum haec est: Celiel Stephanus dicitur, Nasoam vero Nicodemus, Abibas filium Gamalielis significat [Celiel, Nasoam, Gamaliel, Abibas; the words were Hebrew, but in Greek letters. The names translate as follows: Celiel means Stephen, Nasoam Nicodemus, and Abibas means the son of Gamaliel]."[38] As they come upon Stephen's sarcophagus, there is an earthquake (this is in version B only), and "tanta suavitas et fraglantia [sic] odoris inde egressa est quantam nullus hominum sensisse se meminit, ita ut putaremus nos in amoenitate paradisi esse positos [such sweetness and fragrance emerged from there as none of the people there remembered having smelled before, so that we thought we had been placed in the beauty of Paradise]."[39] Miraculous cures occur instantly. Two bishops are present at the event, "cum suo clero." The relics are then translated to Jerusalem in a solemn procession.

In tone, style, and purpose, the *Revelatio* is very different from the English *inventiones* of the twelfth century. But it is clearly the narrative model for most of our texts. It firmly establishes the main plot elements, of which Matthew Paris, much later, furnished the visual rendition; these plot elements, as Heinzelmann has observed, remain fairly constant for centuries, although there is some flexibility to accommodate local circumstances.[40] The relics are found either by coincidence, usually in connection with some construction or renovation project, or by divine guidance, through dreams or visions. The search for the right place and the digging itself are usually much emphasized; it is stressed that the community "earned" the relic through its intense desire and hard work. There must be an audience present, minimally represented by the bishop or other high clerics in charge, but often described as a large crowd of clergy and laity. There will be some confirmation that the relic is genuine: the body may be incorrupt, or at least emit a pleasant fragrance;[41] sometimes there is an inscription or some identifying artifact. The *inventio* is followed by a *translatio*, that is, the body is brought to a more worthy shrine, and its authenticity is further confirmed by miracles.

It seems likely that the *inventio* genre was imported into Anglo-Norman England, together with the *Revelatio* itself, by Continental churchmen. It is not clear if the *Revelatio* was known to the English of the late Anglo-Saxon period. Bede certainly knew it, since he mentions it in several places and in one instance finds it significant enough to treat Orosius's translation of Stephen's relics to the Latin West as one of a handful of milestones of post-Incarnation history. In the twelfth century, both the *Liber Eliensis* and Thomas of Monmouth mention it explicitly, in a way that indicates that they expected their readers to be familiar with it.[42] But not one of the many manuscripts listed by Vanderlinden is English, whereas there is a wealth of them, primarily from the tenth to the twelfth century, in the northern French and Flemish regions that were so influential in English ecclesiastical life in that period. Of the manuscripts extant today, one can be traced to Fleury, another to St. Omer. Fleury is the home of Abbo of Fleury, who, after a visit to Ramsey, wrote the important *Life of St. Edmund* in about 980. From St. Omer came both Folcart and Goscelin of St. Bertin, authors of several saints' lives in the first decades after the Norman Conquest.[43] It is quite possible that the text, like many others known to Bede's contemporaries, was lost during the decline of English monasticism and, unlike many such texts, was not reintroduced during the tenth-century reform. Be that as it may, even if Goscelin and people like him are not responsible for physically reintroducing manuscripts of the *Revelatio* into the British Isles, they do seem to have taught the post-Conquest ecclesiastical community there what one could do with that text, how that model could be adapted to contemporary affairs; in the decades after the conquest, the sense of loss and confusion, as well as the eagerness to reaffirm cultural and historical continuity, may well have provided a fertile ground for the rhetorical possibilities of the genre.[44]

Goscelin, a monk of St. Bertin at St. Omer, is responsible for an *inventio* of St. Yvo (ca. 1080) at Slepe near Ramsey, which clearly shows the influence of the *Revelatio*.[45] It is not without significance that one of the earliest *inventiones* written in post-Conquest England should be associated with Ramsey, which had long-standing connections with the Continent, particularly Fleury.[46] As in the fifth-century text, the remains of a saint (Yvo) and "his companions" are found in an open field, not, as is much more common, in a church. In this case, the discovery is accidental: a peasant comes upon the graves as he plows his field. But the identity of the bodies found is revealed in visions. Again, it is the saint himself who appears to the dreamer, this time an illiterate workman. And again, the dreamer does not act upon the vision until the third night, when the saint becomes angry and strikes him. Two details confirm one's suspicion that Goscelin had the *Revelatio* at his elbow: his extended etymological play on "Aprilis autem quasi Aperilis ab aperiendo [*April*, or 'aperilis,' comes from *aperiendum*, 'to be opened']" is reminiscent of the *Revelatio*'s use of the word "aperire," which occurs almost like a refrain: "quousque non aperis nobis [How much longer will you wait to open (the sarcophagus) for us]?" And Goscelin's odd comparison of the two abbots present at the *translatio* to "gemini boves Christi [the twin oxen of Christ]" was probably suggested by the rather obscure riddle concerning oxen in one of Lucianus's visions, in which it becomes clear to him that the "ox" without which he will not be able to find and move the relics must be St. Stephen himself.[47]

Unlike the *Revelatio*, Goscelin's *inventio* is part of a larger narrative context: it is preceded by a very brief life of Saint Yvo and followed by *miracula*.[48] This arrangement, seen also at St. Albans and fairly typical of monastic local hagiography,[49] indicates a very different function for the later *inventiones*: quite unlike the *Revelatio*, they are part of a local history. It is not surprising, then, that they acquire an additional plot element that is absent in the *Revelatio*: the foundation and endowment of a monastery in the place where the relics were found or translated. Indeed, most medieval inventiones are foundation stories, both in a literal sense (they often serve to motivate the foundation of a monastery, such as St. Albans, or the refoundation of a defunct one) and in a larger sense: *inventiones* serve, in many ways, as the foundation of a monastery's corporate identity and self-definition.

It should be clear even from the brief summaries given so far that the typical *inventio* is to a very large extent a symbolic story. *Inventiones*, like other relic narratives, are stories about the communities that host the relics.[50] Most are inspired by dreams and revelations but are also the result of a strenuous effort by the monks. This suggests a happily balanced interplay between providence and grace on the one hand, and human effort and initiative on the other—surely a portrayal in which a monastic community would like to see its own image.

Set within this balance of the divine and the human, *inventiones* are narrative realizations of two notions that are very important to the monks: the ancient, venerable origin of their community and its continuity over time. Interestingly, an *inventio*, or something approaching an *inventio*, is often constructed in cases where it is not really appropriate or plausible; this would seem to indicate how much prestige or psychological satisfaction there was to be gained from such a story.[51] At St. Albans, for instance, the tradition that the location of Alban's grave had been completely forgotten and was miraculously rediscovered by Offa in 792 seems a little unlikely in light of Bede's testimony—which of course St. Albans also heavily draws on—of a flourishing cult at the time he was writing (731).[52] In the case of St. Edmund, *inventio* is simply not applicable: the saint's cult was uninterrupted from the time of his death. But the way Edmund died—he was beheaded by Viking raiders— permits Abbo, his earliest hagiographer, to use many of the elements of an *inventio* in the search for the saint's severed head:

> utpote socii ad socium alternatim clamantium "Ubi es?," illud [i.e., caput] respondebat designando locum patria lingua dicens "her, her, her," quod interpretatum Latinus sermo exprimit "hic, hic, hic." Nec umquam eadem repetendo clamare destitit quoad omnes ad se perduxit.

> Like friends to a friend, they took turns shouting "Where are you?" to which it [i.e., the head] responded, designating the place in its native language, "here, here, here," which in Latin is "hic, hic, hic." And it never ceased to repeat the same phrase until it had led them all to itself.[53]

St. Æthelthryth of Ely is not, strictly speaking, "invented" either, but the twelfth-century *Liber Eliensis* is careful to approximate the accounts of her successive *translationes* to *inventiones*. This is particularly clear in the account of the first *translatio*, which is adapted and considerably expanded from Bede: although her sister Sexburga is obviously quite aware of the location of Æthelthryth's grave, the element of search and providential discovery is transferred, as it were, to the search for an appropriate sarcophagus. Stone, the *Liber* explains, is not to be found in the island of Ely nor in the surrounding swamps, so the *fratres* who are entrusted with the mission brace themselves for a long search:

> Qui statim, ascensa navi, applicantes venerunt ad civitaculam quandam tunc temporis desolatam, non procul inde sitam, que lingua Anglorum Grantecester vocatur, et, dum nimium solliciti deambularent, mox invenerunt iuxta muros illius civitatis locellum de marmore albo pulcherrime tectum in loco, qui usque hodie Ærmeswerch dicitur, id est opus miseri. Mirantur singuli, negant vicini huiusmodi lapidem se habuisse illo in loco vel aliquando vidisse, et, accedentes propius, non a quolibet illic positum asserebant, sed Dei potius iussione ad ipsorum usus celitus fuisse colatum.

> Once aboard ship, they immediately arrived at a small town, which was abandoned at that time, not far from there [i.e., Ely], named "Grantecester" in English; and, as they walked around, overly concerned, they soon found near the walls of that town a sarcophagus of white marble, with a beautiful covering slab, in the place that until this day is named Ærmeswerch, that is, poor man's work. Everybody is amazed; the locals deny that there has ever been such a stone in that place, or that they have ever seen one; drawing near, they assert that it has not been placed there by just anyone, but rather that it must have been placed there miraculously by divine command, for the use of the monks.[54]

This is then followed by the obligatory assembly of a festive crowd, miracles, and the miraculous appearance of a holy well.

The next *translatio* recorded in the *Liber*, dated 1106, is also not strictly speaking an *inventio*: the relics are merely moved into the new church built by Abbot Richard. But the term "invenire" is frequently used, and the event is compared to the "inventio corporis beati Stephani martyris."[55] An element of the *inventio* model, the solicitous search and the providential finding, is also recognizable in the foundation story of Æthelthryth's search for the right place to found her monastery.[56]

The series of *translationes* or *inventio*like episodes (there is another, minor one in book 2, chapter 52), emphasizes the monastery's historical continuity. Ely, first founded in the seventh century as a double monastery by Æthelthryth and continuing under female leadership for two centuries (this is the subject of book 1), is destroyed during the Danish raids of 866–70 and then refounded by Æthelwold, in the course of the tenth-century monastic revival, as a male monastery.[57] On that occasion, Æthelwold "found" (invenit) the body of St. Æthelthryth where Sexburg had buried it, although, as the *Liber Eliensis* expressly states, he refrained from moving or even inspecting it at that time.[58] As the community abandons its old church for a new one, moving the body of Æthelthryth and the other "sanctae" ensures continuity from the old building to the new.

The use of relics to emphasize material continuity is extremely common. Ailred of Rievaulx wrote a *legenda* for the monastery of Hexham, to be read on the feast of the translations of its saints. The major point of this text is to show that all the early saints were still there after the Danish invasion of 875 and the ensuing long hiatus in the monastery's history until its refoundation in the eleventh century. The pivotal chapter is chapter 11, which narrates the total destruction and later refoundation. Ailred's eloquent lament on the destruction of Hexham and its historical documents is very much that of a scholar and historian:

> Post desolationem Nordahymbrorum, quam irruentibus in Angliam Dacis miserabiliter incurrit, sicut caeterae hujusmodi ecclesiae, haec Haugustaldiensis: ut verbis Propheticis utar, multo tempore sine sacerdote, sine ephod, sine teraphin gemebunda resedit. Tunc *plorans ploravit in nocte et lacrimae ejus in maxillis ejus.* Quidquid de lignis fuerat, ignis absumpsit. Bibliotheca illa nobilissima, quam praesul sanctus condiderat, tota deperiit. In qua denique devastatione monimenta, quae de vita et miraculis Sanctorum sancti patres ad posteritatis notitiam stilo transmiserant, constat esse consumta.

> After the devastation of Northumbria, which it lamentably suffered as the Danes overran England, this church of Hexham, like many others of its kind, sat sighing—to use the words of the Prophet—for a long time without a priest, without an ephod, without teraphin [Hosea 3:4]. Then "she wept in the night, and her tears were on her cheeks" [Lamentations 1:2]. Whatever was made of wood was consumed by fire. That most splendid library, founded by the holy bishop [i.e., Acca], perished entirely. It is clear that in this destruction, all documents about the lives and miracles of the saints, which the holy fathers had transmitted to posterity in writing, were destroyed.[59]

This is followed by five more chapters on the *inventiones* and *translationes* of the old saints, as well as notes on the identity of those no longer well documented (191–203). Similarly, Goscelin devotes a *libellus* to the wholesale *translatio* of all the saints (there were many) of St. Augustine's, Canterbury, when the new choir was built by Abbot Scotland.[60] Gervase of Canterbury begins his history with the great fire at Christ Church in 1174 and the subsequent reconstruction of the cathedral. Apparently this event is significant enough for him to mark the beginning of "recent history," but at the same time he takes great care to emphasize that all the relics are accounted for, so that continuity with the previous Christ Church is ensured.[61]

The body of a patron saint, then, becomes metonymically the "corporate body" of the community, which, like the saint, remains the same, and "incorrupt," despite constant change.[62] The most famous example is St. Cuthbert, whose body was moved from Lindisfarne as the monks fled Viking attacks and accompanied them on their long wanderings from place to place until they finally settled in Durham.[63] The implication is that the Durham community is continuous with the dissolved Lindisfarne community, although neither the place nor, after so many years, the persons remain the same. The body of St. Cuthbert is not only incorrupt, but remains "quasi adhuc viveret integrum, et flexibilibus artuum compagibus multo dormienti quam mortui similius [whole as if he were still alive, and, with all his joints flexible, resembling a sleeping man much more than a dead man]."[64]

St. Edmund's body is similarly well preserved (his nails and hair continue to grow and must be groomed regularly), and he acts as an active defender of his monastery: attacks on the shrine are attacks on the house and vice versa, and St. Edmund, as the collections of his miracles show, will severely punish any offender against shrine or monastery.[65] Barbara Abou-el-Haj has documented how the iconography of the famous illuminated *libellus* of St. Edmund can be traced in almost every particular to a specific political or economic concern of the monastery.[66] But not only does Edmund defend his monastery, he also embodies it. The much emphasized wholeness of Edmund's body is an all-but-explicit metonymy for the wholeness of the community: although the king died a martyr, riddled with Danish arrows and beheaded, his body, when finally reunited with the head, shows no trace of any wounds except for a thin red line around the neck; this is paralleled with the scattered community rallying after the Danish invasion. During a later *translatio*, as Jocelin of Brakelond reports, a bold abbot goes to great lengths to ascertain that the head is indeed firmly attached to the body: he has another monk pull at Edmund's feet, while he himself pulls the head; although the body withstands the test, the abbot is punished for his presumption. (Abbot Samson, remembering this precedent, limits himself to feeling the body through the shroud and counting its toes.)[67]

The metaphor of the saint's inviolate body is carried to even greater lengths at Ely, where the founding saint is a woman who, moreover, founded the monastery expressly in order to preserve her virginity. According to Bede, and the *Liber Eliensis* after him, Æthelthryth's body is incorrupt when Sexburga unearths her sixteen years after her death, and a wound from a surgically removed tumor, which her physician testifies must have been on her neck at the time of her death, is found to have healed without a trace.[68] One particularly interesting detail the *Liber Eliensis* adds to Bede's account of the *inventio* of the sarcophagus (see above) is that after the saint's entombment, the covering slab bonds so firmly with the sarcophagus that no gap or seam ("compago") is visible.[69] (One cannot help thinking of Edmund's head bonding with his body.) The seamless shrine comes to stand, metonymically, for the inviolate body of the saint.

This reading is confirmed when there ensues a series of symbolic rapes or violations of the shrine. During the Danish raids, one of the pagans makes a hole in the shrine. He, of course, is duly punished by the saint, but the hole remains — as does the "wound" inflicted on the monastery by the Vikings. In the 1106 *translatio*, much is made of the fact that Abbot Richard does *not* open the sarcophagus (and neither did Æthelwold a century earlier). But an unfortunate earlier episode is mentioned at that point: a wicked "presbyter" once introduced a cleft stick through the hole in the shrine in order to pull out a piece of the saint's dress. She pulled it back, "cum vigili indignatione." Next, the "temptator," presumably to see what had happened, mounted a candle on his cleft stick and introduced it into the sarcophagus. He dropped the candle, and it flared up, but the relics remained miraculously unharmed. The "temptator," of course, died soon after this adventure.[70] In the 1106 *translatio*, however, in which this episode is embedded, "regia domina Æðeldreða" was translated "intentata et inconspecta [untouched and unseen]."[71] This account occurs in the middle of book 2, which details Ely's possessions, acquisitions, "damna," and attempted encroachments by neighboring nobility. The series of attempted symbolic rapes is emblematic of the attempted "rapes" of the monastery, as the attempts to despoil St. Edmund's shrine are clearly emblematic of attacks on Bury St. Edmunds. What makes the Ely example particularly obvious and vivid is the fact that the metonymy, the transfer from "saint's body" to "monastic community," is anticipated by an intermediate step: the sarcophagus, a smaller "container," comes to stand for the virginal body of the saint, and this container/contained compound in turn stands for the larger "container," the church and the community.[72]

While their psychological and metaphorical aptness is beyond dispute, *inventiones* do, at the same time, purport to be factual historical accounts about the origins of religious houses, and this is where their very aptness (not to mention their sameness) can cause problems. The patent artificiality and impossibility of most *inventiones* has sometimes irritated modern historians; their responses range from apologetics or mild derision to outright condemnation.[73] But irrespective of their factual accuracy, *inventiones* are fascinating historiographical vignettes, not only because they carry with them a rich, suggestive imagery of loss and rediscovery, origins and continuity, but also because their status as truth-telling is extremely interesting. On the one hand, they are almost always made-up history, either outright forgery or a bona fide reconstruction of what might have been. Like all etiological legends — stories that explore causes, that explain how a current state of affairs came about — they are necessarily retroactive: they are projected backward from a present end point to an imagined origin. And the writers know, to varying degrees, that they are "making up" history, in both senses implied by Nancy Partner's punning essay title, "Making Up Lost Time": making up a loss and making up a story. They usually know, at least, and often comment, that they have very little reliable evidence to go on. On the other hand, *inventio* stories make specific, empirically verifiable truth claims about historical dates, places, people, and events; in many cases, indeed, they take on quasi-legal status, and it is of great practical importance that their accounts be understood and accepted as factually referential.

One modern way to account for the dubious truth status of *inventiones* (as well as other historical accounts and the vexed problem of the widespread forgery of documents) is to posit a Christian-Platonic model of truth that differs sharply from our own sense of historical accuracy. In this model, the ultimate standard of truth is conformity to the highest truth, Christian revelation; faithfulness to outside reality, or individual, contingent circumstance, is comparatively less important. The sameness of *inventio* narratives, their conformity to a received narrative type, would therefore not arouse suspicion but inspire trust.[74] It is certainly true that the relic cult in general — including all the rites, legal procedures, and narratives that surround it — constitutes an oddly "closed" system of truth and confirmation, in which the allegorical reference to Christian revealed truth outweighs and sometimes eclipses the everyday reference to physical reality.

Inventio narratives are in themselves authenticating narratives, not only true but told in order to lend truth to something else: the genuineness of the bones they go with and the antiquity and prestige of the monasteries that produced them. The relic cult is centrally about truth. One medieval word for relic is "pignus," a complicated word with many figurative meanings that pull it in different semantic directions, but its basic meaning is "pledge": an object given in pledge, even a pawn; a person given in pledge, that is, a hostage; a guarantee or proof of truth.[75] Relics are pledges left by the saints to prove that they are still present, still actively with those who venerate them; they are material proofs, guarantees of the faith. Relics qua physical objects are therefore little parcels of Truth, which accounts for their widespread use as objects to swear by. This custom is attested as early as the sixth century and still alive in the twelfth; it slowly disappears, first from ecclesiastical then from secular legal practice, in the course of the thirteenth century. Catechumens, novices, newly elected bishops make their *professio* by relics, until oaths on the gospel slowly replace this practice in the later Middle Ages.[76] The Bayeux Tapestry depicts Harold swearing by the relics of Bayeux,[77] and in 1172, Henry II swears both on the gospel and on relics that he did not intend the murder of Thomas Becket.[78]

Rituals and texts concerning relics — showings ("ostentationes"), processions, solemn translations, as well as written miracle collections, *inventiones* and *translationes* — serve, in turn, to authenticate the relics. Before canonization became the sole prerogative of the pope, "elevation" of relics by the bishop, but also all other aspects of the cult — the physical presence of relics, the narratives and rites — served as de facto canonization of a saint. There were earlier instances of papal canonization, but it was not until the Lateran Council of 1215 that Rome began a serious attempt to formalize and monopolize the process.[79] For most of the medieval period, then, canonization was not a onetime judicial proceeding but an ongoing ritual and narrative elaboration. Thus, when there were disputes about relics, refutations — surprisingly for modern readers — often took the form of further narrative elaboration, rather than discrediting the other party's narrative. Matthew Paris, for instance, wrote a wildly inventive tract ("Cum Danorum rabies," which was later inserted into the *Gesta Abbatum*) in order to respond to a claim from Odense in Denmark that the relics of St. Alban had been brought there and were no longer at St. Albans. Matthew does not attempt to disprove Odense's narrative of how the relics got there, but rather tops it with an additional *furtum sacrum*, in which the relics are stolen back by a St. Albans monk.[80] In the late Middle Ages, the increasing importance of papal canonization, as well as the obsolescence of relics in judicial proceedings, changed the status of relics: they became objects of private rather than public devotion. At the same time, suspicion about false relics and fraudulent relic deals increased. Although in the twelfth century there was some debate about true and false relics,[81] there was not yet the cynicism we know from reading Boccaccio or Chaucer's "Pardoner's Tale," where relics are anything but pledges of truth. The twelfth-century relic cult consists of a complex system of mutual, sometimes circular, authentication of stories, objects, and rites. By modern standards, the system is shaky, since it does not seem to be grounded anywhere. To medieval thinking, it was grounded in a shared faith and, on the whole, seems to have been acceptable and sufficient in practice.

The imitative practice mentioned above, of approximating an *inventio* story even where no *inventio* had actually occurred, is partly motivated by the desire for such authentication. The standard *inventio* narrative carries such strong connotations of "truth" that it is worthwhile to adapt the model to gain some of the authority inherent in it. Waltham, for instance, claimed to possess the body of King Harold, who had refounded and endowed it.[82] The canons do not go as far as to claim sanctity for him, but they come very close.[83] The quasi-hagiographic account, "De Inventione Sanctae Crucis . . ." does construct a kind of *inventio* for Harold: two canons, who have observed the battle of Hastings from a distance, obtain the Conqueror's permission to look for Harold's body on the battlefield among the thousands of fallen warriors. With the help of Harold's former mistress, Edith Swanneshals, the king's body is finally identified. The body is brought to Waltham and honorably interred.[84] But all this does not amount to a real *inventio*, or anything clearly hagiographic at all. The remedy is to associate Harold closely with Waltham's founding *inventio*: even before Harold became its patron, Waltham was famous for a miraculous crucifix, which, according to local legend, was discovered during the reign of Cnuth in an *inventio* not at all unlike the one of St. Yvo; thereupon, the owner of the land, Tovi le Prude, founded a small house of canons in the spot miraculously indicated by the cross itself.[85] Before the battle of Hastings, according to the chronicle, Harold came to Waltham to pray and prostrated himself before the cross "in modum crucis [in the form of a cross]." [86] Thus the *inventio* of the cross rubs off on him as well, as it were, both sanctifying him and confirming that his relics are at Waltham.

The most thorough and skillful exploitation of the *inventio* model is seen in Thomas of Monmouth's *Life of St. William of Norwich* (1150), a text that is infamous for being the first recorded instance of the ritual murder accusation against Jews. The story, reminiscent of a modern detective novel, has frequently been recounted:[87] twelve-year-old William, last seen on Good Friday in the company of an unknown young man, is found murdered in the woods on the next morning. That is about all the factual information there is. The theory that Jews were responsible for the murder was slow to develop and to gain acceptance, and the ulterior motives of those who argued it are transparent even in Thomas's partisan account. Nor did the case meet with lasting public interest, and the cult of the "saint" was sluggish for a long time. Thomas, a newcomer at Norwich several years after the murder, finds himself championing the boy saint against significant resistance and well-founded skepticism. The case, which he enthusiastically develops, is weak: in some particulars, it relies on the *absence* of evidence, which is interpreted as a sign of the Jews' cleverness in disguising their crime. One thing Thomas can do to strengthen his case is to pattern the narrative on standard hagiographic models. His account of the unfolding of the case is a series of burials and rediscoveries; the occasional problems of logic and verisimilitude show how hard the author tries to make his story "work" according to the model he has in mind. The word "inventio" is used in rubrics: "Quomodo et a quibus sit inventus"; "Item inventio altera." One of these *inventiones* is modeled on the Easter story—not surprisingly, since the murder is alleged to have happened as part of a gruesome Passover ritual. A nun named Legarda, who (in case we did not catch the Easter allusion) lives next to the church of St. Mary Magdalene, is guided to the boy's body by a vision of celestial light; unfortunately, given the exigencies of real-life chronology, this happens not on Easter Sunday but on Saturday morning. Another *inventio* occurs as the body is finally taken to a churchyard and buried there: no coffin can be found, but suddenly, the diggers miraculously hit upon two empty sarcophagi, which are used to bury the body, one sarcophagus serving as the lid for the other. Again, echoes of the biblical accounts of Christ's burial are unmistakable, for instance in Thomas's remark that the sarcophagi had not been used before.[88] Finally, Thomas himself experiences an *inventio*: the founder of his monastery, Herbert, appears to him, commanding him to tell the abbot that the "martyr" must be translated from the cemetery into the church. But Thomas, instantly reminded of Lucius's vision of Gamaliel, decides to wait for a second and third vision, and only after these are granted and Herbert has pinched his arm very painfully does he comply with his command.[89] Here, as at Waltham, conformity to the narrative model was clearly felt to serve as a strong authentication.

This closed system, in which textual models, ritual practices, and specific historical accounts mutually reinforce each other and have their ultimate guarantee in the Christian faith itself, obviously goes a long way toward explaining the odd truth status of *inventiones*. They strike a peculiar balance between the commonsense referential and the allegorical. In other words, they are doubly anchored: not only "in the countryside," in local landmarks and familiar place names, but also in a higher truth. By conforming in a reassuringly predictable way to an accepted narrative model, they are indirectly plugged into the larger model of salvation history — a concept that seems relatively remote in most of the stories, but by an implicit process of Platonic ladder climbing, we arrive at the one highest Truth, in the light of which individual variations of the narrative model pale and petty objections to minor details lose importance.

There remains, however, the stubborn problem that *inventiones* also claim to refer correctly to physical, historical "outside" reality; they are not ahistorical *exempla* but dated and localized reports. In medieval terms they are "historia," not "fabula," "res gestae," not freely created "integumenta" of doctrine. *Historia* and *fabula* might sometimes be thrown together, as ultimately serving the same purpose of teaching *doctrina*;[90] this helps explain why the boundaries could be somewhat permeable, but it does not obliterate the basic distinction. The concepts of "genuine" as opposed to "fake" and "factual" as opposed to "mendacious" were of course understood, and *inventiones* generally insist that their account is factual. "Odo of Ostia," the alleged — and perhaps real — author of the *inventio* of St. Milburga, makes this point very vehemently.[91] His prologue is entirely on the subject of veracity in saints' lives:

> He therefore, who by extolling the Saints whom he loves passes the bounds of truth, shall verily be seen to gain in their sight not thanks but loathing, and will be punished by God with severer penalties in so far as he is condemned for having spoken as a false witness against Himself. . . . I am speaking the truth. Before Christ I do not lie. . . . Let no man judge that I am arranging anything in this narration by lying. . . . The fact is that I shall be self-pierced with my own sword if, condemning liars, I do not myself escape the charge of lying, according to the well-known saying of the Apostle: "In the way in which you judge another you condemn yourself; for you commit the same fault which you are judging." [92]

While standards of evidence might have been different from ours, monastic historians generally understand the concept of evidence and accept the need for it. Many miracle stories, as well as some *inventiones*, anticipate and carefully forestall objections to the good faith of certain cures or the accuracy of the identification of a relic. In one miracle ascribed to King Edward when he was still alive, the king tests the man who was allegedly cured of blindness, not only on whether he can see now, but also on whether he was truly blind before.[93] Odo of Ostia refuses to vouch for more than his evidence will allow: in the case of a young girl cured of diabolical possession, he can testify, from having spoken to her, that she is now perfectly sane; since he did not know her before her cure, he cannot guarantee with the same degree of certainty that she was indeed possessed, but—second best to personal observation— he has trustworthy witnesses who will attest to that fact.[94] Goscelin, in his epic account of the translation of many saints during the renovation of St. Augustine, Canterbury, appears to concede uncertainty in one case to make the others the more credible: one body that is dug up cannot be identified, and the monks make various guesses. But the unknown saint forestalls further speculation by appearing to one monk in a dream. He thanks the chapter for the reverence shown him but, without revealing his identity, informs them that all previous identifications have been wrong; the monks should be content at this time to remain ignorant of his name. The monks therefore dub him "Deonotus," known to God, and leave it at that.[95] Thomas of Monmouth is virtually obsessed with clues and corroborating detail; the special circumstances of his hagiography make it particularly easy to observe the hagiographer at work and to observe his thinking about evidence and truth. He has obviously been accused of lying, and he counters the accusation not only by threats against those who deny due veneration to the martyr, but also by carefully "proving" the truth of his assertions.[96]

Thus, *inventiones* remain uneasily suspended between referential and allegorical truth claims, gesturing, sometimes skillfully, sometimes helplessly, in both directions. At the same time, however, a third possibility can be glimpsed: traces of a literary self-awareness that at least temporarily supersedes both the referential and the allegorical truth claims, that begins to make textuality the point of reference for the story's validity.

To observe this tendency, it is particularly useful to watch how *inventiones* locate themselves in time and space, or, more precisely, how they sometimes use space to locate themselves in time. We shall see that in some *inventiones* (or, perhaps, in an incipient form in all *inventiones*), the process of localization, of searching and finding, becomes emblematic of the historian's work, and therefore of the text itself.[97] Since *inventiones* claim to tell the truth about local history, they bolster their truth claims by anchoring themselves both in established chronology and in real-life space. They insert themselves into accepted historical texts and attach themselves to well-known historical figures. St. Albans is said to have been founded by King Offa of Mercia, who also discovered the bones of St. Alban. Denis Piramus anchors his life of St. Edmund in a long overview of British history.[98] At Abingdon, the historical frame for the foundation story is the early conversion of Britain as narrated by Bede and Geoffrey of Monmouth, and objects found together with the Nigra Crux, the house's main relic, confirm this association.[99] In a text from Saint Omer (Goscelin's home), Bovo, the abbot of the monastery, relates that the *inventio* of St. Bertin happened accidentally, as the church was being renovated; it was only then that Bovo remembered having read in the life of St. Bertin that the bones had been hidden in that location to be protected from Norman raiders.[100] Most *inventiones* give very precise place names, with local landmarks and authenticating details, inviting readers to go look up the place. In Goscelin's St. Yvo story, for instance, the bodies are said to be found "in the village of Slepe, eight English miles from Ramsey, and three from the town of Huntingdon, right on the river Ouse."[101]

Saints' cults in general are very much localized, intimately connected to their respective locales, as the practice of pilgrimage shows. From the earliest times, as Peter Brown notes, the cult centers established around relics serve as "holy places," as a means to "localize the holy":

> *Hic locus est*: "Here is the place," or simply *hic*, is a refrain that runs through the inscriptions on the early martyrs' shrines of North Africa. The holy was available in one place, and in each such place it was accessible to one group in a manner in which it could not be accessible to anyone situated elsewhere.
>
> By localizing the holy in this manner, late-antique Christianity could feed on the facts of distance and on the joys of proximity. This distance might be physical distance. For this, pilgrimage was the remedy.[102]

Where *inventiones* (or *translationes* or *furta sacra*) are foundation legends, they serve precisely to motivate or confirm the choice of location for a new monastery. St. Albans is constructed above the site where Alban was found.[103] In other cases, such as Waltham, the relic is moved from its original site, but it miraculously indicates where it wants to be translated.[104]

Another foundation story that adapts the *inventio* model—in this case the motif of miraculous confirmation of a building site—concerns Battle Abbey. The abbey is not, of course, founded on the site of an *inventio*, but on the site of the Battle of Hastings. William the Conqueror insists that the altar must be placed on the exact spot where Harold's standard fell. But that location is then confirmed by an *inventio* of sorts. The designated spot is, unfortunately, on a hillside, which presents major problems for building; also, the architects point out that there is no water and no building material anywhere nearby. Grandly brushing aside the water problem, William arranges to have stones imported from Normandy, but this turns out to be unnecessary:

matrone cuidam religiose reuelatum est quatinus in designato sibi per
uisum loco fodientes, ibidem ad opus premeditatum lapidum invenirent
abundantiam. Non longe itaque a presignato ecclesie ambitu, ut ius-
sum fuerat, querentes, tantam ac talem lapidum reppererunt copiam ut
manifeste pateret inibi diuinitus ad predestinatum opus lapidum ab euo
reconditum esse.

It was revealed to a pious lady that if they dug in a place shown her
in a vision, they would find there an abundance of stone for the projected work. Accordingly they searched not far from the boundary that
had been marked out for the church, and there found such a supply of
good stone that it was quite apparent that the Lord had laid up a hidden treasure of stone there from the beginning of time for the predestined work.[105]

In order to introduce the notion of divine sanction, the "inventio" of materials is substituted for the *inventio* of a saint.

The tradition of assembling lists of saints and their cult centers is apparently peculiar to England: the Old English *Secgan* lists saints' names, towns,
and important landmarks such as rivers or hills.[106] William of Malmesbury's
Gesta Pontificum provides a more ambitious topographical survey, with brief
narratives and a critical discussion of sources. But the function would seem
to be the same as in the *Secgan*: to tie the country's collective narrative of its
sacred history firmly to the map or, conversely, to associate real-life landscape
with salvation history.[107]

The spatial organization of such surveys is much more important than their
chronology: the *Secgan* gives no dates, and although William of Malmesbury
occasionally does, time is not the organizing principle for his overview either.
In relic cults, especially those of late antiquity and the earlier Middle Ages,
space, rather than time, is the primary parameter. To put it somewhat reduc-
tively, space supersedes time, or at least neutralizes it. Peter Brown titles his
chapter on localization "Praesentia": by being localized, the saints are made
available in the present; temporal distance, or proximity, is replaced by spatial
distance or proximity. As we shall see, one of the distinctive historiographical
achievements of the twelfth-century local *inventiones* is that they often depart
from the early tradition by reintroducing a strong temporal element, a sense
of historical distance.

In our earliest text, the *Revelatio Sancti Stephani*, the lack of historical distance is very striking. In the vision, Gamaliel does provide some "history"

by explaining the circumstances of each saint's death and burial; but the very fact that these circumstances are narrated in the first person, by one of the saints themselves, creates a peculiar directness and "praesentia." Much of the text consists of conversations between Gamaliel and Lucianus, partly on very practical matters, such as the precise location of the tombs, partly on esoteric visionary material. The saints continue to direct the search-in-progress by sending another elaborate verbal message. Lucianus and his helpers are not so much retrieving a "pignus," a token, from the past; they are searching for persons who are very much alive, who are nearby, although hidden from view. Gamaliel does not promise a find of holy relics (as St. Oswin does, for instance, or St. Fides in a tenth-century French text);[108] he commands, "Aperi nobis!"[109] One almost pictures the saints alive in their sarcophagi, pounding against the slabs from inside and demanding to be let out. The distance the searchers have to overcome is not the distance between their own and a past age; it is the distance between the human and the numinous. In one version, the opening of the sarcophagi is accompanied by thunder and earthquakes. The emphasis in this text is not on history—one is never invited to think of the relics' venerable age or the length of time they have been hidden—but, apart from the practical matter of access to the relics, on the visionary. True to its title, the *Revelatio* flirts with the apocalyptic tradition and even explicitly invokes the precedent of the Revelations of St. John.

Much, though not all, of both the immediacy and the numinosity is lost in the *inventio* of the high Middle Ages. Saints still appear in person to ask to be discovered; the motif of the saint threatening or even physically punishing the dreamer is also quite popular. But first-person narratives have become very rare. Often the *inventio* is narrated significantly after the fact: it is itself a historical event—usually the very founding moment of the monastery and therefore of the chronicle. Even where the reported *inventio* is very recent, it is remarkably rare for the author to describe himself as an eyewitness, let alone the main agent. On the contrary: Odo of Ostia, the narrator of the *inventio* of St. Milburga at Much Wenlock (1102), emphasizes that he has heard the story from trustworthy witnesses. Although the circumstances of his report are not made clear, he casts himself as an independent outside investigator called upon to verify the monastery's claim to have found a saint. He explains that he has carefully inspected the available evidence: he has spoken to persons who claim to have been cured, and he has seen and handled important physical evidence, such as the ancient parchment describing the location of Milburga's grave, and a box containing a "worm" donated as a votive gift by the grateful pilgrim who was cured of it. But he was obviously not present at the event itself.[110] Jocelin of Brakelond, who is very much present as an eye-witness in his entire chronicle, is nevertheless not a witness at the climactic *translatio* of St. Edmund. His painful exclusion from the proceedings, and the complicated narrative device of having an author surrogate secretly spy on the event, is one of Jocelin's major artistic successes in the book.[111] The one notable exception to the "no eyewitness" rule is Thomas of Monmouth, who finds himself as visionary, inventor, champion, and biographer of the saint all in one. This, however, is not a typical *inventio*: it is not the discovery of a historical saint, but an attempt to turn into a saint a contemporary whose sanctity was far from universally accepted. Typically, the high medieval *inventio* clearly distances the act of narration from the event itself. It is true that the *Revelatio Sancti Stephani*, too, had acquired a distancing device by the time it reached the Latin West: the framing letter by Avitus, the translator. But this frame is part of the transaction that occasions it: the passing on of some relics as a gift. As such, it has more to do with the empirewide "network" of relic exchange as tokens of friendship, as described by Peter Brown; this, too, is a mechanism for bridging spatial, not temporal, distance, leaving the relics largely ahistorical.[112] Most of our *inventiones*, far from neutralizing distance as the *Revelatio* does, almost go out of their way to stress it.

One notable effect of the narrative distancing in medieval *inventiones* is the (re-)introduction of a temporal element. To posit a witness, or in some cases even a narrator, at some time between the death and burial of the saint and the time of writing creates a point of reference, and therefore a sense of "depth," in an otherwise undifferentiated past time.[113] The best example is a rather striking text from St. Albans: the *passio* of Saints Alban and Amphibalus by a St. Albans monk named William, written probably in 1177 or 1178, on the occasion of the "discovery" of St. Amphibalus at Redbourn, not far from St. Albans.[114] In the last third of the twelfth century, St. Albans began not only to strengthen the cult of its patron saint, but also to promote a new saint: Alban's mentor, the foreign visitor who lodged with him at Verulamium and converted him. He had received only the briefest of mentions in Gildas, Bede, and other early accounts of Alban's martyrdom;[115] in Geoffrey of Monmouth's *Historia*, he had somehow acquired a name, Amphibalus, and it was mentioned that he, too, had suffered martyrdom.[116] In 1178, the body of Amphibalus was found near the village of Redbourn, a few miles from St. Albans, and was translated to a shrine in the abbey church. William wrote his *passio* of both saints shortly before or shortly after the *inventio*, but at any rate for the occasion.[117] It is the earliest version of the Alban legend we know of that includes a full account of Amphibalus's death. According to William, Amphibalus was followed to Wales by the Romans who had executed Alban. He was brought back to a place near Verulamium and martyred there together with thousands of other Christians. The connection of William's story with the actual *inventio* of Amphibalus is quite clear; the narrator even predicts the discovery: "quidam fidelis in Christo clam beati Martyris corpus auferens, sub terram occuluit diligenter, quandoque (ut confidimus) divino munere in lucem proferendum [a faithful man in Christ took the body away and carefully concealed it under ground, to be, as we trust, brought to light one day by the grace of God]."[118] It is equally clear that both the story and the cult of Amphibalus are new. Despite Geoffrey's earlier mention, it is unlikely that there was a cult of St. Amphibalus at St. Albans prior to 1178, since there were no relics of that saint; besides, Geoffrey, for reasons that have to do with his misread source, associates the saint with Winchester, not St. Albans. Moreover, William emphasizes the newness of his account. He explicitly states that the name Amphibalus, not previously known at St. Albans, comes from Geoffrey ("Gaufridus Arcturus"). More important, he claims that his narrative is a translation from an ancient book "anglico sermone" that he has discovered; although William does not say so, this, too, is obviously borrowed from Geoffrey.[119]

It is this source fiction, developed into an intriguing narrative frame, that makes William's *passio* distinctive. Introduced as a kind of external frame, in the dedication to Abbot Simon, the source fiction automatically provides William with an internal frame, in which the ostensible author of that source speaks in the first person. He is not, as one might expect, a contemporary eyewitness of the two saints' martyrdom. He lives significantly later ("longo post tempore"), though before the Christianization of England: he cannot give his name for fear of persecution by his pagan compatriots. The unnamed narrator cannot, of course, have direct knowledge of the saints. His account of his sources is truly striking—a gold mine for all those interested in historiography, memory, and the passage from orality to literacy:

Cives quondam Verolamii, ob elationem cordis sui declarandam qualiter passus sit beatissimus Albanus in muris suae civitatis sculptum reliquerunt: quam scripturam, longo post tempore, in muris eorum, jam ruinosis et ad ruinam inclinatis, inveni: vidique moenia prae vetustate jam labi, infra quorum ambitum B. Albanus graves in corpore pertulit cruciatus. Vidi locum repleri arborum densitate, in quo Martyr invictus quondam pro Christo sententiam subiit capitalem. Haec inter cetera multorum relatione cognovi, qualiter vir sanctus fontem in vertice montis orando produxerit; ut inimicis siti laborantibus, et jam de vita desperantibus, aquarum beneficio subveniret. Omnem rei seriem diligenter inquisivi, didici, et (ne lateret posteris) in hunc modum stylo memoriaeque mandare curavi.

The then citizens of Verulamium, in order to proclaim the uplifting of their hearts, left sculpted on the walls of their city in what manner the most blessed Alban suffered; this writing I found, much later, on those walls, which were already decaying and about to collapse; and I have seen the town walls collapse with old age, in whose circumference the blessed Alban suffered severe bodily torments. I saw the place in which the undefeated martyr once suffered capital punishment for Christ being overgrown with dense woods. Among other things, I have learnt from the accounts of many how the holy man produced by his prayers a spring on the top of a mountain, in order to assist with the gift of water his thirsting enemies, who were already despairing of their lives. I have diligently researched and learnt the entire sequence of events, and, so that it might not be hidden from posterity, I have taken pains to entrust it in this manner to pen and memory.[120]

While William is not necessarily the most elegant of writers, he performs an astonishing and unusual act of historical imagination, though one that is implicit in his textual model, the *inventio* genre. First of all, like many local hagiographers, he makes use of local landmarks, in his case the ruins of Roman Verulamium, situated across the river from the abbey and still quite visible in his time.[121] But he does so in a far more sophisticated way, imagining the ruins' role in not one but two past epochs and picturing them not only as the backdrop of his narrative but the very medium by which it is transmitted. Secondly, he borrows from Geoffrey the device of the "ancient book in the British language."[122] But he goes farther than any other medieval author I know of in historicizing the pretended content of his fictive source, imagining the writer's situation, his fears and hopes, his ways of learning about the events he describes; and he sustains the borrowed voice throughout his — admittedly brief — narrative, whereas in Geoffrey there are no specific indications past the prologue that we are hearing the voice of the "liber uetustissimus."

One must ask what William gains by employing such a narrator figure. After all, by placing him several centuries after the saints' deaths, William sacrifices the spontaneity and liveliness, not to mention the authority, of an eyewitness account.[123] This is the more remarkable since eye imagery and ocular proof play an important role throughout the narrative.[124] Apparently, William is consciously attempting to create historical depth by staggering time levels, creating, as it were, a three-dimensional rather than a flat picture of the past. What is more, the narrator's position is strategically chosen: he is the perfect link between Alban's time and William's own. He comes at the very end of the era in which the two saints lived: the country is still pagan, but he foresees its imminent conversion. Despite the temporal distance, he still partly shares in Alban's and Amphibalus's experience: like them, he is threatened by a pagan environment and has to keep his faith secret. Since by the end of his narrative he is ready to travel to Rome and be baptized, he could be said to be the last link in the story he narrates, the last in a series of conversions by direct example.[125] At the same time, he is the first to be converted by his narrative, the very text we are reading; in that sense, he also models the reaction of his ideal reader. Despite the immediacy of his reaction to the story, he feels equally isolated and separated, not only from his pagan contemporaries, but also from history: he has to piece the story of the saints together from decaying walls and from fading local memories. This, on the other hand, makes him crucially important. He is the last person to be able literally to read history in the ancient ruins and in the local landscape. He arrives on the scene just in time to salvage an almost lost tradition from unstable written and even more unstable oral witnesses. The narrator even makes his pivotal role explicit by ending with a "prophecy":

> Albani memoria non delebitur, sed ejus laudabile meritum, si quid mea carmina possunt, longe lateque per orbem diffundetur. Tempus erit, ut confidimus, quo viri religiosi, viri Christiani, ad praedicandum Gentibus venient in Britanniam. Isti cum venerint, Dei magnalia hoc modo libris adserta reperient, legent et ad notitiam deferent plurimorum.

> Alban's memory will not be destroyed, but if my poem has any power, his laudable merit will spread far and wide across the earth. I am confident that there will be a time when religious men, Christians, will come to Britain to preach to the pagans. When they come, they will find God's great deeds confirmed by books in this manner; they will read them and make them widely known.[126]

On one level, this is merely a particularly clever way of using referentiality, "real" topographical features, for authentication. A twelfth-century St. Albans reader would be reassured by the reference to the physical realities he or she is familiar with: clearly, despite the temporal distance, this ancient witness shares the same spatial reality as the reader, and since he gets geographical details right, he can presumably be trusted on other matters. There is also a

Fig. 4. *Inventio* of St. Amphibalus. From Matthew Paris's *Chronica Majora*, Corpus Christi College Cambridge Ms. 26, f. 135 v. Photograph provided by the Conway Library, Courtauld Institute of Art. Reproduced by permission of the Master and Fellows of Corpus Christi College, Cambridge, and the Conway Library.

strong "allegorical" element: William once again "sanctifies" the landscape by associating it, feature for feature, with the history of its two principal saints.

Both the authenticating and the allegorizing use of landscape are neatly recaptured in a later St. Albans account of the *inventio* of Amphibalus (fig. 4), first recorded by Roger Wendover (early thirteenth century), then elaborated by Matthew Paris (after 1235).[127] One night in 1177, St. Alban appears to Robert Mercer, a citizen of St. Albans, inviting him to a stroll to St. Amphibalus's grave, which at the time had been completely forgotten. Robert, of course, marks the site pointed out to him, and on the next day informs the monks of St. Albans. Matthew Paris adds some important details to Roger's short account. Unlike the rather spooky story of the *inventio* of the Holy Lance, by which this little episode may well be inspired,[128] the encounter between Alban and Robert Mercer is entirely friendly:

> Obiter colloquebantur, ut solet amicus cum amico co-itinerante, tum de moeniis dirutae civitatis, tum de amne diminuto, tum de strata communi adjacente civitate. . . . Cum autem pervenissent ad medium itineris,

ubi duo arbores in medio stratae fuerant, ait martyr: "Hucusque duxi magistrum meum beatum Amphibalum, cum ultimo in hac vita mundiali lacrimabiliter colloquebamur, tunc ab invicem recessuri."

On the way they conversed, like two friends traveling together, now about the walls of the destroyed city, now about the river that had shrunk so much in size, now about the public street that passed by the city. . . . When they arrived at the halfway mark of their journey, where there were two trees in the middle of the road, the martyr said, "Until here I accompanied my teacher, the blessed Amphibalus, when we tearfully spoke to each other for the last time in this life on earth, as we were about to part."[129]

It is a beautiful touch that the third-century saint and the twelfth-century citizen make this trip in such chummy familiarity: the landscape and the ancient city are a reality that they share across the centuries. Yet the passage of time is also marked, in St. Alban's observations on the changes that have taken place since his own time. The saint casually authenticates his own legend by tying it to landmarks familiar to thirteenth-century readers, by laying it out on the map of their immediate vicinity. Conversely, he sanctifies the landscape by giving it such associations. In fact, he "sanctifies" it so much that at one point the two of them have to get off the road and hide in order not to frighten other travelers: when St. Alban walks on it, the road itself glitters and sparkles.[130] Thus, in both Matthew's and William's stories, references to landscape and topographical features serve a double purpose: they tie the narrative to outside reality, and, via that outside reality, to a higher level of reality, a sacred meaning that is available for all physical reality if one knows how to read it.

At the same time, however, the imagery seems to be working on a different level. William is depicting not only the past and present of his monastery, but also his own work of mediating between them; in other words, the narrative becomes self-referential. William's situation is somewhat analogous to the unnamed pagan's—but also quite different in important ways. Like the narrator, he is cut off from the reality he is trying to describe; he is only thinly connected to it through a series of unstable, almost lost oral and written sources. Like the narrator, he is engaged in a precarious rescue operation: both must salvage this highly endangered tradition before it sinks into oblivion forever. Unlike William, however, the pagan narrator is in the privileged position of still being able to read it in the ruins, in the landscape. This writing is lost to William; the only way he can recapture it is by projecting an ideally positioned alter ego, who is partly uninvolved, partly involved (or becoming involved) in the events he is describing; who is removed in time from his subject, but who, unlike William, is just barely still part of the same historical era.

William is dramatizing the situation of the twelfth-century historian, who is at a threshold between largely oral and largely written modes of historical tradition and therefore more acutely aware than his colleagues at most other times of the precariousness of historical transmission. William conveys a sense of loss frequently articulated in similar hagiographical and historiographical texts: the complaints about forgotten shrines, obliterated inscriptions, and lost records are more than just clumsy excuses for a lack of tangible evidence. At the same time, William's nostalgia, the desire for more direct access to the historical past, is far from simplistic. He does not, after all, imagine a historian figure with unlimited access to the truth. There are no visions, no divine revelations, not even a full, unimpeachable written account: the narrator is piecing the story together as it is about to fade from physical existence. In that sense, too, William's use of the traditional "Schriftauffindung"[131] is unusual. When Geoffrey finds a book "britannici sermonis," that source, though provocative in itself, is not further problematized; although Geoffrey unsettles our faith in his accuracy in other ways, there is no attempt to portray the "liber uetustissimus" as unstable or doubtful in itself. William's "invented" source, however, mirrors his own uncertain and even painful process of investigation. The imagined author, too, experiences nostalgia and loss; he, too, feels the separation between himself and his subject. On the other hand, William can reciprocate, as it were, for the services rendered by his "source": the pagan narrator's greatest sorrow is that he cannot speak out, that he must keep his knowledge hidden, even as he writes it down. William is able to bring the old story to light and finally to provide the narrator with the readership he anticipated so long ago. This, of course, is another quite plausible image of what a historian does: to make the sources speak, to lend a voice to silent witnesses long dead.

The search for the saint — or, rather, in this case, the search for the saint's story — has become a vehicle for a quite different concern: the historian's access to the past. This is where the *inventio* imagery becomes almost indistinguishable from the "Schriftauffindung," the source fiction that consists in the finding of an old book. In fact, William's pagan narrator suggests the equation. Both the saint's body and the book are hidden for posterity to find; and the narrator closes with a double prophecy: both his book and the body will be discovered.[132]

This, it seems to me, is a use of imagery quite different from allegory. It has become a "poetic emblem," a "mirror in the text,"[133] which imagines the origin of the historical narrative itself.[134] Dällenbach recognizes that such "meta-phors of origin" occur in medieval texts, but suggests that their use of such source fictions is different from that of modern texts. The medieval found source, according to Dällenbach, is presented as absolutely authoritative, not open to question or doubt; that, in fact, is its raison d'être. It expresses the Middle Ages' confident "onto-theology," whereas its modern counterpart is more likely to position the reader in a hall of mirrors, an ironic play with in-finite regress.[135] Given the intrinsic "truth value" of relics, *inventiones* would seem to bear out Dällenbach's thesis—but only up to a point. Even a text like the *passio* of Saints Alban and Amphibalus is capable of shaking its own absolute foundations; I shall suggest in subsequent chapters that more fully literary historical narratives go much further in the direction of "affirm[ing] that they alone anticipate and succeed themselves"; Dällenbach in fact sug-gests this possibility for a medieval text in his analysis of *St. Alexis*.[136]

To the extent that the narrative concerns its own intellectual processes, it cannot be verified or falsified outside itself. It is self-referential, coincides with itself. Thus, on that level, the whole question of reference, of truth, of a "back-ing" for the narrative in physical or metaphysical reality is suspended. At that level, the narrative is self-consciously textual, and it derives its meaning from this. To that extent, too, the spatial setting of the narrative and its movements in space (searches, digs, etc.) relinquish some of their primary reference, with-out, of course, ever giving it up: we are still to refer the ruins of Verulamium to the actual stone structures seen across the river Ver from the monastery of St. Albans, even though they have also become a metaphor for historical trans-mission and historical loss. But the narrative still works even if we are not con-scious of such a reference. The spatial references, then, are "pulled inside" the narrative, to serve the internal needs of the text; there is, as Haidu has put it, a partial "withdrawal of the referential function," which permits "littérarité."[137]

In fact, such a mirror metaphor is potentially contained in the very notion of digging for a saint, which presupposes the "archaeological" assumption that by digging deep you can go backward in time—that the layers of soil reproduce, or signify, "layers" of time. Having said this, it is important to qualify the remark: this notion—the most natural metaphorical translation of *inventiones* for us—is not necessarily the first one that comes to mind in the twelfth century. The beginnings of archaeology are usually dated in the eighteenth century, with perhaps a few precocious Renaissance antecedents; conventional wisdom has it that the Middle Ages lacked the "sense of the past" needed for archaeology in the modern sense. Like most such general-izations, this is very largely true. Specifically, medieval historians have little understanding of, or patience for, what Partner has called the "metonymic" aspect of archaeology.[138] Modern archaeology is inferential; it constructs historical insights from small finds, and from many such finds it claims to piece together an entire past epoch, complete with social structures and a "daily life." This detective aspect largely accounts for archaeology's appeal as "nonfiction" reading matter for the general reader. In medieval texts, the diggers, whether real-life or textual, ideally find their past whole: a book or document, for instance, that contains the entire story, or a whole saint, if possible with an identifying inscription. Although partial relics are extremely common in real life, a find of anything less than a complete body is extremely rare in the narratives.[139] Also, in many cases, the identity of the saint is known beforehand and merely confirmed by what is found. Medieval diggers dig deductively, not inductively.

Not surprisingly, then, the primary metaphor *inventiones* suggest to medieval writers is not layers, strata, or depth, but "hidden" versus "revealed," "closed" versus "opened." Many relics, in fact, are said to have been purposely hidden, usually during a time of persecution. Both in English and above all in Continental *inventiones* this is most often associated with Viking or Norman pirate raids.[140] In William of St. Albans' *passio*, a Christian hides Amphibalus's body so that it may be found by later generations (see above at n. 127). In an unusual twist to the motif, Enimia, a French saint, has a vision of her own future *inventio* shortly before her death; so she hides herself or, more precisely, arranges for her grave to be mislabeled in order to deceive her greedy brother, who she knows will attempt to take her relics away.[141]

The imagery of revealing and opening, as we have already seen, is suggested by the *Revelatio Sancti Stephani*, with the saints' insistent demand that their tombs be opened. Goscelin, taking up the suggestion in his *inventio* of St. Yvo, elaborates the "aperire" theme into a rhapsodic Easter hymn, mixing images of opening with images of spring and resurrection:

Facta est autem haec ejus inventio anno Domini millesimo primo, regnante Rege Ethelredo, octavo Kalend. Maji mense Aprilis. Aprilis autem quasi aperilis ab aperiendo appellatur, cum coelum in aestivos soles clarius aperitur, et mundus in flores et foetus animatur; et tunc omnis ager, tunc omnis parturit arbor; tunc frondent silvae, tunc formosissimus annus, tunc vireta floribus, et volatilia cantibus, et omnia rerum gaudia Christi resurrectioni et Paschalibus diebus resultant: tali namque tempore decuit haec beata pignora reperiri, quae in aeternam gloriam novo coelo et nova terra debent resuscitari.

His *inventio* took place in the year 1001, in the reign of King Ethelred, on April 23. Aprilis, or "aperilis," is derived from *aperire*, "to open," when the sky opens up more brightly toward the summer sun, and the earth is enlivened with flowers and fruit; at that time every field, every tree gives birth; then the forests grow leaves, then the year is at its most beautiful; then plants break out in bloom, birds in song, and all things in joy over Christ's resurrection and the day of Easter: for it was fitting that at such a time the holy relics were discovered, which shall be resurrected to heavenly glory with a new heaven and a new earth.[142]

This imagery, too, obviously "mirrors the text," and the writers often make the parallel quite explicit: the text, like the *inventio* itself, opens up and makes manifest something that was previously hidden. Formulaic explanations for writing an *inventio*, like "ne lateret posteris" (lest it be hidden from posterity), are extremely common. But the way this particular "mirror" portrays the historian's work is quite different from the view suggested by digging metaphors. It helps theologize the text, as it were, by turning it into a quasi-sacred text about a "revealed" event, if not a revealed text itself. It puts the text directly into the service of God's salvific plan: it is God (or the saint) who has decided that the relics should be revealed at this point; the narrative, if portrayed in this way, is chiefly an instrument to accomplish this end. In terms of the balance I suggested earlier, of divine providence and human ingenuity, under this model the accent is clearly on providence. This mirror, then, points chiefly in the direction of allegorical truth, as indeed Goscelin's device of etymologizing "Aprilis" suggests: like most medieval etymology, it serves as an allegorical instrument, emphasizing the way in which Yvo's *inventio* fits not only the liturgical calendar but salvation history as well.[143]

But while "archaeological" notions are most often latent, they are there nevertheless. They can be seen most clearly when a dig brings to light not only a saint, but also physical evidence that aids in his or her identification, evidence that must be interpreted inductively. In the *inventio* of St. Milburga, the foundations of the earliest monastic establishment at Wenlock are rediscovered as well. This not only makes the *inventio* and the identification of the saint more plausible, but also, conversely, stresses her intimate connection with the monastery's history. Part of the point of "inventing" Milburga is to reestablish continuity with the almost forgotten early monastery, and this is accomplished symbolically by finding its foundations and the saint with the foundations. Similarly, the *inventio* of the Nigra Crux at Abingdon brings to light several other objects, from which the chronicler infers that the diggers have hit upon the earliest settlement in the time of Lucius—which, as he has just told us, was when the monastery was first founded.[144]

Once again, it is Matthew Paris who brings the motif to perfection. In the *Gesta Abbatum*, he tells of two digs in the ruins of Verulamium, both in the reign of abbots about whom he has little else to report. (He does not give dates, but we must be approximately in the tenth century.) The second of these is a "Schriftauffindung," the discovery of a *Vita* of St. Alban in a mysterious ancient language and in mysterious ancient lettering. The book is perfectly preserved, just like the body of a saint: "Asseres querni, ligamina serica, pristinam in magna parte fortitudinem et decorem retinuerunt [The oak boards and silk bands retained for the most part their original strength and beauty]."[145] A translator is finally found, a very old priest named Unwona; but once he has completed his translation, the book—"quod mirum est dictu"—disintegrates.

While this is unmistakably a medieval *inventio*, with a book substituted for the saint, Matthew's first digging episode comes surprisingly close to the modern concept of archaeology. Abbot Ealdred, having studied "antiquas scripturas" about Verulamium, proceeds to dig there, in part to destroy hiding places for robbers, prostitutes, and even a dragon, and in part to find building materials for a new church; but the dig brings to light other objects, which are viewed "not without interest" (non sine admiratione). Parts of ships, rusty anchors, and shells are found; this proves that there must indeed have been a major waterway there, as the legend of St. Alban suggests. This discovery "unearths" local memories as well: "Unde nomina locis ubi talia reperunt incolae, haec videntes, vel imposuerunt, vel retulerunt se a veteribus relata meminisse: utpote, Oistrehulle, Selleford, et Ancrepol, Fishpol—nomen vivarii regii ex reliquiis aquae diminutae [When they saw this, the locals either gave names to the places where these things had been found, or else remembered having been told these names by their elders: such as Oysterhill, Shellford, and Anchorpool, Fishpool—the name of the royal fishpond made from the remainder of the shrunken waters]."[146]

All these archaeological discoveries do, of course, serve as authenticating devices, often on very specific points (e.g., in the case of Matthew Paris, as a proof that there used to be significantly more water in the river, as Bede's account suggests). But they also show an awareness on the part of the writers of "digging up the past," and they mirror the historian's activity. Again, one can look to Matthew Paris for a particularly striking illustration of the process. In the *Gesta Abbatum* Matthew relates that in the twelfth century, Alban's relics were once again translated. When the sarcophagus was opened, there was a gold circlet around the skull of the saint, which King Offa had put there when he found the relics. It was inscribed, "Hoc est caput Sancti Albani Anglorum protomartyris." Unfortunately, somebody took this circlet and destroyed it — with the best of intentions, of course: the new shrine was still being decorated, and the good monk thought that the gold could be melted down and recycled to the greater glory of the martyr. Needless to say, the abbot was furious. But, says Matthew, a new circlet was made and substituted for the old one.[147] This story, on the one hand, pretty much encapsulates the medieval attitude toward forgery of documents and historical evidence, as outlined by Fuhrmann and Schreiner.[148] By modern standards, the new circlet is all but useless: it no longer fulfills the requirements of historical evidence. For Matthew, the loss of Offa's circlet is grave, but not irreparable. If the original evidence is lost, you can and should replace it. If you *know* that you are telling the truth, and that at some point there was evidence for it, it is not a lie to recreate the evidence. At the same time, the anecdote is a perfect image for what historians like Matthew do when they try to assemble the history and documents of their houses. In fact, the story is so explicit that one might suspect Matthew of drawing attention to what he is doing; in other words, he seems to be conscious of the story as a metaphoric expression of his work as an imaginative historian.

Inventiones, then, refer and make their truth claims in multiple, overlapping and intersecting ways. They undeniably refer to real (or supposedly real) people, shrines, dates, and above all, places. Competent readers of bona fide *inventiones* could reasonably go out and check up on the story by, for instance, verifying that there are ruins of a Roman city near St. Albans and that there is a holy well on top of a hill there; or they could demand to see the actual relics (as pilgrims frequently did).[149] They could check the account against Bede or other historical sources, to see whether there was a St. Alban and a St. Amphibalus, or against the *Liber Eliensis*, to find that its story about the current whereabouts of Alban's relics is incompatible with the version propagated by St. Albans.[150] Such actions would reasonably substantiate or falsify those texts, and that means that part of an *inventio*'s truth claim is historically referential. To that extent, and to that extent only, factually dubious *inventiones* can be (and were) said to be fraudulent.

Side by side with that outside reference, *inventiones* also refer "upward," as it were, to an accepted, standard type of *inventio*. That is, they base their truth claim in part on their conformity to a quasi-canonical textual model; in that respect, all *inventiones sanctorum*, to adapt Gregory of Tours, merge into a single *Inventio Sanctorum*.[151] Small to medium-sized discrepancies between this "upward," Christian-Platonic reference and the "downward" reference to the specific givens of empirical reality were largely tolerated, just as there was a remarkable tolerance for forged documents and charters as long as they reflected a historical truth agreed upon by the textual community they served. This, evidently, is close to what I called "allegorical" reference in the introduction — in the eyes of many medievalists the absolutely predominant, if not the only, concept of textual truth available to the Christian Middle Ages.[152] It is, I hope, becoming clear from my discussion that I regard this model as far less exclusive and pervasive than those scholars do.

Finally, despite their relatively unassuming and prosaic functionality, *inventiones* have self-reference, mirror themselves: they perform, on a different level, the actions they describe. They seek and find, unearth and open up the historical past, and in that sense describe their own function; they both describe and *are* the originary moment of their textual communities' self-understanding. To that extent, their truth claim rests in themselves; and to that extent, they are "textual" in the full sense in which that term is understood by most modern critics. In the *inventiones*, that kind of reference is sometimes present only in traces, sometimes fully developed, as in William's *passio* of Saints Alban and Amphibalus. Where it is present, it is perhaps best understood as an aid to allegorical reference: by throwing us back on the text's own makeup, origin, and logic, it lures us away from a referential reading and, perhaps, opens us up to the allegorical meaning. But, as the following chapters will show, these gestures toward self-reference prepare the way for a further literarization of reference, and therefore of the texts they appear in: a literarization that occurs at the expense of, and largely comes to replace, the "allegorical" level, while playing games with the referential level.

✳ 2 ✳

Gaainable Tere

Foundations, Conquests, and Symbolic

Appropriations of Space and Time

he title phrase, "gaainable tere," is borrowed from Denis
Piramus's *Vie Seint Edmund le Rei*, a late-twelfth-century
Anglo-Norman saint's life which will be examined later in
this chapter. "Gaainable tere" conveniently sums up several
of the aspects of *tere*, or territory, that this chapter is concerned with.[1] The phrase has a precise technical meaning: it means "arable
land," land that can be cultivated and turned to profit.[2] But given the contexts in which "gaainable" appears, one is tempted to hear a trace of another
meaning of "gaagner" — "to win, to acquire" — in the phrase as well: the word
occurs three times in the *Vie Seint Edmund*, each time as someone is conquering a land or taking possession of it. In addition, Denis consistently uses
"gaainable," side by side with more affective terms, in describing the richness, sweetness, and delightfulness of the land: "Le pais trovent delitable /
E la tere bien gaainable"; or, "Riche pais e gaainable / E bon e douz e delitable."[3]
These juxtapositions give the word overtones of "lovely, attractive, desirable."
Therefore, we may read "gaainable tere" not only as "arable land" but also
as "available, conquerable" and "desirable" or "coveted" land, a reading that
has ample support in the way the topos is deployed in Denis's poem and the
other texts considered in this chapter: narratives of conquest and settlement,
of surveying, circumambulating, and taking possession of a territory.

Like the rhetoric surrounding *inventiones*, the *gaainable tere* topos has had
remarkable staying power; to modern readers, it is eerily reminiscent of the
conquest rhetoric associated with the early modern "age of discoveries" or
later colonialism.[4] In short, it seems to come up naturally whenever there is a

mood of expansion, conquest, or colonization, and we need not look far for such a cultural context in twelfth-century Britain. The Norman conquest of England, while receding slowly into the historical background, is still a fresh memory, and its aftermath continues to affect people's lives. In the outlying, Celtic areas of the British Isles, especially in Wales, the Norman takeover has been slower and less complete: throughout the twelfth century, these areas are being not so much conquered as infiltrated, annexed, and colonized by Anglo-Norman aristocrats and ecclesiastics.[5] In the border areas in particular, the process was most likely experienced by those affected by it as a slow conquest, not always military or even openly hostile, but characterized by expansionism, small-scale political jockeying and intense competition for land and influence. Since land, its protection, expansion, and appropriation, is always a concern in twelfth-century English life, it is not surprising that it should play an important role in a variety of historical narratives and that it should also serve as a focus for metaphorical activity in the texts.

Like *inventiones*, too, the *gaainable tere* motif has a wide range of referential modes, from the literal and practical to the metaphorical, self-referential, and often playful. It is this logical progression that this chapter attempts to trace. Chronology is not my primary concern: some texts discussed early in the chapter are chronologically later than Geoffrey of Monmouth, who appears later in the discussion, and in some cases even borrow from him. What interests me is the deployment of similar narrative modes, topoi, and vocabularies in different poetic contexts, ranging from the strictly referential and "straightforward" to the highly self-conscious and literary. As we have seen before, these modes are neither mutually exclusive nor even strictly demarcated; it is more helpful to think of a sliding scale than of clear boundaries. The metaphorical potential of *gaainable tere* is always available, whether or not it is exploited or fully articulated in a given context. On the simplest level, *gaainable tere* narratives fulfill well-defined, utilitarian functions within local historiography: they are foundation stories, origin myths; yet even in such straightforward narratives, the metaphorical potential of the motifs is more or less fully realized. After considering a number of historically referential monastic foundation narratives, with Walter Map's parodic version as an illuminating borderline case, I will examine similar imagery and language in more self-consciously literary texts, where their significance is more clearly metaphorical: Geoffrey of Monmouth's *History of the Kings of Britain* and a number of historicizing narratives inspired by Geoffrey.

What unites the origin stories discussed in this and the previous chapter is their concern with the land as a substratum for any history, with the relationship of historical events and agents to the territory they inhabit. That relationship—the way, to take up Southern's image again, in which the narrative is "anchored in the countryside"—in large part defines the type of historical narrative appropriate to the situation. *Inventiones* stress local continuity, antiquity, the resumption of a broken tradition; *gaainable tere* stories tell of new beginnings, of appropriation of territory and expansions into new lands. Nonetheless, there are substantial affinities, even some overlap, between these two types of origin legends. In fact, it is frequently in the writer's interest to blur the distinction between them. As several of the examples in chapter 1 showed, some monasteries that do not have an *inventio* proper fashion narratives that approximate an *inventio*. New foundations, naturally, are particularly likely to be in that position: there is no question of showing the ancient origins, the continuity of the foundation. But there is nonetheless a desire to show that the new foundation is divinely sanctioned, that it is providential; motifs adapted from the *inventio* model can be helpful in establishing such a legitimization.[6] Battle Abbey, briefly discussed in the previous chapter, is a good example. William chooses the site for his new abbey for a reason that appears quite secular: it symbolizes his military victory, his conquest. But the choice is sanctioned after the fact—and against the odds—by the unexpected find of building stones. Thus the digging motif, complete with a vision, is displaced, as it were: no saint is found—no evidence of past sanctity or a previous founder—but the materials for the abbey itself are. Although Battle Abbey is a brand-new foundation, motivated by a recent event, the author of the chronicle manages to smuggle the temporal element, even the continuity, into his narrative: the stones are said to have been there "forever," "ab euo," waiting only for William the Conqueror.[7]

The most famous creators in the twelfth century of new foundations, and new foundation stories, are the Cistercians. Going out, looking for a site, finding the right location, settling and cultivating the land are part of the Cistercian ideal from the beginning: a narrative of Exodus and Promised Land, though with the difference that the land, although fruitful and suitable for farming, is as yet uncultivated, lonely, and unpromising. A concise version of this story is given in the *Exordium Parvum*, one of the earliest Cistercian documents:

> De egressu cisterciensium monachorum de Molismo, et de
> adventu ipsorum ad Cistercium, et de monasterio quod
> inceperunt. III.
> . . . Qui locus in episcopatu Cabilonensi situs, et pro nemoris spi-

narumque tunc temporis opacitate accessui hominum insolitus, a solis
inhabitabatur feris. Ad quem viri Dei venientes, locumque illum religioni
quam animo iamiamque conceperant, et propter quam illuc advenerant,
tanto habiliorem, quanto saecularibus despicabiliorem et inaccessibilem
intelligentes: nemoris et spinarum densitate praecisa ac remota, monas-
terium ibidem voluntate Cabilonensis episcopi, et consensu illius cujus
ipse locus erat, construere coeperunt.

> The departure of the Cistercian monks from Molême, and their
> arrival at Cîteaux, and the monastery they started there.
> ... This place is situated in the see of Chalon, and, because of the density
> of its woods and thorns, it was at that time unfrequented by humans, in-
> habited only by wild beasts. The men of God understood that the more
> worthless and inaccessible the place was to worldly people, the more
> suitable it was for the religious life they had envisioned and for which
> they had come; so, on their arrival, they cut and removed the woods and
> brambles, and, with the consent of the bishop and the owner of the land,
> they began to build a monastery there.[8]

This story is repeated in all kinds of variations in many Cistercian foundation
stories; it becomes part of the order's self-definition. Being Cistercian *means*
going to "horrible places," settling them, making them habitable, reclaiming
land and cultivating it: "locum habitabilem ex inhabitabili reddiderunt [they
made a habitable place out of an uninhabitable one]."[9] The foundation narrative becomes a "text" for the Cistercians in the sense Brian Stock has defined
it: a document that informs and organizes the lives of a "textual community."
The Cistercians are, in fact, one of Stock's prime examples of a movement
"based on texts, which played a predominant role in the internal and external relationships of the members."[10]

Two examples will serve to familiarize us further with the vocabulary and
rhetorical gestures of the Cistercian "text" and many other foundation stories.
In England, the "northern revival" of the mid- and late twelfth century inspired many new foundations and foundation narratives, predominantly but
not exclusively Cistercian.[11] One of those is the "Fundacio Abbathie de Kyrke-
stall," possibly by Hugh de Kirkstall.[12] During the reign of King Stephen,
Prior Alexander of Fountains Abbey sets out with twelve monks (a typical
number) and ten lay brothers to found a new house. Their first foundation,
on land granted by a local nobleman, is not successful, partly because of a
series of bad crops, partly because the monks antagonized the locals early

on: they razed the parish church, "licet minus consulte [it may be with some want of consideration]," since the lay parishioners "erant molesti monasterio et fratribus ibidem commorantibus [became a nuisance to the monastery and the brethren there residing]."[13] The new location that the abbot selects after a few years of bad luck is described as a "locus amoenus" and promised land. The abbot travels in search of a new site and finds it in the wooded, shaded valley of Airedale. In contrast to other foundation narratives, there is no mention of supernatural guidance in the abbot's choice, but the motif is not absent, merely shifted: the hermits he finds already settled in the valley report that they were directed there by the Virgin Mary. Their leader explains, in an interesting mix of biblical and Virgilian echoes, the latter possibly mediated by Geoffrey of Monmouth:

> Nam cum essem in terra natiuitatis mee facta est ad me vox per somp-num tercio dicens, Surge Seleth et vade in prouinciam eboracensem et quere diligenter in valle que vocatur Aierdale locum quendam qui dici-tur Kirkestal. Ibi enim preuidebis habitacionem futuram fratribus ad seruiendum filio meo.

> For when I was in the land of my birth, a voice came to me in my sleep, saying thrice, "Arise, Seleth, and go into the province of York, and seek diligently in the valley which is called Airedale for a certain spot named Kirkstall. For there wilt thou provide a habitation which shall be for the brethren for serving my Son."[14]

The hermit's narrative arouses the new abbot's interest:

> Audiens hec abbas cogitare secum cepit de situ loci et circumstantijs eius, de vallis amenitate et aqua ibidem preterfluente, de siluis adiacenti-bus ad fabricas erigendas. Et visum est ei quod locus satis amenus est et oportunus ad abbathiam inibi construendam.

> Upon hearing these things the abbot began to ponder in his mind concerning the site of the place and its conditions, the pleasant character of the valley and the river there flowing past, and the woods adjacent as being suitable for the erection of workshops. And it seemed to him that the place was fair enough and fit for building an abbey upon it.[15]

He obtains permission from the local lord, buys out those hermits who do not choose to become Cistercians ("accepta pecunia suum ei ius cesserunt et habitacionem [they took money and ceded to him their right and habitation]")[16] and proceeds to build Kirkstall Abbey. The monks then do what Cistercians are supposed to do: "locum habitabilem ex inhabitabili reddunt"; they cultivate the place and make it their own:

> Anno incarnacionis dominice M° C° quinquagesimo ij . . . venit conuentus monachorum de sede prima iam in grangiam redacta ad locum qui nunc Kirkestal nominatur locum nemorosum et frugibus infecundum, locum bonis fere destitutum preter ligna et lapides et vallem amenam cum aqua fluminis que vallis medium preterfluebat. . . . Arrepto igitur ferro succiderunt siluas et noualia sibi nouantes cum filijs Effraym fecerunt sibi locum ad habitandum et spineta condensa ad cultum redigentes auaram glebam letis frugibus luxuriare cogebant. Et vidit dominus labores eorum et benedixit eis et multiplicati sunt in breui numero fratrum et nomine possessionum.

> In the year of our Lord's Incarnation, 1152 . . . came the convent of monks from their first seat (now reduced to a grange) to the place which is now called Kirkstall; a place covered with woods and unproductive of crops, a place well nigh destitute of good things save timber and stone and a pleasant valley with the water of a river which flowed down its centre. . . . So taking their axe in hand they felled the woods and broke up their fallow ground; like the sons of Ephraim [Joshuah 17:14–18] they made unto themselves a place for a habitation, and reducing the thick bush to cultivation brought the niggard soil to grow rich with flourishing crops. And the Lord saw their labours and blessed them, and they were multiplied in a short while in the number of brethren and the tale of their possessions.[17]

The second exhibit is a particularly charming foundation story, though not a Cistercian one: the foundation of the Benedictine monastery of Selby.[18] Selby was founded in 1069 by William the Conqueror, a fact that the *Historia* plays down for the sake of a Virgilian — and biblical — adventure story.[19] (The Abraham parallel is explicit [p. 6]; the Aeneas parallel is not.) The monastery of Selby was begun by Benedict, a monk from Auxerre; this gives the author an opportunity to have the new settler arrive by ship. Benedict is instructed by St. Germain in a vision to sail to a place named Selby and found a new monastery there. By the saint's explicit permission, he takes a Germain relic from Auxerre for the new foundation. First, misled by well-meaning Englishmen, he ends up in Salisbury, where he is well received; but he cannot find the place where he is supposed to found the monastery. St. Germain appears to him again and chides him for his mistake: "non dixi tibi Salesbyriam, sed vt requireres Selebeiam, quod nomen beatus Germanus septus syllabarum producendo repetens: verum, inquit, ne tibi rursus elapso loci nomine error auertat a peruio, iam tibi locum ipsum ostendam ['I didn't say Salisbury, I told you to look for Selby' — and Blessed Germanus repeated that name by pronouncing each syllable separately: 'but,' he said, 'lest the name slip your memory again and you be led astray again, I shall show you the place']." The saint shows Benedict the promised land in a vision, "siue in corpore, siue extra corpus, nescio, Deus scit [whether in the body or out of the body, I cannot tell, God knows]."[20] Benedict and some companions finally find the place, erect a cross there, and build a hut. Then Benedict takes possession of his new home in a passage that merits an extended quotation:

> Loci deinde situm vniuersum vsquequaque Benedictus explorando perlustrans, territorium, confinia, praediorumque et possessionum metas et terminos perambulans, quid cuiuis adiaceret dominio diligenter addidicit, vidensque, locum amoenissimum tam frequenti nemore consitum, tam abundanti diuersoque flumine coronatum, tanquam terrenam quendam Paradisum, illum amplexatus, non minus de illius vtili opportunitate, quam ex inuentione celeri congaudebat.

> Then, exploring and surveying the entire site from all sides, walking around the entire territory and all borderlines, and the limits and boundary stones of all estates and possessions, Benedict learned carefully what bordered on each property. He saw that the place was lovely, planted with dense woods and surrounded by abundant rivers, like a terrestrial paradise; he embraced [or, walked around; or, occupied] it, rejoicing no less in the usefulness and fitness of the place than in its speedy discovery.

The location is described: Selby is on the river Ouse, about ten miles from York; it is surrounded by forests. In fact, the site is graced with three resources, "quae amoeno loco multum decoris conferunt, plus tamen vtilitatis impendunt [which confer much beauty on the lovely place, but provide even more utility]": besides the forests and the water — several rivers, but also "lakes and ponds which abound in fish"; the rivers, too, abound in freshwater fish — there is stone, "lapidis . . . insignissimi copia ad omnem structuram nobilissimi, ad omnem caelaturam aptissimi [a great quantity of high-quality stone, most excellent for any kind of building, most suitable for any kind of sculpture]."[21] One aim of the narrative is presumably to stress that the abbey's original possessions and their exact boundaries are well established and well remembered; but this account colors the most prosaic practical motions of taking possession of a new site with an affective, even jubilant, tone; the word "amplexatus" captures both aspects very neatly. (It even appears in the heading for this chapter in the initial "capitula": "Quam gaudenter locum illum amplexatus sit et de ipsius loci situ [How joyously he took possession of the place, and of its location].")[22] Not surprisingly, a narrative model with such strong and immediate affective possibilities lends itself to a literarization not unlike that of the *inventiones*.

Although Walter Map will be discussed more fully in chapter 3, it is useful at this point to glance briefly at his anti-Cistercian diatribe, since parodies and playful variations are a good indication that a textual model is firmly established as a "genre" or a set piece, that its images and conventions are easily recognized by contemporary readers. The story of Cistercian settlement is told in essentially the same form by modern as well as medieval historians: the central elements of finding, appropriating, and cultivating "horrible places" are present in all accounts.[23] But modern historians, as well as medieval critics of the Cistercian order, also stress that the ideal expressed in the narratives did not necessarily correspond to reality. Cistercian settlements were often not all that remote or "horrible," and in fact not always uninhabited; one of the major complaints about Cistercian foundations was that they frequently displaced the local population.[24] Medieval Cistercian texts, of course, tend to pass over this problem, although a text like the Kirkstall narrative comes surprisingly close to acknowledging it. Their critics are less reticent. *Distinctio* 1 of Walter's *De Nugis Curialium* contains what may originally have been a separate pamphlet, entitled "Incidencia magistri Gauteri Mahap de monachia [A Digression of Master Walter Map on Monkery]."[25] In a vicious parody, Walter Map, not a friend of the Cistercian order (see also chapter 3), systematically perverts all the essential elements of the Cistercian foundation narrative. He brings the common accusation—partly confirmed by modern historians—that the Cistercians do not find but create their wilderness by driving people off the land, causing unrelieved misery:

> et quia parrochianos regere non habent secundum regulam, eradicant uillas, ecclesias parrochianos eiciunt euertunt, altaria deicere non abhorrent et ad uiam uomeris omnia complanare, ut si uideas que uideras, dicere possis "Nunc seges est ubi Troia fuit." Et, ut soli sint, solitudinem faciunt.

And because their rule does not allow them to govern parishioners, they proceed to raze villages, they overthrow churches, and turn out parishioners, not scrupling to cast down the altars and level everything before the ploughshare, so that if you looked on a place that you knew previously, you could say, "And grass now grows where Troy once stood." As I say, they make a solitude that they may be solitary.[26]

In the last section of the tract, Walter does a Cistercian foundation story in reverse: his Cistercians (he calls them "Hebrews," alluding to their own perception that they alone are the "children of light," as opposed to the "Egyptians," i.e., everybody else) make uninhabitable places out of habitable ones. Not only do they move boundary trees and forge charters to gain land; in one incident, Walter charges, they destroyed a neighbor's field with salt to coerce him into selling it—so much for making barren land bear fruit. In another case, they do just that: they manure a field that does not belong to them and then adduce their own expenditure of time and labor to argue that the field must be theirs—a neat twist to the narrative convention by which settlers earn a right to a place by cultivating it.[27] In the most outrageous story, the "Hebrews" hire thugs to kill a recalcitrant neighbor who will not move and then force his family to flee. In the few days it takes the victim's wife to return with a band of kinsmen, they have destroyed every trace of human habitation on the neighbor's estate: "et ubi fuerant edificia, sepes et arbores magne, planissimum inuenit et bene aratum campum, et nullam rei humane apparenciam [and where they knew there were buildings, enclosures, and old trees, they found an absolutely level, well-ploughed field, no appearance of human occupation]."[28] The only evidence that gives away the perpetrators is the large quantity of freshly cut wood that is neatly stacked in the monastery's precinct.

Walter's sharp criticism, I think, is only in part motivated by the social injustice he observed. The Cistercians are not the only order he accuses of expansionism; in his lengthy overview of new religious movements, one of his chief criteria for judging an order is whether or not it will stay within its original boundaries, both literally and figuratively. He praises the order of Grandmont for stipulating specifically that they may never exceed their original land grant: "minorem facere licet, maiorem non [they may make it smaller, but not larger]."[29] He approves of the Carthusians in principle, but after describing the successful foundation of the original house, he blasts Saint-Jean de Maurienne, a daughter house, which has turned into an ugly parody of the "mother":

que cupiditatis instinctu diabolum sequens, amenitate pascorum et uber-
tate notata, censum ex quibuscunque potuit auarissime collegit . . .
locuplex pessimi proposti pruritus implere non desistit; inuasit uicinos
terminos. . . . Sed impinguata dilatata recalcitrauit. Recessit, et sibi simi-
lem matrem domum Cisterciensem aduocauit, que sibi uiscera cupidis-
sime caritatis aperuit, et in iniuriam prioris matris in specialem filiam
adoptauit.

But this, impelled by covetousness, has followed the devil. It is famed for
the pleasantness and fertility of its pastures; it has greedily got together
property from every possible quarter; . . . fertile in evil purpose, it has
not been slack to satisfy its itching. It has overstepped its neighbors'
bounds. . . . It has waxed fat and kicked, and now has broken away and
adopted a mother like to itself in the shape of the house of Cîteaux. She
has opened to it the bowels of a most covetous charity, and adopted it as
her own daughter, to the prejudice of the former mother.[30]

This litany of sins — which, not surprisingly, ends with the culprit going Cistercian — turns around all the images of abundance, fertility, and richness of
the foundation narratives. The final image, of Cîteaux "adopting" Saint-Jean,
is suggestively ambiguous: it is not clear whether the metaphor is one of eat-
ing or a kind of reverse (and perverse) birth.

The perverted birth image is fitting because Walter is worried, above all,
about the proliferation of new observances and, for that matter, about the
proliferation of almost anything else. As we shall see, Walter tends to feel
encroached upon: where other writers discussed in this chapter are expan-
sionists and conquerors, Walter wants to contain the world around him and
guard what space he has. The first *distinctio* of *De Nugis* ends with a curious
anecdote about three hermits, a Frenchman, an Englishman, and an Irishman, and their respective disciplines. The story may be an afterthought to the
distinctio, as the editors suggest, but it is not irrelevant to what came before.
Of the three, we are told, the Frenchman is so perfect that his life cannot even
be described; the Irishman, the only one of the three we actually see, is a wild
man of the woods, barely human. The Englishman — "sed angelicus" — represents the Golden Mean. He wears a seven-foot-long chain around his ankle,
and he carries a stake and a hammer. Every Saturday he moves camp, literally
fixing his radius for the week to come: "ibi comedens quod repperit, sab-
bato castra mouet, non uagus sed loci querens amenitatem, non ubertatem,
non remotum ab aeris importunitate sinum; ubi uictus aliquid secus aquam
obuenerit, cum gaudio metatur [He eats what he finds there, and moves his

camp on the Saturday, not at random, but looking for a pleasant place, not specially fertile, nor yet for a nook sheltered from the weather; and, wherever he may find food in the neighbourhood of water, gratefully gathers]." [31] This anecdote, with its implicit moralization of "expansion" or "staying within bounds," suggests that Walter is not concerned solely with the literal level of the Cistercian narrative. In his hands, the topoi of containment or expansion, fruitfulness or barrenness, moderation or monstrous proliferation receive a metaphoric extension that turns them into images of the modern condition as Walter sees it. In an additional step, which will be more fully discussed in chapter 3, these same topoi turn into a metaphor for Walter's own situation and his task as a writer: he is attempting, with comic desperation, to manage the uncontrollable wealth of materials, stories, nuggets of wisdom that come his way—a losing battle.

The next group of historical and historicizing texts—Geoffrey of Monmouth's *Historia Regum Britanniae* and several vernacular narratives that depend on it—also employ *gaainable tere*, the imagery of expansion and appropriation. Although they do not share Walter's cynical humor, their use of the topos is conceptually not very different from Walter's: they, too, use the themes of wealth and plenty, conquest and expansion, and the settlers' shaky "rights" to their new territory in a way that goes beyond the historically referential and turns *gaainable tere* into a self-reflexive representation of the writers' own situation.

Geoffrey of Monmouth is very much the centerpiece, and even (chronologically speaking) the starting point of this chapter, for the theme of *gaainable tere*, in the wider sense used here, was first fully developed in his *Historia Regum Britanniae*. Geography, real and metaphoric, is an important element in Geoffrey's historiography, and the many uses of place names, topography, and space in the *Historia* form a resonant, coherent motif pattern that is a key to Geoffrey's poetics. It is not so much that he is interested in the actual map of Britain, in fixing the precise locations of events or tracing in detail the geographical movements of his characters. In the *Historia*, time and space form an imaginative synthesis (a chronotope, as Bakhtin would call it) that goes far beyond the referential. The image of "anchoring one's narrative in the countryside" fits no one better than Geoffrey. In the early part of the *History*, toponymical legends and stories of strange burial customs abound. The earliest history of Britain consists of successive divisions of the land, in each of which the parts are eponymically named: first Brutus and Corineus create Britain and Cornwall. In the generation after Brutus, the island of Britain is divided among his sons, and the three parts are named for them: Loegria for Locrinus, Kambria for Kamber, and Albania for Albanactus.[32] Thus the early generations that settle on the island define the map on which future history will happen. Even more intimately connected with the British topography are characters like Humber, Habren, or Leir, who drown in rivers, are buried in underwater chambers, or otherwise merge with the land, leaving their names behind in the form of toponyms as a lasting contribution to the British landscape. Leir's grave under the river becomes an annual meeting point for craftsmen to plan the year's projects, thus literally giving rise to activities aboveground.[33] Bladud, a magician-king who dies in an early attempt at aviation, "grounds" the narrative in yet another way: his sad end, in which he crashes on the temple of Apollo and is "in multa frusta contritus" (dashed in many pieces), comes between several episodes of fragmentation of the realm and right before the story of Leir's foolish division of his realm. By merging with the countryside in this particular way, Bladud not only parallels metaphorically what the other kings have done, but also provides a link back to the countryside where many other characters have already been metamorphosed into names and memories.[34] The overall effect of all the episodes is to create a "storied" landscape, a kind of spatial deployment of collective memory: the landscape becomes a substratum for the whole history, which is created by the characters who live on it — in fact, it consists of them — and at the same time underlies, supports, and brings forth their further activities.

On the other hand, Geoffrey also undermines this substratum. This is one of the most important metaphors in the central episode of Merlin's prophecies: Vortigern's tower turns out to be unstable because it is built above an underground pool, which in turn rests on a cave containing two dragons, asleep but always on the verge of awakening and fighting each other; the prophecy itself is full of images of terrain changing color or shape, shaking or melting.[35] Like everything Merlin says, these details must be decoded: it is, of course, the kingdom of Britain that is at risk of "shaking" or "melting"; it is not only the physical structure Vortigern is trying to build, but his power over the land that is precariously placed and indeed "undermined" by the constant threat of hostilities between the white and red dragons. Beyond these necessary translations into political reality, though, Merlin's apocalyptic images invite another reading: his sensationally obscure and vaguely menacing voice both supports and undermines the straightforward historical account presented in the rest of the *Historia*, gives it authority and at the same time threatens to explode the kind of referentiality one expects from a "history." At that point, then—and, though less spectacularly, elsewhere in the narrative—the text of the *Historia* reflects itself.

Like these images, the *gaainable tere* topos lends itself to self-reflexive metaphorization, complete or partial; it alludes self-consciously and ironically to Geoffrey's own poetic undertaking. This trick contributes significantly to the notorious difficulty of assessing Geoffrey's tone and purpose. Like Merlin, Geoffrey is a trickster; like Merlin's Britain, the *Historia* is somewhat unstable terrain.

Geoffrey develops *gaainable tere* out of an older tradition. In imitation of Orosius's geographical introduction, many early British historians like to begin their work with a "descriptio Britanniae," a brief topographical description and panegyric of Britain. The sixth-century historian Gildas as well as Bede writing in the eighth century and the ninth-century *Historia Britonum* commonly attributed to "Nennius" all follow this tradition, as does, for instance, Geoffrey's contemporary Henry of Huntingdon.[36] The function of the *descriptio* and its relationship to the work as a whole is different in each case. But certain distinctive features remain constant. All the *descriptiones*, including Geoffrey's, emphasize the beauty and, above all, the convenience and utility of the land, its suitability for farming, and its rich natural resources: "Quicquid mortalium usui congruit indeficienti fertilitate ministrat," says Geoffrey. (It provides in unfailing plenty everything that is suited to the use of human beings.)[37] In keeping with medieval notions of aesthetics, the panegyrists stress harmony, measure, balance. They have a predilection for clear-cut numbers: two (or three) major rivers; four (or five) nationalities; twenty-eight ("twice-ten and twice-four") major towns. Unstructured, untouched nature is not described, and the land seems unthinkable apart from its use and cultivation by humans.

What distinguishes the *Historia* from all previous instances of the topos is that Geoffrey integrates the *descriptio* of the desirable land into his historical narrative. In the *Historia*, the *descriptio* is no longer merely prefatory and no longer static. Geoffrey sets it in motion, as it were. Even as he unfolds the laudatory description, he inserts small diachronic movements and gestures toward narrative. The whole passage not only leads directly, seamlessly, into the narrative proper, but appears to launch and motivate it. Most important, the *descriptio* is recalled in various echoes and transformations as part of the narrative. These correspondences between auctorial, editorializing comment and the narrative proper create important parallels between the characters' actions (especially Brutus's) and the narrator's activity in arranging and commenting on his narrative.

Although Geoffrey culls his *descriptio* largely from Bede and Gildas, he changes its emphasis and function in an innovative way. He adopts the key concepts of his sources: plenitude (*fertilitas, fecundus, ubertas*) and suitability (*aptus, congruere, conuenire*). Like Gildas and Bede, he lists "perfect numbers" (three principal rivers, five nations), but he soon swerves from the course suggested by his sources. With the mention of "twice-ten and twice-four" cities, he suddenly leaves the synchronic plane, the map, as it were, and launches into narrative:

> Bis denis etiam bisque quaternis ciuitatibus olim decorata erat quarum quaedam dirutis meniis in desertis locis squalescunt quaedam uero adhuc integre templa sanctorum cum turribus perpulcra proceritate erectis continent in quibus religiosi cetus uirorum ac mulierum obsequium deo iuxta christianam traditionem prestant.

> In earlier times Britain was graced by twenty-eight cities. Some of these, in the depopulated areas, are now mouldering away, with their walls broken. Others remain whole and have in them the shrines of saints, with towers built up to a noble height, where [religious communities] of men and women offer praise to God according to the Christian tradition.[38]

This emphasis on historical change is a new element in the essentially synchronic tableau offered in Geoffrey's sources.

Similarly, his mention of the "five nations" that inhabit Britain (Normans, Britons, Saxons, Picts, and Scots) immediately gives rise to a narrative start that leads right into the history proper:

> Ex quibus britones olim ante ceteros a mari usque ad mare insederunt. donec ultione diuina propter ipsorum superbiam superueniente. pictis. & saxonibus cesserunt. Qualiter uero & unde applicuerunt. restat nunc parare ut in subsequentibus explicabitur.

> Of these the Britons once occupied the land from sea to sea, before the others came. Then the vengeance of God overtook them because of their arrogance and they submitted to the Picts and the Saxons. It now remains for me to tell how they came and from where, and this will be made clear in what follows.[39]

Bede, too, has a historical excursus at this point, but the differences are instructive. Bede's historical note is retrospective and explanatory: it serves merely to explain how the current distribution of Celtic peoples came about. In the body of the work, this material is not taken up again. Moreover,

Bede emphasizes harmony and unity: Latin is a language common to all; the study of Truth is a common pursuit that unifies the disparate ethnic groups.[40] Geoffrey, by contrast, deliberately injects a note of conflict, creating a starting point for narrative development. His passage is proleptic: his narrative, as he says, will serve to expand this short preview.

The next step in the narrative transformation of the *descriptio* is the episode in which the expatriate Trojans, under Brutus's leadership, consult the ancient oracle of Diana on the island of Leogetia.[41] The island is deserted; its towns and temples are in ruins. This not only harks back to the twenty-eight towns of the initial *descriptio*, but anticipates the repeated mention of destroyed, rebuilt, rededicated temples, a major image of change and continuity in the *Historia*[42] In response to Brutus's elaborate ritual, Diana promises Brutus a land

> habitata gigantibus olim.
> Nunc deserta quidem gentibus apta tuis.
> Illa tibi fietque tuis locus aptus in aeuum.
> Hec erit & natis altera troia tuis.

> once occupied by giants. Now it is empty and ready [*apta*] for your folk. Down the years [*in aeuum*] this will prove an abode suited [*locus aptus*] to you and to your people; and for your descendants it will be a second Troy.[43]

This obviously prepares and legitimizes Brutus's appropriation of Britain, in terms that are already familiar and will be echoed again later on. The word "aptus" appears twice, but it has become somewhat more pointed in meaning. It describes not merely the land's general suitability for various agricultural and economic pursuits, but its fitness, even predestination, for this specific conqueror and his people, "in aeuum," forever. This is a kind of "manifest destiny" reasoning, here sanctioned by divine authority and—through the strong Virgilian flavor of the entire episode—the classical tradition. If one thinks of the later, familiar instances of settlers appropriating a new land, it comes as no surprise that the island is described as "deserted," its only inhabitants being "giants," that is, nonhuman creatures whose very nature disqualifies them from having a serious moral or legal claim to the land.

The extraordinarily rich and dense passage that describes Brutus's arrival in Britain and his taking possession of the land is a succinct account not only of a conquest and its legitimization, of settlement and cultivation, but also of a different kind of appropriation: the process by which the settlers make the land morally, or shall we say historically, their own.[44] The Trojans land and deal with what little resistance they encounter from the "few giants."[45] They settle and cultivate the land, spontaneously instituting a kind of feudal system under which Brutus apportions lands to his retainers. ("Patriam donante duce sortiuntur [they divide the land among themselves, with their leader giving it].")[46] Brutus names the land for himself ("Britannia"). Corineus, his second-in-command, does the same for his portion of land ("Corinea," or Cornwall), and kills the giant Goemagog. Brutus then chooses a site for his capital, builds it, and names it New Troy, a name suggested by the Diana oracle.[47]

Many aspects of this account deserve comment. The semantic field of "aptus" is represented in terms like "amoenus," "congruus," "perspicuus." But now there is an even stronger emphasis on the persons to whom the land is thus "attractive" or "suitable." This emphasis is created in part by the characters' movements in space. Brutus and his followers travel around the new country, surveying, appreciating, parceling it: an obvious gesture of taking possession. But their active participation is not limited to accepting what makes itself available to them. They are also engaged in a quest: the ideal location for the capital does not simply present itself by destiny, but has to be sought out in order for the ideal site and its predestined conqueror to come together. The process is given affective coloring in a new key word to complement "aptus": "affectus." The beauty and suitability of the land immediately induces "affectus habitandi" in the travelers—the desire to inhabit it. Soon after, "*affectauit* brutus ciuitatem edificare. *Affectum* itaque suum exequens circuiuit totius patrie situm. ut congruum locum inueniret [Brutus desired to build a city. Therefore, carrying out his desire, he traveled over the whole country to find an appropriate site]."[48] "Aptitude," an objective quality of the place, is now matched by the "affectus" of the settler, the perceiving and appropriating subject.

The settlers immediately begin to cultivate the land and build houses on it; that is, they begin to civilize it. This theme is a necessary part of the "empty land" justification, which argues that the conquerors acquired a right to the territory by being the first to put it to civilized use (unlike the giants or whatever other natives they might find). But, interestingly, Geoffrey pushes this civilizing act back in time, supplementing Diana's future prophecy, "in aeuum," with a backward-looking "ab euo": "ita ut breui tempore terram ab euo inhabitatam censeres [so that in a short time you would have thought that the land had always (*ab euo*) been inhabited]."[49] The Trojans, as it were, establish their right retroactively. This also explains why the land is immediately referred to as "patria," a term that otherwise makes little sense for first-generation immigrants just off the boat. The usage clearly echoes Virgil, but whereas the *Aeneid* makes the transference of "patria" from Troy to Italy an explicit and emotional issue, Geoffrey makes the switch quite casually, appropriating the new land for his settlers not only for the present and future, but for the past as well.[50]

While all this bears an almost uncanny resemblance to colonialist rhetoric of later ages,[51] the purpose here would seem to be somewhat different. Unlike earlier instances of the "fall of Britain" theme, Geoffrey's *Historia* does not draw up simple, didactic parallels between a contemporary conquest of Britain and an earlier, paradigmatic one; instead, he seems interested in making the pattern of conquest and all that leads up to it available for a more inclusive, and less univocal, reflection: that is, his mode of referring is broader, more diffuse. Conquests of various sorts are close to the contemporary experience. The aftermath of 1066 still shapes political realities in England; and Wales, to which Geoffrey has a strong connection, is being taken over by a slower, more desultory Anglo-Norman conquest. Yet it is unlikely that Geoffrey's conquest rhetoric is in the business of justifying any particular conquest, or taking sides; nor can it be said to "refer" to any one of those contemporary or recent events in a direct, readily identifiable manner. While the *Historia* is in many ways deeply and consciously political, and has a number of strong political points to make, it is not, unlike the foundation stories surveyed earlier, directly in the service of a single institution or faction.[52]

It is clear that Geoffrey, even as he talks about Troy and Brutus or about Arthur and the coming of the Saxons, invites his readers to think of the political events that shaped their own time. More than anything else, Merlin's prophecies open up the narrative: they are set apart, with the strongest possible textual signals, as a differently voiced interpolation; they look into the future and invite, even demand, speculation and interpretation from all readers. Merlin challenges readers to equate the events described in his prophecy with events in their known history, thereby inviting them to perform a similar operation for the *Historia* as a whole.[53] Yet this does not take the form of a simple equation, along the lines of "Normans are to Anglo-Saxons as Saxons are to Britons"; rather, the correspondences are multiple, often partial, overlapping, even contradictory. The *Historia* is not anti-Norman, as the logic of such an equation would suggest; and even though some recent "pro-Celtic" readings throw much light on Geoffrey's background and sources, they fall short of fully characterizing the *Historia* as a political or literary document.[54] As Robert Hanning argues, the *Historia* makes the pattern of conquest, and the political alliances and human behaviors associated with it, available to contemporary reflection in a broad, analytical, sometimes ironic, and not always univocal way; its most overt political agenda is a warning against disunity.[55] To begin with, in the simple equation offered above, the "English" (Anglo-Saxons) occupy a somewhat uncomfortable position as the middle term, both aggressors and victims. This is a recurring phenomenon in the *Historia*, sometimes articulated and sometimes not: peoples will rise and fall, and the mechanisms that helped their ascendancy are usually not that different from the ones that spell their own end. The Trojans, as Hanning points out, owe their liberation from Greek captivity to an act of treason (by Anacletus) not so very different from the one that brings down Arthur's reign (Mordred's adultery and insurrection).[56] The "Britons" in the *Historia* are, in some ways, the "Britons" (Welsh) of Geoffrey's own day (and the *Historia* was gladly adopted by Welsh historiography); but they are also the vanquished English and also the conquering Normans. Hanning observes that the attributes of the Normans (cruel, aggressive, tyrannical; heroic, empire-building) are split between the Romans and Arthur's Britons.[57] The *Historia* is a topical and politically engaged work; it even alludes quite clearly to the contemporary troubles concerning the succession to the English throne.[58] It also seeks to rehabilitate the Celtic past; perhaps it even champions the Welsh, although it is hard to determine how far that goes. Nonetheless, it does not appear to be partisan along ethnic lines, although the importance of the conquest theme would suggest such partisanship to modern readers. (In fact, that would have been somewhat atypical at the time, when evaluation of the Normans was equivocal, when any individual identification with an ethnic group might easily be overridden by other alliances or shared interests across ethnic lines.)[59] This is not to say that the *Historia* is harmonizing — it is, after all, full of conflict; or that it is not being provocative in giving the British a glorious history, of greater antiquity and distinction than that of either the English or the Normans; or that it does not sometimes "subversively" champion the lowly Welsh against the Anglo-Norman establishment, as when Geoffrey, in his famous epilogue, favors the obscure provincial hagiographer Caradoc of Llancarfan over the most prominent historians of his time:

> Reges autem eorum qui ab illo tempore in gualiis successerunt. karadoco lancarbanensi contemporaneo meo in materia scribendi permitto. Reges uero saxonum. Willelmo malmesberiensi. & henrico huntendonensi. quos de regibus britonum tacere iubeo. cum non habeant librum istum

britannici sermonis. quem Gvalterus oxenefordensis archidiaconus ex britannia aduexit.

The task of describing their kings, who succeeded from that moment onwards in Wales, I leave to my contemporary Caradoc of Llancarfan. The kings of the Saxons I leave to William of Malmesbury and Henry of Huntingdon. I order these last to say nothing at all about the kings of the Britons, seeing that they do not have in their possession the book in the British language which Walter, Archdeacon of Oxford, brought from Wales [or Britanny?].[60]

The Caradoc reference, with its playful warning to Henry of Huntington and William of Malmesbury, is the most aggressively "partisan" signal in the book. But had Geoffrey wanted to favor the Celts or the Normans or any other group, he could, as Brooke observes, have made his intentions clearer. While the *Historia* narrates "British" (i.e., Welsh) history, it is dedicated to several Norman patrons; and even the "ancient book in the British language," on which Geoffrey founds his claim to sole ownership of British history, was allegedly given to Geoffrey by a Norman friend.[61] What evidence there is of the *Historia*'s early reception does not indicate that the book was regarded as divisive. By the time Wace wrote his French verse adaptation (1155), the *Historia* could clearly be regarded as the "ancestral" history of an Angevin king and his court ("de rei en rei et de eir en eir").[62] Even earlier, probably within a few years of the completion of Geoffrey's work, Ralph FitzGilbert and his wife Custance, Anglo-Norman aristocrats and literary patrons, went to considerable trouble to obtain a copy of Geoffrey's text for the poet Gaimar to incorporate into his French verse history of England. Gaimar's translation of Geoffrey is now lost, having been supplanted in popularity by Wace's; but Gaimar's sequel, the *Estoire des Engleis*, is extant. Both together, for him and his patrons, evidently formed a history of the island that Anglo-Norman readers could adopt as their own.[63] Similarly, Henry of Huntington and Robert of Torigni, whose reactions to the *Historia* are perhaps the earliest documented, seem to regard Geoffrey's British history as distinct from other "histories," but not as divisive or alarming. In the prologue to his continuation of Sigebert of Gembloux's universal chronicle, Robert describes the *Historia* as one of "three histories" (i.e., Norman, English, and British) that he will use to supplement Sigebert's account. His language suggests that Robert saw them as separate but of equal value. Henry of Huntington's letter about his discovery of the *Historia* is in a tone of pleasant surprise at having found this important source so unexpectedly. It is addressed to one "Warin Brito," that is, presumably a Celt (Breton or Welsh), though one with a Norman given name. This implies that Henry did regard the *Historia* as a Celtic history, of special interest to someone of Celtic descent; yet he repeatedly mentions the importance of this new source to the history of "our island." If he sees any contradiction in doing so, or if he sees the *Historia* as subversive or ideologically unpalatable, he does not show it.[64] Thus there are some objections and nervous reactions to the *Historia*; William of Newburgh, writing at the end of the twelfth century, accuses it, among other things, of pandering to the Welsh.[65] The "first variant version" smoothes out some potentially offensive details.[66] Yet on the whole, in Anglo-Norman society, the *Historia* appears to have been thought suitable for all audiences and indeed considered a unifying contribution to a common insular historical heritage.

A similar picture of neutrality emerges when one looks at Geoffrey's treatment of contemporary Welsh issues, especially the ecclesiastical politics that, as an archdeacon (in the diocese of Llandaff), he would have found particularly close to his professional interests. Geoffrey, given his surname Monmoutensis and his relatively wide knowledge of Welsh traditions, must in some way have been identified with Wales and the Marches, and he held ecclesiastical offices in Wales.[67] Yet even within the immediate context of Welsh and border politics, Geoffrey is hard to place. Symptomatic is his much discussed assertion that Caerleon-on-Usk was one of the original archiepiscopal sees of Britain, when he must have been well aware of the bitter dispute over that honor between two ambitious Welsh sees, St. David's and Llandaff. By nominating a third, quite unlikely contender, Geoffrey both acknowledges the contemporary controversy and refuses to take sides in it.[68]

Both C. N. L. Brooke and Kathleen Hughes locate Geoffrey—accurately, I think—in the general context of postconquest Welsh historiographical activity.[69] In Wales and the Marches, conquest, cultural clashes, and ethnic strife are in the air throughout the twelfth and into the thirteenth century, though not in neatly defined camps of conquerors versus conquered; the political landscape must have looked diffuse and chaotic to the contemporary observer. As R. R. Davies has shown in convincing detail, the Anglo-Norman "conquest" of Wales was a slow, uneven procedure, driven more by private initiative than by central planning and characterized by collaboration and compromise as well as resistance and tension.[70] Among other things, it brought not only an influx of Norman churchmen, but also a very noticeable though gradual restructuring of ecclesiastical organization.[71] In ecclesiastical circles especially, the cultural contact as well as the political instability created a fertile climate for historical and pseudohistorical inquiry: in some cases, the Celtic old guard felt defensive or elegiac; more practically, old Welsh monastic houses or their new English proprietors or partners needed to defend old privileges and possessions and saw a chance to obtain more in the general reorganization. Anglo-Norman newcomers, too, took an interest in the traditions of their new surroundings and sometimes wished to champion those traditions either for their own career advancement or out of genuine concern for those newly in their care. Thus lives of Celtic saints were composed or rewritten, and there was an effort from several sides to establish a (spurious) tradition of a Welsh episcopal or even metropolitan see, a movement to which Geoffrey was to give a decisive (though indirect) boost and which, as we shall see, was later taken up again by Gerald of Wales. The best-known piece of historical forgery, or imaginative historiography, from that environment is the *Book of Llandaff*, a collection of tendentiously rewritten saints' lives, charters—edited to suit present concerns—and other materials, compiled probably in the 1130s in order to bolster and support Llandaff's archiepiscopal ambitions.[72]

Unlike the *Book of Llandaff*, however, with its clear political agenda, the *Historia* is not partisan, and while it can be co-opted to the interests of various parties, it is not immediately utilitarian. In the absence of the "serious" purpose that characterizes partisan works such as the *Book of Llandaff*, or historically researched works such as William of Malmesbury's *Gesta Pontificum*, the *Historia* is thus best seen as a parody. This does not necessarily mean that it is primarily a comic, irreverent spoof, though C. N. L. Brooke and Valerie I. J. Flint, among others, have suspected it is.[73] Whether or not Geoffrey meant to be amusing, and what flavor that humor would have had to him or his contemporary readers, is largely unrecoverable. Too many nuances, too many allusions and their valences, are lost to us; though it is worth remembering that many if not most readers in Geoffrey's time and in succeeding centuries took the *Historia* perfectly seriously, though possibly not in the same way as they took histories like William of Malmesbury's seriously. But this does not invalidate or even very much affect the notion that Geoffrey's work is parodic in the sense that Haidu uses the term.[74] The *Historia*, as many commentators have noted, imitates the formal structures used by such great contemporaries as William of Malmesbury and Henry of Huntingdon;[75] yet it is "emptied" of the referentiality and the truth claims that normally adhere to the form. Nonetheless, it is not devoid of serious intentions: like Hanning, I take the *Historia* seriously as "a comprehensive and spectacular vision of the British past largely free of Christian assumptions" in pursuit of serious questions: the role of the individual in history; "human greatness and historical recurrence."[76] While it parodies contemporary historians like William of Malmesbury, it rethinks their structure in new — secular — terms.[77]

It should be noted that such "emptying" has only very little to do with the facticity of the account. Somewhat paradoxically, the *Book of Llandaff* is referential in this sense, even though many of its central narrative entities do not in fact have a referent: there never actually was an archbishop of Llandaff, and some of the saints said to have held that office have no documentable link to Llandaff.[78] It is "referential" in that it wishes to be taken as such, that it makes specific claims regarding its relationship to historical reality and hopes that those claims will be accepted and even acted upon. Geoffrey, though of equally dubious facticity, is less referential in that sense. He imitates the concerns of such topical works as the *Book of Llandaff* and the methods and narrative stance of more "serious" fellow historians, like William of Malmesbury and Henry of Huntingdon, whom he also playfully addresses in the epilogue. But he does not have nearly as much invested in the referentiality of his narrative, its ties to historical reality. The energies freed up by the loosening of those ties are, once again, available for reinvestment elsewhere. This also makes his narrative susceptible to play and irony, wherever he chooses.

Thus, Brutus's conquest, as the parallel between the narrator and his warrior characters implies, is at least in part a metaphoric one. Geoffrey doubles the initial *descriptio*, repeats it at the level of character action, and turns the static, taxonomic description into a dynamic account of historical development; thus he creates verbal and thematic parallels between the narrator's and the characters' perspectives. The parallel says something about Geoffrey's understanding of himself as a historian. Early twelfth-century historians, such as Eadmer or William of Malmesbury, are highly self-conscious about their roles; Geoffrey, as a parodist must be, is more self-conscious than most.[79] Many of them express their awareness that they are pioneering into new historiographical territory: no history of any magnitude had been attempted since Bede, as William points out, and Geoffrey, of course, takes his history back in time before the period covered by Bede.[80] "Historiographical territory" is not necessarily an imported metaphor here: some twelfth-century writers speak of history in spatial terms. These historians seem to have a strong sense of linearity in history: they are not so much concerned with showing typological patterns in history or providing a store of exempla for contemporary conduct, but with presenting an uninterrupted line of development, a *series temporum*.[81] Gaps in chronology disturb them profoundly: William is concerned that English history "limps" in the middle, having nothing to support it for the entire long stretch from Bede to Eadmer, and he promises to "patch up the interrupted sequence of time" (interruptam temporum seriem sarcire).[82]

Geoffrey himself, it is true, does not offer any such picturesque metaphors in his prologue; but he, too, presents himself as filling in gaps, as extending the line of historical knowledge farther backward than had been previously attempted.[83] He is, therefore, a kind of explorer or conqueror himself, and occasionally a ruthless one at that. His historical fictions are sometimes so audacious that even some skeptical twelfth-century readers, whose means of verifying his claims were naturally limited, accused him of lying.[84] The most important fiction concerns his source. In his dedicatory prologue, Geoffrey makes a much imitated and much discussed claim: he says he has discovered his history in a "very ancient book [*liber uetustissimus*] written in the British language." [85] Thus his narrative is not invented, not even compiled, but has been waiting as a self-contained whole to be discovered by an enterprising (and linguistically privileged) translator. This makes Geoffrey the sole proprietor of early British history, as he gleefully points out in the famous epilogue, where he warns Henry of Huntingdon and William of Malmesbury off his historiographical turf and magnanimously leaves later Welsh history to his friend Caradoc. He shrewdly strengthens the source fiction by peppering his narrative with "effet de réel" elements: there are numerous loose ends and incomplete casual references of the kind one might expect to find in a chronicle that was compiled at a different time. In an "old book" one would naturally come across events and names for which one can no longer supply the context; Geoffrey appears to "antique" his narrative deliberately by artificially creating such remnants.[86] The genealogical lists that alternate with more worked-out narrative passages occasionally contain a half-sentence of biographical information, like a "reminder," in a tone that implies that the information is generally known. He also cryptically alludes (twice) to the prophetic "eagle of Shaftesbury," [87] a legend that, to my knowledge, has never been traced. One cannot, of course, base too much of an argument on the absence of sources; but even if the eagle once had a referent in local legend, Geoffrey teases his readers by pretending that everyone knows the eagle's prophecies, a playful challenge that stumped even his first translators, Wace and Laȝamon.[88]

Perhaps the very boldness of such devices as the ancient book or the mysterious eagle suggests that they may be not so much an attempt to deceive as a playful challenge to the reader to enter into the game of making up history retroactively; that, at any rate, seems to be how many of his readers used Geoffrey. We have seen some texts influenced by Geoffrey already; some mention him explicitly. The *Historia Monasterii de Abingdon* (late twelfth century), for instance, uses the general outline of Bede's and Geoffrey's histories to insert the figure of the monastery's own legendary founder, "Abennus," and a foundation myth concerning the finding of the Black Cross. This episode is of course modeled on St. Helen's finding of the True Cross, which, on Geoffrey's authority, is connected to England; it is also embedded in a description of the monastery's site that sounds distinctly like *gaainable tere*.[89] William of St. Albans, whom we encountered in the previous chapter, even acknowledges Geoffrey's influence as he uses a similar source fiction. In the mid-thirteenth century, St. Albans' most famous historian, Matthew Paris, takes the book image one step further by having his predecessors literally dig up an ancient book "antiquo Anglico, vel Britannico, idiomate" in the ruins of an old Roman town.[90] The example of *Fouke le Fitz Waryn* will be discussed below. If I am correct in hearing Geoffrey through the Virgilian material in the *Fundacio* of Kirkstall and even more in the "Historia Selebiensis Monasterii," we can add these works to the list, too.[91] Whatever the conscious intentions of any or all of these historiographers, Geoffrey seems to have inspired, or sanctioned, historical inventiveness in a way that Bede or William of Malmesbury, for instance, did not. Whatever his contemporaries or near-contemporaries called this phenomenon in their own minds—fiction, lies, or something else—it suggests that they had at least a semiconscious sense that Geoffrey was not the same kind of source as Bede, a source perhaps more to be imitated and appropriated than quoted.

They understood, that is, one metaphorical implication of the "liber uetus-tissimus": like his prototypical settler Brutus, Geoffrey seeks out the territory that has been waiting only for him; he covets, then occupies his *gaainable tere*; he makes himself at home in it and boldly pretends that he has always possessed it. The Diana oracle is another emblem for this attitude: it has been waiting for many years in a deserted island, "si forte ab aliquo peteretur [in case somebody were to seek it out]."[92] Reactivating traditions, real or pretended (rededicating temples or naming places after an abandoned homeland or inventing a national history) is an activity common to both the historian and his hero.

At the same time, there is an implied awareness, or at least an uneasy hunch, that the land thus appropriated is not in fact quite the conqueror's for the taking. The uneasiness is illustrated by the fact that the giants in Britain are not completely vanquished but driven underground—an unstable solution at best, given both the giants' mythological associations and other instances in the *Historia* of unsuccessful containment of trouble "underground."[93] Geoffrey repeatedly draws attention to the extreme, and in many cases gratuitous, violence of the conquerors; that would seem to be one of the major functions of the semicomical character Corineus. Corineus willfully provokes a bloody and ultimately quite useless war in Gaul, and he engages in giant-killing because he enjoys it as a sport. This is not necessarily a critique of excessive violence, let alone a pacifist sentiment; but even as one may enjoy the drama or the slapstick humor of such scenes, one is not allowed to forget that the conquerors have victims.[94]

There is no such thing, it seems, as an unoccupied territory. In fact, the literary imagination of the historians seems unable to conceive of untouched land; it is always imagined as already cultivated, or at least so "apta" to cultivation that it has no true existence apart from the cultivators and their desires. In extending their histories backward, the twelfth-century historians have to draw on earlier literary models (Virgil, the Bible), but they are also imposing their postconquest, school-trained literary sensibilities and scholarly needs on an earlier, indigenous historical culture that they use and describe, but whose separate value and importance they have to deny. Geoffrey, who, as R. William Leckie has shown, skillfully exploits both the narrative traditions and the gaps in earlier historiography to insert his own account, is presumably quite aware of the process.[95] The historian is a pioneer, but the land is not entirely pristine; appropriating a space of one's own involves both exploitation and denial of what came before.[96] The "liber uetustissimus" Geoffrey claims to be using embodies this dual awareness. Geoffrey's work is both innovative and derivative; he "discovers," or invents, history, but he imagines it as already in book form.[97]

Geoffrey, by his own bold and almost explicit appropriation of territory, not only encourages others to do their own retroactive historicizing, but has thrown himself open to appropriation by others to their own purposes. A brief look at some vernacular writers influenced by Geoffrey — even though they take us somewhat beyond the time frame of this book — will illustrate the shapes such an appropriation can take. The three examples come from three quite different spheres; this suggests the flexibility and range of applicability of the topos. Furthermore, they are interesting precisely as vernacular transformations of Geoffrey's motif. Since I am arguing here that *gaainable tere* has poetological significance, one might expect to find different accentuations of the theme specific to the poetological situation of vernacular historical writing. In the remainder of this chapter I will sketch, first of all, a monastic and hagiographic version of *gaainable tere*. Denis Piramus's *Vie Seint Edmund* is a late-twelfth-century Anglo-Norman verse life based on Abbo of Fleury's life of St. Edmund and Galfridus de Fontibus's romancelike account of St.

Edmund's childhood. The Anglo-Norman romance *Fouke le Fitz Waryn*, from the cultural and political milieu of the baronial families in the Welsh Marches, is extant only in a fourteenth-century prose *remaniement*, but preserves traces of an earlier (thirteenth-century) verse narrative. Finally, I will look at Laʒamon's *Brut*, an idiosyncratic adaptation of Wace's translation of Geoffrey in an archaizing alliterative English verse. They have in common that they understand and creatively develop the poetics of Geoffrey's *Historia*. While the *Vie Seint Edmund* remains close to the referential use of the topos (the claim to ownership of a land) but adapts the "conquest" to hagiographic purposes, the other two texts go beyond the referential to a metaphorical use: the author's ownership of his subject.

It is appropriate to begin with Denis's *Vie Seint Edmund* (late twelfth century), which, after all, contributed the phrase and notion of *gaainable tere* to this discussion. In order to understand Denis's use of the motif, it is necessary to be aware of the important role the Edmund legend played in the rhetoric and politics of Denis's monastic house, the influential abbey of Bury St. Edmunds. As one of the major landlords in East Anglia, the monastery used the figure of its patron saint to establish and defend its land claims, its jurisdiction, its royal privileges, and its independence from the diocesan bishops. Hence its virtual obsession with the "terra Sancti Edmundi" in its historiography and documents. The fact that Edmund was a king as well as a saint proved eminently useful in this enterprise. By carefully legitimizing Edmund's right to the land—after his death as well as before—the monks bolstered their claim to spiritual as well as political "ownership" of their lands.[98]

Part of the long-term hagiographic project at Bury, besides developing the Edmund legend internally, was to fit it into known and accepted historiography. There are beginnings of this in the earliest major hagiography of St. Edmund, the tenth-century *passio* of the saint by Abbo of Fleury, which begins with a brief historical introduction and a short version of the familiar *descriptio Britannie*.[99] Denis has no *descriptio* at the beginning, but instead carefully places his *vita* in a large historical context derived not only from Abbo but from Geoffrey as well. What is more, he turns the *descriptio* of his source into a full-fledged, quite complex Geoffreyan appropriation topos with important structural and thematic functions.

In the *Vie Seint Edmund*, the phrase "gaainable tere" always occurs in connection with conquests. Denis uses it to set up an interesting pattern of parallels and contrasts in his story. The first invasion he describes is that of the

Saxons. (Brutus is only briefly alluded to.) The Saxons arrive at a time when the Britons have left their land because of a famine; therefore, they find the land empty. The stages of the appropriation are by now familiar: "Le pais trovent delitable / E la tere bien gainable [They find the country delightful, and the land very *gaainable*]."[100] Before long, the Saxons begin to build fortifications, then a town. They successfully cultivate the land. (It should be noted that the Britons, who were forced into exile by a famine, apparently were unable to do this.) When the Britons return to reclaim "lur dreit et lur heritage [their right and their heritage]," the Saxons explain that their right to "lur tere e lur conquest [their land and their conquest]"[101] supersedes the Britons':

Kar, kant il en la tere entrerent,
Homme ne femme n'i troverent
Ki de rien lur contredeist,
Ne qui a reisun les meist,
Kar en la tere dunc vivant
N'out homme ne femme n'enfant.

For, when they entered the country, they found neither man nor woman there who lodged any protest or asked for any justification; for at that time, neither man nor woman nor child lived in the land.[102]

The Saxons' victory in a fair battle confirms this interpretation and settles the question once and for all. As the conquered land is divided among the victors, the story zeroes in on the place that will be important for the further development of the story, East Anglia, and dutifully repeats the steps of appropriation for this "rich and *gaainable*, good, sweet, delightful land."[103]

Edmund's arrival as the designated successor of the childless King Offa is entirely peaceful. But it strikingly echoes that of the military invaders: he lands on a plain that is "pleasing and beautiful and green and delightful [acceptable / E bele e vert e delitable]."[104] Like other newcomers, he "cultivates" and improves the land to make it his own, but after his own fashion: on his arrival, he kneels and prays, with the effect that the area, to this very day, is "more *gaainable* and more plentiful in all good things [plus gaainable / E de tuz biens fusunable]"[105] than the surrounding territory. Like Brutus, he travels his new land, and he marks his territory by leaving miraculous transformations in his wake. Denis goes out of his chronological way to tell us that later, immediately after his coronation, Edmund built a hall and a chapel— a secular and a religious building—near his landing place.[106] He is elected king peacefully and unanimously, since there is no legitimate heir; again, not unlike the Angles and Saxons, he gains power by default, taking over an un-claimed realm.[107]

The viciously brutal Danish raids that lead to Edmund's martyrdom read like a cruel, semicomic parody of the Saxons' legitimate conquest and Edmund's peaceful arrival. The raiders are driven not so much by greed as by their envy of Edmund's effortless "conquest," the nature of which they thoroughly misunderstand: King Lothebroc taunts his sons with Edmund's achievement,[108] whereupon they take the land by force, slaughter its inhabi-tants, and execute the legitimate ruler, King Edmund.

This series of "conquests" is only the beginning of the careful legitimiza-tion of Edmund's rights to the land. His reign does not end with his death. Denis could hardly make this point more clearly than when he reports that East Anglia was without a king for a while after Edmund's death, because no one dared to take "segnurie":

Kar en lur curages noterent
Que bien deit estre e reis e sire
Del pais ou suffrit martire,
Kar mult l'en aveit deservi
Vers Dampnedeu e bien meri.

For they acknowledged in their hearts that he well ought to be king and lord of the land where he suffered martyrdom, for he had well deserved it before the Lord God.[109]

There are, however, legitimate successors of two kinds: first, those kings who respect Edmund's lordship and are endorsed by him; second, the reli-gious community that forms around the martyr's burial place. Edmund con-tinues his church-building activities after death. As we saw in chapter 1, it is his body that brings the scattered English back together after the devastat-ing raids. In the most famous episode of the Edmund legend, they scour the forest for Edmund's severed head, and the head assists them in their search by shouting "here, here, here."[110] The body, like the community, miraculously comes back together,[111] and Edmund's incorrupt body is later found to be free of any wounds, except for a thin red line around the neck.[112] One is tempted to interpret this as a parallel to the hagiographer's enterprise: he is, after all, trying to close gaps in the history of his house, to create a seamless account.

The chapel that is constructed above Edmund's tomb is soon felt to be in-adequate.[113] The next step is to house the *corseint* better. A second search is mounted that is not unlike the search for the head—and not unlike Brutus's search for the ideal spot to found Troia Nova:

> Tant unt cerchié par le pais,
> Tant unt demandé e enquis,
> Qu'il unt trové liu acceptable
> E bel e bon e convenable
> En une grant vile real.

They searched throughout the land, they asked and inquired, until they found a pleasing, good, beautiful place in a great royal city.[114]

As Brutus the conqueror must find (and earn by his painstaking search) the place that is "aptus" for him, so St. Edmund's followers find a regal city for their royal saint that is "convenable." The remainder of the poem emphasizes the growth and continuity of the early ecclesiastical establishment around the relics of the saint, his almost-live presence within it ("en char, en os, cum il fust vifs [in flesh and bones, as if he were alive]")[115]—and his continued influence on daily life as defender, ruler, and judge.

On a much more modest scale, the thirteenth-century Anglo-Norman verse romance *Fouke le Fitz Waryn* is a secular counterpart to Denis's narrative.[116] *Fouke*, of which only a fourteenth-century prose version survives, is one of the insular vernacular narratives that have been dubbed "ancestral romances."[117] The story traces the early history of the Fitz Waryns, an influential family in the Welsh march, and, by implication, the history of the Welsh border barons in general. *Fouke* begins with the Norman Conquest: the Conqueror, in a gesture familiar from Brutus, travels through the region, dotting it with castles and with loyal barons.[118] There is considerable genealogical detail to show that several contemporary families descend from these early barons. Since most of the families named do not in fact go back as far as William the Conqueror, this is in itself a bit of retroactive historicizing, similar to Geoffrey's observation that one might have thought the settlers had been on the land forever.[119] But that is by no means the only Geoffreyan reminiscence. Like many ancestral romances, *Fouke* pillages other well-known texts for narrative motifs and works the scraps into a wild and playful pastiche of literary echoes and real-life history and topography. *Fouke*'s chief quarry is Geoffrey of Monmouth. In the course of the Conqueror's first land-taking trip, Payn Peverel, a Fitz Waryn ancestor, performs a replay of Corineus's fight with Geomagog in a deserted and haunted city called La Blaunche Launde.[120] This is no mere allusion: we are explicitly told that Payn's adversary is an evil spirit in Geomagog's body. To make sure that Geoffrey's account is present to us in all relevant details, a local peasant reminds the conquerors (and readers) of Geoffrey's original episode. First the peasant, later the ghost himself, vanquished by Payn and interrogated at sword-point, fill us in on the intervening history: Corineus won the place by his victory, but after his death demons reclaimed it. King Bran attempted to rebuild the city, but the devils continually destroyed his buildings overnight. St. Augustine was more successful in appropriating the land by building a chapel on it, but again the devils were able to take it back. It is now, as the ghost all but admits, high time for Payn Peverel to take over. La Blaunche Launde, or Whittington, becomes the Fitz Waryns' pet property: a hard-won possession, wrested from the forces of evil, that is therefore morally as well as legally theirs.

Although the precise political context of *Fouke* is open to debate, its general drift is clear enough: the Payn episode, like much else in the story, legitimizes the land claims of the Marcher lords in general, and perhaps of one family in particular.[121] But here, as in Geoffrey, the *gaainable tere* topos takes on a poetological meaning. The self-reflexive aspect of the "appropriation" lies in the very derivativeness, the pastiche character of *Fouke*. The text not only does not disguise its artificiality, but flaunts it: the allusions to the Tristan story, to Geoffrey, and to other texts are so obvious that the pleasure of recognizing them and observing their almost grotesque transformations must account for part of the effect of *Fouke*. There is one odd detail in Payn's interrogation of the ghost that seems to speak to this fact. The giants, says the ghost, have left behind a buried treasure of golden animal figures. Payn demands to be led to the site, but the ghost warns him not to attempt it: the treasure is not meant for him but for someone yet to come.[122] That is all; the motif is dropped here and never picked up again. This treasure—another possession left unclaimed waiting to be taken—is an apt image not only of the riches awaiting the Fitz Waryns, but also of the narrative possibilities open to a romance like *Fouke*. As I shall argue in the following two chapters, there are parallels—similar "golden worlds," underground treasures of ambiguous moral origin and difficult accessibility—in Latin historiography, clearly with self-referential significance. The *Fouke* narrator is describing himself, through the Geoffreyan echo, as a latecomer on the romance scene: while implying, with sly self-mockery, that all good stories have been told before, he also suggests something about the riches available to him who can find the treasure. He, too, is appropriating an earlier literary tradition, but, given the looser demands and different ambitions of vernacular romance writing, appears to do so with little anxiety and little need for concealment; he can afford to be frank and playful about his borrowings and, as it were, to establish his story's "genealogy" along with that of the Fitz Waryns. Patent artificiality, or lack of verisimilitude, does not appear to have detracted from the practical usefulness of a family genealogical legend, as the extraordinary success of the Mélusine legend for the Lusignan family shows.[123] Perhaps readers were willing to suspend disbelief; perhaps what mattered was the prestige of having an origin legend at all, and its artificiality and "literariness" were savored and valued.

Vernacular adaptation and appropriation, and the author's claim to his "territory," are overt concerns in Laȝamon's *Brut*, dated variously between ca. 1185 and 1275, a work whose immediate audience, patronage, and literary context remain hard to determine.[124] But Laȝamon's version of the *gaainable tere* motif helps to throw some light on his view of himself and his position as a poet. The *Brut* is, of course, the most directly "Geoffreyan" of the texts studied here: it is the English adaptation of Wace's French adaptation of Geoffrey's *Historia*. Since Wace does not translate Geoffrey's prefatory material, it is not surprising that Laȝamon does not have a *descriptio Britanniae* either. But later in the narrative, there is a beautiful appropriation passage; we see Brutus lovingly surveying the country he has brought under his control — much like the Creator, seeing that it was good:

Brutus hine bi-þohte · 7 þis folc bi-heold.
bi-heold he þa muntes · feire 7 muchele
bi-heold he þa medewan · þat weoren swiðe maere
bi-heold he þa wateres · 7 þa wilde deor.
bi-heold he þa fisches · bi-heold he þa fuȝeles.
bi-heold he þa leswa · 7 þene leofliche wode
bi-heold he þene wode hu he bleou · bi-heold he þat
                    corn hu hit greu.
al he iseih on leoden · þat him leof was on heorten.

Brutus looked out upon this multitude; he beheld the fair, tall mountains, the broad meadows, the rivers, the wild game, the fish, the birds, the pastures, and the lovely forests. He saw how the woods flowered and the grain grew; all he gazed at in that land was dear to his heart.[125]

This contemplation makes him so nostalgic for Troy that it induces him to found "Troye þe Newe" (line 1017). Like Geoffrey's Brutus, he is led by his *affectus* to reestablish an interrupted tradition, to close a gap in his history. As in Geoffrey, this *gaainable tere* or *affectus habitandi* passage harks back to the prologue, although Laȝamon's prologue material is quite different: instead of a *descriptio Britanniae*, he names himself, formally announces his project, and describes his search for appropriate sources. But Brutus looking at his land sounds strikingly like Laȝamon looking at his books. Laȝamon, too, has had to travel and search to find his treasured possessions:

> Laȝamon gon liðen · wide ȝond þas leode.
> 7 bi-won þa aeðela boc · þa he to bisne nom.

Then,

> Laȝamon leide þeos boc · 7 þa leaf wende.
> he heom leofliche bi-heold · liðe him beo Drihte
> Feðeren he nom mid fingren · 7 fiede on boc-felle.

Layamon traveled widely throughout the land acquiring the honored books he used as exemplars. — Layamon laid open these books, turned their leaves, and viewed them fondly — may the lord be merciful to him. [He took] a pen with his fingers and [wrote] on parchment.[126]

Both Brutus's and Laȝamon's emotional response to the land they survey is reminiscent of the Selby foundation story, with the monk Benedict's circumambulation and joyful "embracing" of his new property: "Quam gaudenter locum illum amplexatus sit."[127]

As in *Fouke*, it is interesting to consider Laȝamon's "conquest" in terms of his self-conscious role as a vernacular writer. E. G. Stanley and, more recently, Daniel Donoghue have argued that Laȝamon is deliberately returning to Anglo-Saxon literary models and language, in an "antiquarian" or "archaistic" move, in a conscious effort to stress the gap between the old and the new, the Anglo-Saxon and the Anglo-Norman.[128] In this effort, his self-presentation as priest and poet, as well as the affective coloring of that presentation, is crucial. In the prologue, the priest-turned-historian is surveying his "territory," with an unmistakable, almost sensuous *affectus*. Like Geoffrey's Brutus, Denis's Edmund, or William the Conqueror in *Fouke*, he immediately proceeds to make this land his own by leaving his mark on it — in this case, with a quill. Through this image, Laȝamon casts himself as a clerkly narrator, as a facilitator or mediator who researches the sources and makes learned materials available to a less literate, or even illiterate, audience. In view of this mediating position, it is not without significance that he refers to three books — Latin, English, and French — and that the French one is placed between the other two, as if to mediate between literate Latin and popular English, which by Laȝamon's time had been virtually stripped of all literate and written functions and thus had become more radically "vernacular," more radically oral than French.[129]

At the same time, especially in the long Arthurian section of the poem, Laȝamon stresses his close links to an oral, bardic tradition. Although he is in fact following a written source fairly closely, he refers to a wealth of oral tales, suggesting that he is collecting these stories and consolidating them into a written work, not unlike Chrétien in the *Erec* prologue or Thomas in his *Tristan*, who portray themselves as making a similar transition from oral traditions to a new vernacular literacy.[130] In contrast to these writers, however, Laȝamon does his job without any polemics or any assertions of superiority. There is no contempt for the lesser efforts of "cil qui de conter vivre vuelent [those who would make a living by telling stories],"[131] or competition for the correct version of the story. Arthurian history is a collaborative venture. Laȝamon's Round Table is not so much a school for courtly civility, as is Wace's, but a Eucharist for bards:

> swa him saeide Merlin · þe witeȝe wes maere.
> þat a king sculde cume · of Vðere Pendragune.
> þat gleomen sculden wurchen burd · of þas kinges
> > breosten.
> and þer-to sitten · scopes swiðe sele.
> and eten heore wullen · aer heo þenne fusden.
> and winscenches ut teon · of þeos kinges tungen.
> and drinken 7 dreomen · daies 7 nihtes.
> þis gomen heom sculde i-lasten · to þere weorlde
> > longe.

Thus was it prophesied by the famous Merlin before Arthur's birth that a king would come of Uther Pendragon, and that bards would make a table of that king's breast at which noble poets would eat their fill before going hence; from this king's tongue they would draw wine and drink to make merry the days and nights in game as long as the world endures.

> of him scullen gleomen · godliche singen.
> of his breosten scullen aeten · aðele scopes.
> scullen of his blode · beornes beon drunke.

Gleemen will artfully sing of him, noble poets will eat of his breast, and knights will be intoxicated by his blood.[132]

The bookish Laȝamon, in another guise, is also not unlike a bard: in a second start, after his clerkly prologue, he begins, Caedmon-like: "NV seið mid loft-songe þe wes on leoden preost. / al swa þe boc spekeð [Now speaks with lofty song he who was priest in the land / all that the book speaks]."[133] Occupying a middle ground between bard and cleric, using learned written sources yet "saying" and "singing" what his sources "speak," he could be said to officiate as the priest at the Round Table Eucharist. In order to do that, he, like Brutus, and like all the other authors, has to seek out, conquer, and appropriate his own space as a historian and narrator, his own *gaainable tere*.

From Laȝamon's affective embracing of his material to the *Fouke* author's casual playfulness, we see that Geoffrey of Monmouth spawned a tradition of *gaainable tere* as a locus for representing the writer's role, his attitude toward his text. This interest in the author's role and the freedom to shape it creatively are, as Bäuml and others have shown, inseparably bound up with textuality. The "fixity" of the written text and the absence of the storyteller automatically render the "author" an abstraction, a "fiction." This in turn allows for variations in the fictional author's distance from and stance toward his material. It permits irony, playfulness, truth claims of various degrees of seriousness, and different kinds and degrees of self-dramatization. The importance of this for the development of vernacular romance has been discussed extensively by literary critics.[134] For a historian, on the other hand, the necessary "fictionality" of the author is an unsettling insight: it calls into question the authority of the author and therefore the truth of the text. In the next two chapters I will examine four authors' responses to that insight. In all of them, the historian-author's role is a central concern (sometimes associated with the *gaainable tere* motif, sometimes going beyond it). Two of the authors are by and large "straightforward" historians (William of Malmesbury and William of Newburgh), who raise the possibility of fictionality and examine it briefly, only to leave it aside as an unresolved, contrapuntal segment of their chronicles. The other two (Walter Map and, in chapter 4, Gerald of Wales) make such inquiry a central principle of their narrative poetics.

⇥{ 3 }⇤

Underground Treasures

The "Other Worlds" of William of Malmesbury,

William of Newburgh, and Walter Map

ne of the most apt and memorable images in Auerbach's *Mimesis*, to my mind, is his characterization of Gregory of Tours's writing: "What he relates is his own and his only world. He has no other, and he lives in it."[1] Whether or not this does full justice to Gregory, the image of Gregory enclosed in his own self-sufficient world can serve as a useful starting point for a discussion of twelfth-century historiographers, though only by contrast: strange as it may sound, they are cognizant of "other worlds" than their own, or at least seem to feel compelled to invoke the possibility of other worlds. And at least one of them, Walter Map, is almost obsessed with the problem of having to describe "his own and his only world," of living in the very world he is trying to describe.

I shall argue that both Map's epistemological problem and the excursions to, or visits from, "other worlds" signal the narrative self-awareness that is often considered a necessary condition for fictionality.[2] In the introduction to this book, I proposed that we reexamine two kinds of referentiality in medieval historiography: "realistic" outside reference and allegorical reference; I suggested that our sample texts navigate between these two and strain against both. The "other world" episodes discussed in this chapter create playful spaces that permit writers to articulate the hypothetical, the ironic, the uncertain, and at the same time to reflect on and play with such intrusive voices in their texts. They are designed to shake the firm construct of referentiality, of both sorts, and to allow for doubt, whether serious or playful. Most often, the vehicle for such play with reference is an author figure. Whether we are dealing with an author stand-in descending to a hidden world (a *gaainable tere* underground) or a narrator trapped in his own world and assaulted by inexplicable intrusions from outside, the author ironically undermines his own stance, and his own credibility, in a way that casts doubt on referentiality and truth.

The authors discussed in this chapter and the next test the limits of referentiality and historicity by inviting in phenomena and episodes that strain belief, often, it seems, for the sole purpose of raising the question of what should be done with such troublesome intruders. Miraculous though some of these episodes are, they are not, as is often said, examples of naive credulity or the lack of firm standards of evidence. Nor are they signals that these histories are tied, at the expense of factual accuracy, into a firm theological system of thought that pulls in and absorbs all history and predetermines its interpretations. When they avoid one of these extreme interpretations, modern readers often resort to the other. John O. Ward, for instance, argues that medieval historians, at least the more ambitious ones, know their work to be "rhetorical," or textual; outside reference, mere factuality, is too ephemeral and contingent to be a major standard for their historiographical practice. Yet to make up for that loss of firm anchoring in reality, Ward posits a rigid theological ideology, which holds all historiography in a secure grip of accepted doctrine; that, indeed, is to him the distinguishing mark of medieval, as opposed to Renaissance, uses of rhetoric: "For Leonardo Bruni, rhetoric opens, keeps dialogue open, and prevents factional tyranny; and rhetorical history erects this into a principle of interpretation. In the twelfth century, however, rhetorical history functioned, like liturgy, to close out doubt and encourage certainty."[3]

It is this widespread assessment of medieval historiography—based in part, I believe, on our own doctrinal orthodoxies about the Middle Ages and the Renaissance—that I want to question; it seems to me that the writers under discussion here are capable of precisely that openness which Ward and other critics explicitly deny them. Twelfth-century writers such as William of Malmesbury, William of Newburgh, and Walter Map certainly recognize the textuality of their work and the problems of simple referentiality that come with it; that is one of the insights their startling "adventures underground" dramatize. At the same time, they feel that the quiet assurance of a religious referentiality supporting their texts is slipping away from them; the unifying voice of a consensual doctrine ("like liturgy") often seems elusive or inaccessible. In that space between referentialities in which they find themselves as a result, there arises that "freedom" (although they probably experienced it more as insecurity or loss of certainty) that historians of fictionality talk about.

Although in the historiographic texts discussed here, the "question of importance" or "meaning" is never entirely set aside, we shall see that Haidu's ludic, parodic model of fictionalization as well as the notion of withdrawal of the religious function of writing are applicable and helpful. But my findings will also challenge Haidu's half-stated assumption that Latin writing does not participate in this process, does not emancipate itself but is the standard the vernaculars emancipate themselves from, since it is by definition bound up in a theological worldview.[4] The episodes discussed in this chapter, and the analysis of Gerald's *Itinerarium Kambriae* in the next, show that the secular spirit which makes vernacular fiction possible is also present in some of the Latin historiographers.

Geoffrey of Monmouth, of course, has inspired reflections on the boundaries between history and fiction from a very early time. In William of Newburgh's celebrated attack on Geoffrey of Monmouth's *Historia Regum Britannie*, the central argument is that there is simply no room in the accepted history of the country for Geoffrey's Arthurian stories. Geoffrey's chronology clashes with Bede's: Bede says that Ethelbert was king when Augustine arrived; if we believe Geoffrey, "regnum Arturi et ingressus in Britanniam Augustini concurrere debuerunt [Arthur's reign and Augustine's arrival in Britain ought to have coincided]"; obviously both cannot be right.[5] At any rate, there are not as many kingdoms in the known world as Geoffrey claims Arthur has conquered. William scoffs: "An alium orbem somniat infinita regna habentem, in quo ea contigerunt quae supra memoravit? quippe in orbe nostro numquam talia contigerunt [Is he dreaming of another world, containing kingdoms without number, in which the events took place which are mentioned by him earlier? Certainly in our world nothing of this kind took place]."[6] In a sense, of course, William is exactly right: Geoffrey does "dream" another universe in which there is plenty of room for all his "fictions" and "fabulae," as William contemptuously calls them; he is creating, as Bäuml would put it, a "coherent pseudo-reality," or fiction. As art historians are fond of remarking of a similar attack, that of St. Bernard against fantastic images in Romanesque sculpture: deep down, William had to understand his target fairly well, even appreciate it, in order to characterize it so well.[7] William even has a very brief, almost disconcertingly out-of-place section on "other worlds" himself. But more on that later.

William of Newburgh objects to Geoffrey because his own view of history is strictly linear. Like William of Malmesbury, he is fond of sequence, of order. He speaks of a "series temporum," an "ordo historiae," as something that can be, and has to be, covered completely by the historian. He plans to "run briefly through the time" (tempora succincte percurram) from the Norman Conquest to Stephen, and then to give a "fuller narration" to the present. He situates himself in the time line, less, it seems, for self-advertisement than for easier orientation:

> Quoniam vero Anglicanae ordinem historiae quibusdam usque ad decessum regis Henrici primi novimus esse deductum, sumpto ab adventu Normannorum in Angliam exordio media tempora succincte percurram, ut a successore ejusdem Henrici Stephano, cuius anno primo ego Willelmus servorum Christi minimus et in Adam primo ad mortem sum natus et in secundo ad vitam renatus, narrationem Deo volente producere pleniorem.

> Since we are aware that the sequence of English history has been taken by certain writers as far as the death of King Henry I, I shall begin with the arrival of the Normans in England and run briefly through the intermediate period, so that God willing I can begin to extend a fuller narrative from the time of Henry's successor Stephen. In the first year of his reign, I, the least of Christ's servants, was born in the first Adam to death, and was reborn in the second Adam to life.[8]

William of Malmesbury, about sixty years earlier, had surveyed the previous "coverage" of history in the prologue to his *Gesta Regum Anglorum*, identified the areas that needed work, and announced his intention to "patch up the interrupted sequence of time" (interruptam temporum seriem sarcire).[9] His sequentiality is not that of annals, though: annals, as he observes, are selective and leave many gaps. In his kind of historiography, there is a sense of filling in a space, and doing so conclusively, ideally with no gaps and no alternatives. This, like fictionality or other kinds of literariness, is obviously a consequence of widespread literacy.[10] It presupposes history as books, written text; it even presupposes the existence of some form of research library, however primitive, in which these written histories can be retrieved at will. We are no longer in an age where history has to be told repeatedly in order to remain in the collective memory. Such a literate history is also, at least ideally, much less malleable than an oral history would be.[11] When William of Newburgh stakes out his territory, he implies that whatever has already been "covered" can be left alone; on the other hand, nothing must be left uncovered, and therefore, to be on the safe side, he will undertake to write a history of recent times even though he is not certain that someone else is not already doing so. Gaps disturb these writers. Yet, as in the much repeated axiom of medieval physics (and of intuitive common sense), only one body can occupy any given space at any given time.

Applied to historiography, this commonsense principle comes with the assumption that history is a direct, uncomplicated, "transparent" record of facts: if the facts have been recorded once, further historiography would be redundant. Obviously, even a rather modest theoretical reflection shows this assumption to be naive.[12] If historical narrative records facts straightforwardly and "transparently," then historical narratives on the same subject, the same period, ought to supersede each other. Of course they do not, or at least not entirely; it is perfectly possible for several different narrative accounts of the same historical subject to coexist, perhaps not peacefully but with equal claims to a serious readership. (And, one might add, when a historical narrative is superseded, it is frequently not because new facts have come to light but because its "emplotment" [H. White], its "relevance criteria" [Stierle], its narrative configuration no longer meet the needs of a new generation of readers and historians.)[13] But, at least as an initial stance in their prologues, William of Malmesbury and William of Newburgh seem to present just that naive, commonsense view of written history.

Geoffrey of Monmouth both exploits and violates the principle of "transparent," linear history. As Leckie has shown, Geoffrey finds a gap in accepted historiography into which he can splice his own vision of the past; thus, at least on the surface, he subscribes to the notion of linearity held by the two Williams. On the other hand, he also violates the principle — and this is what provokes William of Newburgh's anger — by overstuffing the gap, so that his material spills over and begins to compete with received historical opinion. Since there are bodies in those spaces already, Geoffrey must be wrong; he must be a liar; or, as William suggests, he must be bypassing the *series temporum* altogether and "dreaming another world." Yet even writers like William of Newburgh and William of Malmesbury are willing to leave the *series temporum* and "dream" another world, or at least earnestly try to account for another world as it is presented to them — with interesting consequences for their entire narrative.

William of Malmesbury has frequently been praised for his judicious treatment of sources and his serious attempt to sort out just which body occupied which space at any given time.[14] It has been pointed out that to do this, he developed, single-handedly, brilliantly, a more sophisticated sense of source criticism than most of his contemporaries were capable of; he employs what Spiegel calls "a sort of primitive historiographic *sic et non*."[15] William's almost scientific, "modern" methodology is certainly one of his greatest achievements. Much to the surprise of many modern readers, however, William opens up his account to quite different "realities": legends, ghost stories, miracles.[16] We could again look to Spiegel and remark that this is what medieval historiography was doomed to do: if the chief criterion for authenticity is reliable testimony, and the only criterion for source criticism is conflict between sources, medieval historiography is left with "practically no sound theoretical grounds" for excluding anything it finds in its sources.[17] This, however, shows only why the miraculous does not need to be excluded; it does not provide a sufficient explanation for the *in*clusion of such material, at least not for William of Malmesbury. Apart from the useful axiom of linguistic pragmatics, that the mere fact that something is true can never adequately explain why it is being said, William can be quite selective when he wants to; moreover, in many cases, he goes out of his way to include a source that is apparently quite unrelated to the business at hand. Although in such cases he typically apologizes for digressing, or gives some lame reason, such as the "edifying" or entertaining character of the material, on closer inspection there frequently turns out to be a much better motivation, and the episode is much better integrated into the structure of the narrative than might at first appear.

The most remarkable sequence of miraculous stories occurs in book 2. It is organized around the legend of Gerbert of Aurillac, the mathematician, philosopher, reputed necromancer, and later Pope Silvester II, a legend that is told in different versions in a number of sources, but which William of Malmesbury is generally credited with having brought to its fullest, most substantial form.[18] The digression, in addition to being very long, draws attention to itself as a digression; it demands to be accounted for rather than dismissed.[19]

In William of Malmesbury's version, Gerbert, trained in the liberal arts and in magic by Saracens in Spain, is led to an underground treasure by a statue in Rome that is inscribed "percute hic" (strike here). Many have tried doing so, to no avail. Gerbert, in his ingenuity, is the only reader to interpret that message correctly: you must not strike the statue itself, but follow the shadow made by its outstretched finger at noon. Together with a servant, he digs at the spot so indicated, and finds ingentem regiam, aureos parietes, aurea lacunaria, aurea omnia; milites aureos aureis tesseris quasi animum oblectantes; regem metallicum cum regina discumbentem, apposita obsonia, astantes ministros, pateras multi ponderis et pretii, ubi naturam vincebat opus.

a vast palace with golden walls, golden roofs, everything of gold; golden soldiers, amusing themselves, as it were, with golden dice; a king of the same metal, at table with his queen; delicacies set before them, and servants waiting; vessels of great weight and value, where the sculpture surpassed art.[20]

They cannot, however, touch anything in this underground realm, for it is uneasily poised, ready to go away: the bright light that illuminates it comes from a carbuncle, at which one of the golden figures is pointing a drawn bow and arrow. If anything is disturbed, the archer shoots the carbuncle, and everything goes dark. This is precisely what happens: while Gerbert immediately understands the situation and refrains from touching anything, his servant attempts to steal a golden knife. They barely manage to save themselves, having to leave the knife behind, of course. William comments that Gerbert's ingenuity is inspired by the devil, but points out that Solomon, too, practiced the magical arts.

Next, William brings this story closer to home, and out of the books into firsthand oral testimony: "dicam quod a quodam loci nostri monacho, genere Aquitanico, aetate provecto, arte medico, in pueritia audisse me memini [I shall relate what I recollect having heard, when I was a boy, from a certain monk of our house, a native of Aquitaine, a man in years, and a physician by profession]."[21] The story is given in direct speech, as told by the monk himself. Traveling in Italy as a young man, this monk discovered "montem perforatum, ultra quem accolae ab antiquo aestimabant thesauros Octoviani reconditos [a perforated mountain, beyond which the inhabitants supposed the treasures of Octavian were hidden]."[22] Together with twelve companions, he ventures into the cave, which turns out to be a labyrinth strewn with skeletons of previous explorers. The young men, however, are better equipped, since "Daedali secuti ingenium," they have brought a ball of thread to guide them back out. Finally, they arrive at a lake with a bridge; on the other side "visebantur mirae magnitudinis equi aurei, cum assessoribus aeque aureis, et cetera quae de Gerberto dicta sunt [were seen golden horses of great size, mounted by golden riders, and all those other things which are related of Gerbert]." (The cross-reference to the Gerbert story is the more striking since the stories differ irreconcilably in significant details. The story of the Aquitanian monk is rather vaguely localized; there is absolutely no reason to think that the monk's hollow mountain is supposed to be in Rome, and in fact, one gets the impression that it is not. The point seems to be that the "treasures of Gerbert" are everywhere, which signals their metaphoric status.) [23] As in the previous tale, however, the golden world has mechanisms — almost comically mechanical ones — that protect it against intrusion: whenever one of the explorers sets foot on the end of the bridge, it tilts, "producens rusticum aereum cum aereo malleo, quo ille undas verberans, ita obnubilavit aera ut diem caelumque subtexeret [bringing forward a rustic of brass with a brazen club, with which, dashing the waters, he so clouded the air, as completely to obscure both the day and the heavens]." [24] The young men return disappointed, but not ready to give up. A necromancer teaches them the unutterable name of God, against which all magic is powerless. As they return to the mountain, "exitum ulteriorem a daemonibus credo obstipatum offendimus, invidentibus scilicet nomini Domini, quod eorum commenta refelleret [We found the farther outlet beset, as I believe, with devils, hating, forsooth, the name of God because it was able to destroy (more exactly: refute) their inventions]." [25] It is not entirely clear from the narrative why the young men do not proceed with their plan to force their way in with their new magical knowledge.[26] Instead, a Jewish necromancer, who has heard of their enterprise and asks to be part of it, enters the mountain easily and brings up several of the objects the young men remember seeing beyond the lake, as well as some of the dust that turns everything it touches into gold: "non quod ita pro vero esset, sed quia ita videretur, quoad aqua dilueretur: nihil enim quod per nigromantiam fit potest in aqua aspectum intuentium fallere [not that it was really so, but only retained this appearance until washed with water; for nothing effected by necromancy can, when put into water, deceive the sight of the beholder]." This assertion is backed up by another anecdote in which a young actor is turned, Apuleius-fashion, into an ass, and after a short career as a circus animal escapes by plunging himself into a lake.[27]

Thus prepared — after all this, as William observes, Gerbert's story should no longer seem quite so unbelievable — we hear of Gerbert's death. Gerbert, now pope, is fooled by one of his own creations, a brass head that can answer all his questions. When Gerbert asks it whether he will die before he says mass in Jerusalem, the head — truthfully, it turns out, but also ambiguously — answers "no." Gerbert has overlooked the fact that there is a church in Rome popularly known as "Jerusalem," where the pope says mass three times a year. He realizes his mistake too late. On his deathbed, he confesses his sins and attempts to save his soul by having himself maimed and his limbs thrown to the devils waiting to pick up his soul.[28]

Gerbert and the Aquitanian monk are clearly author stand-ins, which allows William to use them for oblique commentary on his own epistemological situation by way of a mise-en-abyme.[29] The monk is biographically linked to William—an expedient we will encounter again. As magicians and explorers, both the monk and Gerbert also meet the qualifications outlined by Dällenbach for such "authorial substitutes." Though neither job description figures directly in Dällenbach's list of "qualified personnel from among those who specialize in, or make their living from, the truth," whom authors tend to "recruit" as stand-ins, they fit in well with "(a) the novelist; (b) the artist; (c) the critic; (d) the scientist; (e) the clergyman; (f) the librarian; (g) the bookseller;—but also (h) the madman; (i) the innocent; (j) the drunkard; and (k) the dreamer." [30] William's underground episodes are, therefore, "mirrors" of the text; this leads to important questions about their implications for the historiographic work they appear in.

There are unmistakable parallels between these narratives about the finding of underground treasures and the *gaainable tere* motif described in the previous chapter. The theme of plenty reappears, though exaggerated almost beyond recognition. There is a hero who merits access to this world through his personal qualities: here, it is Gerbert's "ingenuity" in correctly reading the instructions on the statue; the young monk's perseverance in pursuing the treasures; the magician's special knowledge. But in these stories, the land the characters desire and find is not just naturally "suitable," exploitable, and waiting to be taken: it is overrich, otherworldly, and forbidden. And this time there is no successful appropriation; the providence/*ingenium* balance no longer seems to work. In no case, here or in the analogues elsewhere in medieval historiography, is the intruder able to maintain his right of access to the buried world or to bring up anything of lasting value from there.

But if, at the center of the book, we are made to descend with the historian into his lab and watch him fail, we have to doubt the foundations of the narrative itself. Massimo Oldoni argues convincingly that in Gerbert's "frozen" underground world, a world of automata, we have the historical "facts" *in potentia*, so to speak, to be animated by the historian/magician's touch.[31] But in the narratives themselves, at least, this never appears to work. In one case, the material must not be touched at all: the whole underground world is poised to self-destruct if disturbed, and it is not entirely clear whether there is also a threat to the intruder who would presume to touch an object. In the other case, material is brought to light, though by a character marked as "suspect" by his religion, and with forbidden methods; but the object disappears upon contact with water, as do, according to the narrator, all objects produced by magic. The obvious implication is that the material was not real, at least not after it was lifted from the cave. The *demones*, in fact, are up in arms not because they fear that their property may be stolen, but because their "inventions" (=frauds, phantasms) might be "refuted." The magic performed by Gerbert is thus of a dubious nature—not only in its morality, as Oldoni argues, but also in its efficacy, in the degree of reality of anything it can produce. The magician figures are dubious, the methods are dubious, the nature of the material retrieved—if any—is dubious.[32]

William of Newburgh, who also deals in underground adventures, though not Gerbertian ones, directly addresses this problem. Despite (or perhaps because of?) his dismissal of Geoffrey's "other world," he himself includes brief excursions to these worlds, or visitors from them. The chief objective seems to be to raise and discuss, but ultimately leave open, the questions about reality that come with such "marvels." It is important to keep in mind that not all of the episodes that involve supernatural phenomena (by our definition) are ipso facto in contradiction with the "rationalist" position William stakes out for himself at the beginning; that would be to superimpose our own dichotomy where he may have seen none. His objection to Geoffrey's stories is, after all, not on the basis of any "supernaturalness" or inherent improbability but chiefly on the basis of their conflict with received historical opinion. It is not surprising, then, that his first approach to the problem of marvels is to invoke "trustworthy witnesses":

> Et quidem diu super hoc, cum tamen a multis praedicaretur, hesitavi, remque vel nullius vel abditissimae rationis in idem recipere ridiculum mihi videbatur, donec tantorum et talium pondere testium ita sum obrutus ut cogerer credere et mirari quod nullis animi viribus possum attingere vel rimari.

> I myself had protracted doubts over this, though it was reported by many, and it seemed to me absurd to accept as genuine an event whose rational basis was non-existent or most obscure. But finally I was so overwhelmed with the weighty testimony of so many reliable people that I was compelled to believe and marvel at what I cannot grasp or investigate by any powers of the mind.[33]

As Nancy Partner sums it up: "the theme of the passage is doubt; the resolution is testimony."[34] Nonetheless, William keeps returning to such marvels, to ponder and "solve" the problem of their trustworthiness, as if to scratch an itch.

William always tries to find a rational explanation for his ghost stories, or at least never gives up the hope that there must be one. In one incident, several workers died while cleaning out an old well: this, says William, can be explained naturally—perhaps there was a poisonous substance down there—and therefore is not really a marvel.[35] Other marvels, such as William's vampire stories, can be rationalized in a different way.[36] They lend themselves to metaphoric readings, fitting in with their immediate context but raising it to a different level. The series of vampire tales is preceded by the story of Longbeard, a popular rebel and champion of the poor, whom the king has executed. It is only after Longbeard's death that the extent of the popular support for him becomes fully visible. There is talk about miracles at his grave, and a spontaneous cult is starting, but the bishop forbids the cult and disciplines the priest who encouraged it.[37] William seems not unsympathetic toward Longbeard, but he does approve of the bishop's action: Longbeard was not a saint, if only because he was an adulterer. The first vampire story, which immediately follows this, is clearly parallel to Longbeard's story, except for the ending. An unquiet corpse is a plausible metaphoric translation for a man who stirs up trouble after death by attracting a crowd of naive followers. Here a man who died excommunicated comes back from the grave. This time, in contrast to Longbeard's case, the bishop's solution is conciliatory: he writes a letter of absolution and pins it to the corpse's shroud. The subsequent vampire stories move away from this initial model—they also get grislier each time—but not so far as to make impossible such associations with the surrounding account of political and social turmoil. These marvels, therefore, both the ones that are capable of rational explanation and those that work well on a metaphorical level, pose no real threat to William's rationality and explanatory categories.

But in the short, self-contained, two-chapter segment on marvels near the beginning, explanation fails. The tales are clearly marked as a digression. They are set off from the surrounding narrative by auctorial musings on their reality, and when he is finished, William explicitly returns to the *series temporum* ("ut autem jam ad seriem historiae narrationis redeam").[38] The first episode is about the "green children," a boy and a girl of green complexion and strange, uncivilized language and dietary habits, who emerge one day from a ditch in Suffolk.[39] Once they get used to an ordinary English diet (which also makes their strange skin color go away) and acquire some fluency in the local language, they report that they came from a country that was almost devoid of sunlight but otherwise much like England; they even report it to be Christian. They cannot say where the land is located, nor do they have any recollection of how they got to Suffolk. The boy soon dies, but the girl grows up, "nec in modico a nostri generis feminis discrepante [differing not even in the slightest way from a woman of our own kind]," and marries a man in the village of Lynn.[40] The touching banality of this ending is doubly significant in light of the subsequent stories, which present different variations on it.[41] The first concerns two hairless, smelly greyhounds found in a closed, airtight cavity in a quarry. Their fierceness, bad smell, and unnatural survival skills make one suspect that they may be somehow demonic in origin, although this is not explicitly said. But, while one of them dies soon, the bishop keeps the other as a pet for a while, with no apparent adverse effects. By contrast, a similar "marvel" found elsewhere—a toad with a gold chain, which also was enclosed in a hollow rock in a quarry—is reburied by order of the local bishop: "praecepit episcopus iterum signari lapidem et lapidicinae altitudini redditum ruderibus in perpetuum operiri [The bishop ordered the stone to be sealed up again, returned to the depths of the quarry, and buried with rubble forever]."[42] Some details in these stories about entirely secular "digs" evoke hagiographic *inventiones*: for instance, a bishop is present to judge the nature of the find and to determine what is to be done with it.[43]

Finally there is the story of a peasant from William of Newburgh's native village, who, to his surprise, finds an open door in a nearby hillside. When he enters, he comes upon a brightly lit, lively dance party. He is handed a drink, but he has the presence of mind to discard the contents and run with the cup ("effuso contento et continente retento concitus abiit"). The theft is noticed, he is pursued, but, in contrast to most analogues to this story, he escapes unharmed with his booty. The further fate of the otherworldly cup, however, seems oddly anticlimactic and quite characteristic of William of Newburgh:

Denique hoc vasculum materiae incognitae, coloris insoliti, et formae inusitatae Henrico seniori Anglorum regi pro magno munere oblatum est, ac deinde fratri reginae, David scilicet regi Scottorum, contraditum annis plurimis in thesauris Scotiae servatum est; et ante annos aliquot, sicut veraci relatione cognovimus, Henrico secundo illud aspicere cupienti a rege Scotorum Willelmo resignatum est.

Eventually this cup of unknown material, unusual colour, and strange shape was offered as a splendid gift to the elder Henry, king of England. Subsequently it was passed on to the queen's brother, David king of Scots, and kept for very many years among the treasures of Scotland. Some years ago, I learned from a reliable account, Henry II wished to see it, and it was surrendered to him by William king of Scots.[44]

For the sake of just such a memento from an underground world, Gerbert's servant risks his own life and his master's; his counterpart in the *Gesta Romanorum* version of the story loses his life;[45] the boy Elidyr in Gerald of Wales's *Itinerarium Kambriae* loses the happy land of his childhood.[46] Here somebody succeeds in bringing the treasure to the surface, and it is merely traded back and forth between the kings, as an interesting "marvel" to be sure, but primarily an oddity, quite unconnected to their world: "of unknown material, unusual colour, and strange shape." It is interesting to compare this last detail to similar stories in Walter Map, where the motif of royal inspection of a prodigy ("the king insisted on seeing it") often serves as a means of authentication. By contrast, in William of Newburgh, the impression one gets is one of bafflement, almost embarrassment: the kings involved do not know what to do with this intruder from another reality. That is all. The contents are gone; only the container remains. It is not even said to possess magical qualities; neither is the green child, who grows up to be a perfectly normal woman, or the greyhound, which, anticlimactically, ends its life as a harmless pet in the bishop's household.

This sounds more comfortable, more at home with the miraculous, than it is; in fact, William is rather perturbed by the ability of such found objects to survive and adapt themselves to their new, everyday contexts. He seals off this troubling segment of his narrative with systematic but inconclusive reflections about the reality of such phenomena. He is somewhat apologetic about including them in the first place. In contrast to some other marvels, where he clearly suggests that the story has an interpretation the reader is invited to find, it is not clear that he is doing so here.[47] If he is, he fails to deliver any interpretation himself: not one of the marvels in this section (unlike others elsewhere in the book) is moralized or successfully explained.

To conclude the section, William attempts, a little desperately perhaps, to introduce some order into the debate. First, he reaffirms that the factual truth of these tales is not in question: there are trustworthy witnesses ("dignis fide testibus contigisse probarentur"). Next, he quotes Augustine on magic and magicians: Augustine says that, although magicians may produce all kinds of things, they do not really *create*; whatever creative power they have is derivative of God's and results at best in a kind of second-class reality. In William's paraphrase,

> aliud est enim ex intimo et summo causarum cardine condere atque administrare creaturam, quod qui facit solus est creator Deus, aliud autem pro distributis ab illo viribus et facultatibus aliquam operationem forinsecus admovere, ut tunc vel tunc, sic vel sic exeat quod creatur, quod non solum mali angeli sed etiam mali homines possunt.

> For it is one thing to fashion and to sustain created things from the innermost and highest nexus of causes—God the Creator alone does this—and quite another thing to use the powers and abilities assigned by God to perform some external action on them, so that a created thing appears at a particular time or in a particular form; not only wicked angels, but also wicked men can do this.[48]

This explanation appears to reassure William considerably. It easily accounts, he thinks, for phenomena like the dance inside the hill, which are achieved merely "praestigialiter et fantastice" (by trickery and illusions). Those cases that involve objects that exist, and remain, "in veritate," such as the dogs, the toad, or the cup, present more of a problem, and William of Newburgh begins to flounder in his exposition. He merely dismisses them as futile puzzles, "in quibus homines stupore inutili teneantur": devils, he suggests, will go to great lengths to distract humans from their true purpose. The most intractable of the stories, however, is that of the green children, and he throws up his hands (I am not sure why he thinks of this story as in a separate category—perhaps because it is too benign to be ascribed to evil forces): "Porro puerorum illorum viridium, qui de terra emersisse dicuntur, abstrusior ratio est, quam utique nostri sensus tenuitate non sufficit indagare [But an explanation (*ratio*) of the green children, who are said to have come forth from the earth, is more puzzling; the frailty of our intelligence is quite incapable of unearthing this]."[49]

The drift of William of Newburgh's thought is fairly clear. The entire section, from the appearance of the green children to the Gerbert-like treasure story, begins with confident assurance that the stories are sufficiently shored up by testimony and that, though their "ratio" may be "occulta," they can somehow be accommodated in the order of things; it ends with a certain embarrassment. Magic is not *supposed* to produce any lasting or fully real effects, but nonetheless, there are tangible reminders of each of these stories: objects or people that will not go away (unlike William of Malmesbury's, which are not waterproof) and often do not even signal their dubious origin, but simply blend indistinguishably into banal everyday reality—by marrying, for instance. The alternative course of action taken by the bishop in the toad story (the middle one of the three anecdotes in chapter 28, and a neat counterpoint to the other two, in which the strange finds are salvaged and kept), namely, to rebury the marvel and hide it forever, only serves to highlight the stubbornness of such "real toads." Reversing the process of discovery does not undo it; covering up the object obviously does not make it go away.

The two Williams' approaches to marvelous intrusions may appear radically different. After all, the objects in Malmesbury's stories quite readily obey Augustine's (and Newburgh's) rules, by being "tunc vel tunc, sic vel sic," and tending to go away when transposed or treated the wrong way, whereas Newburgh insists on worrying himself and us about objects that exceed these comforting stipulations.[50] But since both leave their stories ultimately open and refuse to settle on any particular interpretation, they are perhaps not so far apart as one might think. If we read the two sequences as emblems, as mises-en-abyme of the entire historical enterprise, they in fact point to a similar kind of uncertainty. Both recognize that the historian/narrator, although he does not, perhaps, "create," does "make appear" persons, objects, events that belong to another level of reality from our everyday world—here literalized as "other worlds" underground. In other words, they recognize, in the simplest and most conservative interpretation, that there is a referential complexity to historical narrative. One cannot simply assume that narrated events correspond one-to-one to real-life events. There intervenes, at the very least, a process of selection, of retrieval, or transposition, if not creative adaptation. Malmesbury quite explicitly states this toward the end of his *Gesta Regum*:

Et quidem erunt multi fortassis, in diversis regionibus Angliae, qui quaedam aliter ac ego dixi se dicant audisse vel legisse: veruntamen, si recto aguntur judicio, non ideo me censorio expungent stilo; ego enim, veram legem secutus historiae, nihil umquam posui nisi quod a fidelibus relatoribus vel scriptoribus addidici. Porro, quoque modo haec se habeant, privatim ipse mihi sub ope Christi gratulor, quod continuam Anglorum historiam ordinarverim post Bedam vel solus vel primus: si quis ergo, sicut jam susurrari audio, post me scribendi de talibus munus attemptaverit, mihi debeat collectionis gratiam, sibi habeat electionis materiam.

There will perhaps be many in different parts of England, who may say, that they have heard and read some things differently related from the mode in which I have recorded them; but if they judge candidly, they will not, on this account, brand me with censure: since, following the strict laws of history, I have asserted nothing but what I have learned either from relators, or writers, of veracity. But be these matters as they may, I especially congratulate myself on being, through Christ's assistance, the only person, or at least the first, who, since Bede, have arranged a continued history of the English. Should any one, therefore, as I already hear it intimated, undertake, after me, a work of a similar nature, he may be indebted to me for having collected materials, though the selection from them must depend on himself.[51]

What comes between the text and the *res gesta* is, in short, an act of narration, which, in both Williams' episodes of underground exploration, is figured as "magic." The historical world to be narrated is not immediately accessible — in part because it is past (which would seem to be the point of the "romanitas" in the Gerbert story and its analogues), in part because no configuration of facts, events, raw materials is thus accessible; *historia* is always a *narratio rerum gestarum*, an instrument to apprehend the *res gestae*, which is clearly differentiated from the *res gestae* themselves.[52] The material to be apprehended is and remains foreign and intractable: this is the uneasy insight dramatized by the otherwise "pointless" otherworld anecdotes.

Newburgh's policy in dealing with the otherworldliness of his material is one of compromise and containment. He begins his work by banning "other worlds" (perhaps like the bishop who ordered the toad to be put back in its capsule and reburied); that is, at least in part, why he begins by attacking Geoffrey. But he knows he cannot let it rest there: the other worlds will surface again and burden the narrative with unassimilable items (or, on the contrary, items that assimilate so well that one cannot tell them from the legitimate ones) if its system of explanation is not equipped to deal with them. So he will allow them in small doses, carefully packaged with explanations — although of course the explanations eventually break down.

While in Newburgh the intrusion of "other worlds" remains framed and contained and amounts to little more than an ironic awareness of the intrinsic difficulties of the trade, Malmesbury takes the ironies, and the awareness, a step further. If Gerbert and the Aquitainian monk are to be read as stand-ins for the historian at work, the historian is always brought up short. He must descend to the world of lifelessly preserved historical "facts"; he must use his *ingenium* and special knowledge to get there. But for all his erudition and *ingenium*, he cannot do much more than gaze; he cannot simply transmit the reality he finds wholesale — if it is, in fact, a reality: enough demonic stage business surrounds these discoveries to cast their very reality into serious doubt. The account of his travels that he does offer is essentially a recreation, out of his own head; we have to take it on trust, since he has no physical evidence to show for his labors.[53]

Interestingly, in Malmesbury's version Gerbert's talking head can only answer yes-no questions. Therefore, the misleading "Jerusalem" prophecy, which in Walter Map and other versions is volunteered by some prescient interlocutor (the brass head or, in Walter Map's version, the fairy Meridiana), is in its substance of Gerbert's own making; the ambiguity is his and, ultimately, so is the trap. The head merely confirms. If it can be said to be deceptive at all, it is so only indirectly, *because* it is entirely dependent on the questions it is asked and will not volunteer any information in its own terms. We may think back to the inert golden figures and objects, which it is the historian's task to "animate."[54] In the case of the brass head, the magical trick consists in animating and eliciting information from an inert object. But the "animation" turns out to be largely illusory. The head's contribution is slight; it merely answers back what the magician suggests to it by his own questioning. The historian's job, then, is strangely self-enclosed, almost circular. The head, after all, is his own creation; so are the questions, and so, in very large part, are the answers. In this frustrating circularity, he is cut off from the material he wishes to present. It is this limitation that makes Gerbert and the Aquitainian monk such poignant, ultimately powerless figures. On the other hand, it is true that the magician figure also has a peculiar kind of authority, what Oldoni refers to as "shamanism." But this would seem to be an authority born of the storyteller's freedom: whatever he offers to us, we have to accept because he says so. It is this, maybe more than his special access or his power to create things (which, after all, do not seem to work very well) that makes the image of a conjurer so appropriate for the historian.[55]

In these episodes, we are very far from Malmesbury's assurance in the prologue that we will be presented with well-sifted, well-ordered facts from reputable sources and nothing else. The world we glimpse is, in fact, definitely outside the *series temporum* — outside normal geography and clearly outside time. Malmesbury indirectly draws attention to this by observing that these stories take the place of something else that is *in* the *series*: "Melius est interim spatiari in talibus, quam immorari in ejus rebus et ignavis et tristibus [It is better to dilate on such matters than to dwell on Ethelred's indolence and calamities]."[56] The stories imagine, among other things, a past world that has its own independent reality, one of the hallmarks of historical imagination in a literate culture.[57] With the right methods of access, one can, at least potentially, go "there" and view it. (For any such notion to be presented in narrative form, the temporal dimension obviously has to be translated into a spatial one: the past has to be a place.) But that past is inert: static, lifeless, endowed at best with the artificial life of automata; it is waiting, as Oldoni argues, for the magic touch of the historian.[58] It is, however, extremely doubtful whether the historian *can* revitalize the world he finds; he never seems to succeed in the stories. And even if he can, there are still substantial doubts about what the status of such a reanimated world would be.

This is a dangerous literary game in something so dependent on truth claims as a history; it has the effect of undermining referentiality, both to an outside world (what, after all, constitutes the "outside world" in the case of historiography?) and to a higher plane of meaning. To be sure, the effect of these interpolated stories, these mises-en-abyme, is fairly local. They do not keep us from regarding the surrounding narrative as a historical account; they merely momentarily disturb our assurance about the truth of such an account. They are an acknowledgment that the reference situation in historiography is far from easy and thus complicate our reading of the narrative.

At the same time, the historian puts on the line his authority, his trustworthiness as a narrator. Although authority and a commitment to telling the truth are essential to the auctorial persona of a historian, these historians are willing to call that pose into doubt, if only temporarily. This brings us to another facet of the Gerbert story—indeed, I would argue, one of the reasons for its popularity. Arturo Graf observes that the early (twelfth-century) versions of the Gerbert legend express much more doubt about its veracity than later versions.[59] This may well indicate, as Graf suggests, that the story simply gained authority with age. But perhaps it indicates, more than any "rationality" on the part of the writers, the story's function at that time, a function it later lost: it is supposed to unsettle one's assumptions about the truth of the narrative; hence highlighting its doubtful status is helpful. In other words, the Gerbert story is "born" with a semantic element of doubt, so to speak; in the early versions, it keeps that element, whether or not the writer is fully aware of it or fully exploits it. Many, if not most, early sources that tell the story, or even parts thereof, almost automatically append a disclaimer, refusing to commit themselves to the truth of the story, and sometimes take the opportunity to excuse themselves of errors in general.[60]

Moreover, in his capacity as mathematician-wizard, Gerbert apparently came to be associated with a certain type of logical brainteasers, the fore-runners of the *insolubilia* of the later Middle Ages. Oldoni quotes a twelfth-century math book for school use, where a modest logical puzzle for young students ends with the challenge, "Dic tu, Girbertista, quot . . . ?" (You tell me, Gerbertist, how many . . . ?). The puzzle itself is termed "indissolubilis," although it does not appear to be a paradox in the strict logical sense. In the late thirteenth century, Rudolph of Lonchamps reports that there is a certain type of puzzle that Gerbert's famous talking head was unable to solve, thus forcing Gerbert to skip over the difficulty: "Inde est, quod locus ille inexpositus 'Saltus Gilberti' appellatur [and therefore this unexplained *locus* is known as 'Gerbert's Leap']."[61] Gerbert, therefore, may well stand for a kind of Faustian ingenuity, as Oldoni argues. But one could equally well conclude that Gerbert stands for perplexity, for the limits of logic.

This makes him an intriguing historian figure indeed. In William of Malmesbury, he appears as the concrete embodiment of both the historian's ingenuity and his powerlessness, and of the urge common to both Williams to test the limits of historical representation by going "underground." This self-undercutting by proxy flirts with the famous "Cretan Liar" paradox, the logical puzzle involving a Cretan who asserts that all Cretans are liars. The real vogue of such *insolubilia* in the Middle Ages, and their serious discussion as a philosophical problem, does not start until the thirteenth century, but there is good evidence that puzzles of the Liar type were known, and understood for the logical problems they are, in the mid-twelfth century.[62] Our case, in which the historian suggests that he is a liar, is not of course a paradox in the strict logical sense; that applies only for strict self-reference, that is, if it is absolutely clear that the assertion that a sentence is a lie is itself being termed a lie. In one twelfth-century formulation, the question is "an verum dicat qui nichil nisi se mentiri dicet [whether he says true who says nothing but that he is lying]."[63] All the historian suggests here is that he is untrustworthy, that he may or may not be lying in any given utterance. But that still makes for an "insoluble" (idest difficile solubilis)[64] contrast with the historian's persona in the prologue and elsewhere in the history. The circularity of Gerbert's conversation with the brass head in Malmesbury's version is a striking image of the intriguing (though logically imperfect) self-reference these twelfth-century chroniclers uneasily toy with.

A fuller, more properly self-referential use of the Liar is one of the major premises of Walter Map's *De Nugis Curialium*. Walter can be called a historian only in a rather loose sense. *De Nugis Curialium*, his only surviving work, is a collection of anecdotes, facetiae, and short tracts.[65] But Walter, as we have already seen, is interested in definitions of history, and his ambition in *De Nugis* is to be a chronicler of sorts, though primarily of *modernitas*, not of the past.[66] Above all, he is interested in, and perplexed by, a narrative problem that bears very much on our discussion. In playing out his philosophical concern — in a rather covert and playful fashion — Walter not only allows us to revisit many of the issues dealt with in this chapter (the Gerbert legend, "underground" episodes, intruders from other realities, and Liar jokes), but helps us contextualize them through his description of the royal court and the anomie of the courtier-cleric.

De Nugis Curialium survives in a single, late manuscript, and the text shows clear signs of incompleteness, or clumsy interference, or both. Some anecdotes appear twice, sometimes with major differences; the repetitions are so clumsy that one suspects one of the versions was meant to be edited out but was not. The prologue reappears, almost verbatim, at the end of the book. (I am less sure that this is an error; the exact repetition is odd, but it makes a certain amount of sense to open and close the book with a vision of "hell.") The chapter rubrics are far from satisfactory, sometimes splitting up a story that clearly is one unit, introducing "epilogues" near the beginning of a *distinctio*, and generally showing little consistency or logic. In the end, what looks superficially like a meticulously systematic outline — the book is divided into five *distinctiones*, which are in turn subdivided into *capitula* — does not amount to much of an order at all. Although there are thematic connections of various kinds, it is not easy to pinpoint a consistent theme for any one *distinctio*, let alone to find an organizing principle for the work as a whole. Textual scholars have tried their hand at sorting out the mess. James Hinton suggested that the rubrics, as well as the arrangement of the work as we know it, is the work of a later adapter or scribe; Walter, according to Hinton, could not have left much more than unsorted loose-leaf drafts, compiled over a considerable length of time, possibly two decades. Hinton attempted — influenced, one suspects, by *Canterbury Tales* scholarship — to identify continuous "fragments" of connected tales that Walter himself might have ordered.[67] In his introduction to the text, C. N. L. Brooke refutes much of Hinton's conjecture, especially his views on the status of the rubrics. He concludes, quite plausibly, that the rubrics are Walter's, and that the work was substantially written in the early 1180s and cast more or less in the form that we have now. Walter, he surmises, kept updating the book for another fifteen years or so, and many of these insertions may indeed have been in loose-leaf form; these were later copied into the text, "on occasion with startling incompetence" by a redactor or scribe.[68] At any rate, he concludes, no matter to what precise extent Walter is responsible for the work's final form, it is "the untidy legacy of an untidy mind," and one cannot entirely disagree with him.[69] Even if the exact shape in which the "untidy legacy" has come down to us may be a historical accident, it fits in very well with Walter's auctorial persona and the conceit that underlies the whole work: that the royal court is hell and that Walter is therefore stuck in a "hell" characterized by disorder and restlessness.

Some of the auctorial comments create the impression that even under ideal circumstances, with no scribal interference and with Walter's full attention, the book would not have been significantly less untidy. Only a few pages into the work, Walter apologizes for his inability to stay on the subject, as so many tangentially related matters intrude themselves on him: "De curia nobis origo sermonis, et quo iam deuenit? Sic incidunt semper aliqua que licet non multum ad rem, tamen differri nolunt [Well, the court was the subject with which I started, and see the point at which I have arrived! Such topics are always liable to emerge, perhaps not much to the purpose, yet refusing to be put aside]."[70] The opening of distinctio 2 announces two tales on "Dei iudicium et misericordiam [the mercy and judgment of God]," only to dismiss them, untold, since they "non solum non delectant sed tediosa sunt [are not only not pleasant but are even tiresome]."[71] This looks as if Walter has lost control of his scholastic system: the narrator does have a plan but lacks the patience or seriousness to execute it.

Walter is an extremely self-aware narrator: he constantly comments on what he is doing, and, as Shepherd observes, the work is not only a collection of stories but "also a book about stories and their status."[72] Brooke aptly characterizes Walter's witty, colloquial, offhanded stance as "bravado." But Walter's boast does not consist in superior craftsmanship and control, in anything like Chrétien's "conjointure," but rather the lack of it. Most of his auctorial comments form a kind of large-scale, ongoing modesty topos. Distinctio 2 ends with a virtuoso disclaimer:

> *Conclusio premissorum*
> Siluam uobis et materiam, non dico fabularum sed faminum appono; cultui etenim sermonum non intendo, nec si studeam consequar. Singuli lectores appositam ruditatem exculpant, ut eorum industria bona facie prodeat in publicum. Venator uester sum: feras uobis affero, fercula faciatis.

The Conclusion of what has gone Before.

I set before you here a whole forest and timberyard, I will not say of stories, but of jottings; for I do not spend time upon the cultivation of style, nor, if I did, should I attain to it. Every reader must cut into shape the rough material that is here served up to him, that thanks to their pains it may go forth into the world with a fair outside. I am but your huntsman. I bring you the game, it is for you to make dainty dishes out of it.[73]

Thus, in apparent confusion, the narrator turns his raw materials over to "singuli lectores," abdicating all responsibility for the final "meal."

The reason for his confusion, as he explains at length in distinctio 1—by far the most unified and streamlined of the *distinctiones*—is his situation as a writer at court.[74] The book begins with an "Assimilacio Curie Regis ad infernum [A Comparison of the Court with the Infernal Regions]." With the owlish mock-scholasticism that characterizes much of the book, the narrator sets out to examine the proposition that the court is hell:

Infernum aiunt locum penalem. Quid si presumem audax effectus, et temerarie dicam curiam non infernum, sed locum penarum? Hic tamen dubito an eam recte diffinerim; locus tamen uidetur esse, nec ergo infernus. Immo certe quicquid aliquid uel aliqua in se continet, locus dici potest. Sit ergo locus; uideamus si penalis.

Hell, it is said, is a penal place, and if I may presume so far, in an access of boldness, I would rashly say that the court is, not hell, but a place of punishment. Yet I doubt whether I have defined it rightly: a place it does seem to be, but it is not therefore hell. Nay, it is certain that whatever contains a thing or things in itself, is a place. Grant, then, that it is a place: let us see whether it be a penal one.[75]

As if the definition of "place" had been at issue! And he concludes:

et sufficit ex hiis secundum dictas concludere raciones, quod curia locus penalis est. Non dico tamen quod infernus, quia non sequitur, sed fere tamen habet ad ipsum similitudinem quantam equi ferrum ad eque.

It is enough to conclude from the above, according to the reasons here set forth, that the court is a place of punishment. I do not however say that it is hell; that does not follow: only it is almost as much like hell as a horse's shoe is like a mare's.[76]

One effect of this long and witty meditation is to establish and reinforce the secularity of the work. This may seem like an odd assessment, given the large proportion of stories and comments that deal with religious matters of all kinds. Walter is deeply concerned about the moral and spiritual degeneration of the contemporary world. He frequently expresses the view that stories can and should serve moral instruction.[77] Many stories are concerned with religious orders, with the church and ecclesiastical politics, and while Walter's stance is satirical, he seems genuinely interested in according praise where it is due and in mitigating his criticism whenever he can. Then again, the seriousness of some of these remarks is also open to question. For instance, the introduction to distinctio 2, quoted above, where moral tales are announced but immediately withdrawn, may conceal a self-deprecating joke. It begins with a moral *sententia*: "Victoria carnis est aduersus racionem, quod que Dei sunt minus appetit homo, que mundi maxime. Racio uero, cum tenetur, anime triumphus est; reddit que Cesaris Cesari, Deique Deo [The victory of the flesh is against reason, for man desires the things of God little and those of the world much. But reason, when it is held to, is the triumph of the soul, for it renders to Caesar the things that are Caesar's and to God the things that are God's]."[78] The rejection of tales about God's mercy as "not pleasing" and "tedious," which immediately follows this *sententia*, would seem to illustrate the "victory of the flesh against reason."

On the whole, then, the tone of the work is not antireligious but cynically resigned to a world in which divine things are remote and almost impossible to attain. The long critical overview of new monastic orders—a distinctive sign of the times in twelfth-century religious life—seems to serve, among other things, to illustrate this point. Apart from his specific objections against each order (intermingled with occasional praise), Walter begins and ends the section with highly skeptical remarks on the usefulness of so many new rules: "Suffecerunt due femine mouere Dominum paucis etiam precibus ad suscitationem quadriduani; tot autem hominum et feminarum milia noui uel ueteris ordinis quem suscitant [A few prayers uttered by two women were enough to move the Lord to raise a man four days dead: but so many thousands of men and women, whether they belong to an old order or a new, whom do they avail to raise]?"[79] He continues to argue that the religious—not unlike the courtiers—are squandering their energies in hectic and multifarious pursuits and have sided with Martha rather than Mary. We can be "raised," he suggests, not by relying on the orders, but by pursuing our salvation "quisque pro se."

As if to underscore the sterility of the new orders, a series of uncharitable and sometimes off-color jokes, among other things about unsuccessful "miracles" by Bernard of Clairvaux, echoes the question, "quem suscitant?" When Bernard throws himself on a boy who has just died, trying to resurrect him, nothing happens — although, as Walter quips, "Numquam enim audiui quod aliquis monachus super puerum incubuisset, quin statim post ipsum surrexisset puer [I have heard before now of a monk throwing himself upon a boy, but always, when the monk got up, the boy promptly got up too]."[80] On another occasion, Bernard unsuccessfully tries to resurrect his recently deceased friend, the count of Nevers, by shouting, "Galtere, ueni foras."[81] Not only is Bernard unable to raise the dead, but his attempts to model himself on the Lord result in utter ludicrousness.[82] The only way the modern church seems to be able to "raise" anything or anyone is by corruption: Jocelin, bishop of Salisbury, advises his son to get a bishopric by bribing the pope: " 'ipsique bursa grandi paca bonam alapam, et uacillabit quocunque uolueris.' Iuit ergo; percussit hic, uacillauit ille; cecidit papa, surrexit pontifex ['Give him a good smack with a heavy purse, and he will tumble which way you like.' He went: one smote; the other tumbled. Down fell the Pope, up rose the bishop]."[83]

The subject of simony is of course a staple of ecclesiastical satire, and the Bernard jokes are prompted in part by Walter's intense dislike of Bernard of Clairvaux. But there is a note of real urgency, even despair, in Walter's comments on the godlessness of his world. Toward the end of the section on the orders, Walter complains: "et cum omnibus modis hec tempora Deum attrahere contendant, minus nobis adesse uidetur quam cum de corde simplici sine uestium aut cultus artificio petebatur [And though these times vie in drawing God to them in every fashion, he seems to be less with us than in days when he was sought out of a simple heart without peculiarity of dress or worship]."[84] All the attempts to "draw God into the world" — some of which, Walter is quite ready to admit, are perfectly sincere — are not very successful. God is now "less present" than in an earlier, simpler age.[85] The secularism one senses in Walter — and in other writers of his time — does not consist in an absence of religious concerns, or general rejection of the religious life, but in a painful sense that God and, by extension, transcendent sources of meaning are inaccessible.[86]

Being thus isolated, trapped within the visible world and its shortcomings, the narrator's power to comprehend his world is of necessity limited. Imprisonment — in court, in "hell," in time — is the real theme of the prologue and, in a sense, of the entire first *distinctio*:

"IN tempore sum et de tempore loquor," ait Augustinus, et adiecit: "nescio quid sit tempus." Ego simili possum admiracione dicere quod in curia sum, et de curia loquor, et nescio, Deus scit, quid sit curia. Scio tamen quod curia non est tempus; temporalis quidem est, mutabilis et uaria, localis et erratica, nunquam in eodem statu permanens. In recessu meo totam agnosco, in reditu nichil aut modicum inuenio quod dereli-querim; extraneam uideo factus alienus. Eadem est curia, sed mutata sunt membra. Si descripsero curiam ut Porphirius diffinit genus, forte non menciar, ut dicam eam multitudinem quodammodo se habentem ad unum principium. Multitudo certe sumus infinita, uni soli placere contendens: et hodie sumus una multitudo, cras erimus alia; curia uero non mutatur, eadem semper est.

"IN time I exist, and of time I speak," said Augustine: and added, "What time is I know not." In a like spirit of perplexity I may say that in the court I exist and of the court I speak, and what the court is, God knows, I know not. I do know however that the court is not time; but temporal it is, changeable and various, space-bound and wandering, never con-tinuing in one state. When I leave it, I know it perfectly: when I come back to it I find nothing or but little of what I left there: I am become a stranger to it, and it to me. The court is the same, its members are changed. I shall perhaps be within the bounds of truth if I describe it in the terms which Porphyry uses to define a genus, and call it a number of objects bearing a certain relation to one principle. We courtiers are assuredly a number, and an infinite one, and all striving to please one individual. But to-day we are one number, to-morrow we shall be a dif-ferent one: yet the court is not changed; it remains always the same.[87]

It is not hard to see that this can be a description of the world as well as of the court and that Walter, in offering this opening statement, is aiming at no less than a representation of the world, of reality. The passage establishes the large metaphor on which the whole book depends: the court is the world, and the book, with its scholastic-sounding division into *distinctiones*, undertakes to be a kind of secular *summa*, a more or less systematic exposition of the world from the school-trained courtier's — not the cleric's — point of view. Walter does concede that the court is *not* the world; but a little later, he argues, with similar seriousness, that the court is not hell — only almost indistinguishable from it. The quotation from Augustine, however lightly handled, makes the equation inevitable.[88] It outlines his theme, facetiously but also quite seriously: being inside time, one cannot describe time; being inside the court, or the world, one cannot describe the court or the world: one lacks an Archimedean point. Walter complains to his friend Galfridus, who commissioned the *Nugae*, that writing at court is almost impossible. The reason he gives is chiefly the restlessness and noise, which are not conducive to serious thought. But the theme of enclosure, of imprisonment, is also clearly sounded:

> Et me, karissime mi Galfride, curialem . . . in hac si uere descripta curia religatum et ad hanc relegatum hinc philosophari iubes, qui me Tantalum huius inferni fateor? Quomodo possum propinare qui sicio? . . . Unde non minus a me poscis miraculum, hinc scilicet hominem ydiotam et imperitum scribere, quam si ab alterius Nabugodonosor fornace nouos pueros cantare iubeas.

> And you, my dear Geoffrey, would have me courtly . . . ? Yet, I repeat, you bid me, me who am bound in and banished to this court which I have here truly described, me who confess myself the Tantalus of this hell, to philosophize. How can I, who thirst, give you to drink? . . . You are asking an inexperienced and unskilled man to write, and to write from the court: it is to demand no less of a miracle than if you bade a fresh set of Hebrew children to sing out of the burning fiery furnace of a fresh Nebuchadnezzar.[89]

Walter's repeated complaints to Galfridus are a modesty topos, but at the same time they confirm that Walter's ambitions go far beyond a loose collection of *nugae*. The word "philosophari" in the passage above is a signal. Walter becomes even more explicit in chapter 12, where he again complains to Galfridus that the task laid upon him is too hard. The weighty complaints— "materiam michi tam copiosam eligis, ut nullo possit opere superari, nullis equari laboribus [the subject you choose for me is so vast that no toil can master it, no effort cope with it]"—are perhaps designed to look comically disproportionate with the assignment; Galfridus, it seems, simply asked Walter to write down his best jokes and anecdotes. Walter manages, and not necessarily for comic purposes, to rephrase the assignment so as to make it seem weighty indeed: "dicta scilicet et facta que nondum littere tradita sunt, quecunque didici conspeccius habere miraculum, ut recitacio placeat et ad mores tendat instruccio [it is just the sayings and doings which have not yet been committed to writing, anything I have heard that is more than ordinarily inspiring: all this to be set down, that the reading of it may amuse, and its teaching tend to moral improvement]."[90] This is indeed a potentially limitless assignment; taken seriously, it amounts to depicting all past *dicta* and *facta* as far as one can know them — the task, in other words, that a historian faces. Not surprisingly, Walter ends this paragraph with a historian's traditional statement of intention: "Meum autem inde propositum est nichil noui cudere, nichil falsitatis inferre; sed quecunque scio ex uisu uel credo ex auditu pro uiribus explicare [My own purpose in the matter is to invent nothing new, and introduce nothing untrue, but to narrate as well as I can what, having seen, I know, or what, having heard, I believe]."[91] In the chapter's final paragraph, he compares himself to Gilbert Foliot, Bartholomew, bishop of Exeter, and Baldwin, bishop of Worcester, "temporis huius philosophi" (today's philosophers). Although the comparison may be tongue-in-cheek, and although it is negative — unlike them, he does not have the leisure and tranquility to write — he is indicating in what league he intends to play. But at the same time, he has set the tone for a rather skeptical "history," since, being inside the world, he cannot know what it is.

Within Walter's world, too, any certain knowledge, especially knowledge of other people and their intentions, is nearly impossible. Immediately after the hell prologue, Walter embarks upon a lengthy defense of King Henry. Using himself as an exemplum of a paterfamilias who cannot hold his own against his household,[92] Walter concludes that the king, whose household is so much greater, cannot be held responsible for the state of his court:

> Quod in tanta tot milium et diuersorum cordium aula multus error multusque tumultus est, cum singulorum nec ipse nec alius possit nomina retinere, nedum corda agnoscere; et nemo preualeat ad plenum temperare familiam cuius ignorat cogitaciones aut linguam, id est, quid eorum corda loquantur.

> For in a hall (palace) that holds many thousand diverse minds there must be much error and much confusion; neither he [the King] nor any other man can remember the name of each individual, much less know their hearts; and no one can entirely control a household whose thought and speech — I mean the speech of their hearts — he knows not.[93]

God alone is a "scrutator cordium," a searcher of hearts; the king cannot be. Humans wear various disguises, and since a higher vantage point is not possible, other humans cannot penetrate these disguises. This, incidentally, seems to be one of Walter's main objections, later in distinctio 1, to the proliferation of new orders. It adds a new set of disguises, one that is unnecessary with respect to God, "cordium scrutator . . . , non pannorum" (a searcher of hearts, not clothes),[94] and threatening to fellow human beings: Walter, as we have seen, is highly suspicious of the true intentions of each order.

The description of Henry's court is followed by two stories that illustrate both the hectic madness of the court and the impossibility of knowing people's intentions in such an environment. King Herla, whose "wild hunt" was well known in Wales until, it seems, the Herla court metamorphosed into Henry's court, is the innocent victim of a trick. He follows an invitation from a "pygmy" king to attend a feast at his court; he has no way of knowing that his host intends to take him and his attendants out of human time, detain them much past their natural life span, and thus force them to wander about eternally on horseback, on pain of disintegrating immediately if they alight, for under real-world conditions they have been dead for centuries.[95]

The King of Portugal is even more obviously a victim of disguised intentions. This king's problem, like Henry's, is that he cannot see through the people who surround him; thus he falls victim to some courtiers' intrigue: they falsely accuse the queen and a fellow courtier of adultery, thus inciting the king to plot the courtier's murder and to kill, in a fit of rage, both his pregnant wife and the child she carries. When he later learns of the treason, he becomes profoundly depressed and never recovers. But this tale also turns into a story about the production of rumor — equally relevant to court life, one assumes, as intrigue and disguised intentions. Rumor is an inevitable, irrepressible phenomenon. Walter describes it as both a communal and an individual process: "Est autem rumor uetitus licito sermone uelocior cum erumpit, et propagata uiritim admiracio, quo priuacius dicitur, eo multiplicius pubblicatur [A forbidden tale, when it does break out, travels swifter than words which are licensed, and a wonder, passed from mouth to mouth, gains the wider publicity from the secrecy of its propagation]."[96] In an ironically "scientific" tone, he both blames and exculpates each individual who participates in the rumor mill: everybody feels perfectly within his or her rights to entrust the secret to just one other person; while this is, of course, selfish and shortsighted on the part of each individual, the process is, on the other hand, quite inevitable. Rumor is the mode of communication most suited to Walter's world. It is created and propagated by individuals; but these individuals are tied into an amorphous (yet almost personified) structure, so that the origin of all communicated information, as well as any responsibility for it, appears uncertain and diffuse.

The world of the *Nugae*, then, almost of necessity breeds the loose collection of short tales as its most appropriate narrative expression. There is no stability and no order.[97] There is no vantage point outside the "hell" in which the narrator is trapped. Although there is a God who is a "scrutator cordium," He is "less present" than he used to be; and to humans, "searching the heart" of others is not possible. For that very reason, there is no central authority—or, even if there is (such as a king, a head of household like Walter, or a narrator like Walter), the authority is passive and powerless, no more able to impose order on the madhouse that surrounds him than anyone else. The shapelessness of the work is thus a necessary consequence of its moral and epistemological premises; the futile attempt to impose a rigid formal organization on the material only underscores this fact. Walter, as we have seen in chapter 2, uses and plays with *gaainable tere* imagery; but unlike Geoffrey and other writers discussed in that chapter, he is no conqueror, no resolute appropriator of territory. He tends to feel encroached upon, overwhelmed, for instance by all the religious orders whose expansionism he fears. His sly self-portrait near the beginning of the work as the clear-sighted yet benignly incompetent paterfamilias, who knows that all his servants and all his nephews take advantage of him but is powerless to stop them, is a very telling image for his narrative stance.[98]

In this context Walter's constant preoccupation with "apparitions" becomes understandable. Distinctiones 2 and 4 in particular are full of anecdotes about supernatural creatures who enter the lives of humans, usually disappear as mysteriously as they have arrived, but often leave tangible reminders of their visit to human reality. Eadricus Wilde, for instance, falls madly in love with a fairy; he abducts and rapes her, and she consents to become his wife, but on condition that he never mention her origin. Of course the condition is violated, and the fairy-wife disappears. Eadric dies of grief soon after. "Reliquit autem heredem filium suum et illius pro qua decessit, Alnodum [He left, however, an heir—his son, borne by her for whose sake he died—Alnoth]."[99] Walter provides a somewhat remarkable story about this Alnoth—a miraculous cure at St. Ethelbert's shrine; but, considering his mysterious origin, Alnoth is a model not only of Christian piety but of normality. After his cure,

> cum graciarum accione donauit in perpetuam elemosinam Deo et beate Virgini et sancto regi Edelberto Ledebiriam suam, que in terris Wallie sita est, cum omnibus pertinenciis suis, que adhuc nunc in dominio episcopi Herefordensis est, diciturque triginta libras annuas facere dominis suis.

> With thanksgiving [he] presented in perpetual alms to God and the Blessed Virgin and St. Ethelbert the King, his manor of Lydbury, which

is in the Welsh country, with all its appurtenances, and it is to this day in the lordship of the bishop of Hereford, and is said to yield its lord thirty pounds a year.[100]

This is an astonishingly down-to-earth ending for a fairy tale, with its remarkable geographic precision and exact money amount. Walter then goes on to remark on the oddity of the story: "Audiuimus demones incubos et succubos, et concubitus eorum periculosos; heredes autem eorum aut sobolem felici fine beatam in antiquis hystoriis aut raro aut numquam legimus [We have heard of demons that are incubi and succubi, and of the dangers of unions with them; but rarely or never do we read in the old stories of heirs or offspring of them, who end their days prosperously]."[101] The next short chapter is devoted entirely to the question of what to make of such real children of imaginary parents (or real donations by imaginary donors), and Walter cannot solve the problem any more than William of Newburgh can:

> A fantasia, quod est aparicio transiens, dicitur fantasma; ille enim aparencie quas aliquibus interdum demones per se faciunt a Deo prius accepta licencia, aut innocenter transeunt aut nocenter, secundum quod Dominus inducens eas aut conseruat aut deserit et temptari permittit. Et quid de his fantasticis dicendum casibus, qui manent et bona se successione perpetuant, ut hic Alnodi et ille Britonum de quo superius, in quo dicitur miles quidam uxorem suam sepelisse reuera mortuam, et a corea redibuisse raptam, et postmodum ex ea filios et nepotes suscepisse, et perdurare sobolem in diem istum, et eos qui traxerunt inde originem in multitudinem factos, qui omnes ideo "Filii mortue" dicuntur?

> Fantasma is derived from fantasia, i.e. a passing apparition, for the appearances which occasionally devils make to some by their own power (first receiving leave of God), pass by with or without doing harm, according as the lord who brings them either protects or forsakes us or allows us to be tempted. But what are we to say of those cases of "fantasy" which endure and propagate themselves in a good succession, as this of Alnoth and the other narrative of the Britains [sic] told above, in which a knight is said to have buried his wife, who was really dead, and to have recovered her by snatching her out of a dance, and after that to have got sons and grandsons by her, and that the line lasts to this day, and those who come of it have grown to a great number and are in consequence called "sons of the dead mother."[102]

The only answer Walter can offer is that God is to be praised in all his works, and such phenomena elude our understanding.

Oldoni rightly sees these tales of "personaggi senz'autore" as central to Walter's world picture: according to him, Walter's world is vulnerable to irruptions, usually harmful, from other realities, since it is tempted to *curiositas*, to reliance on secular intelligence, to a kind of intellectual gluttony.[103] Yet I do not think that Walter is presenting a morally weighted alternative between a religious worldview and secular intellectualism. His problem seems to be primarily epistemological. From Walter's perspective — imprisoned in "hell" — the origin and reality of anything around him cannot be judged; hence the constant irruption of "characters without author," some of which, as he remarks, are harmless, others quite dangerous. From Walter's perspective, all reality is "authorless," since he cannot see beyond the confines of his hell, world, or time. The brief discussion of "fantasmata" he offers extends this image to history as well: some realities around us, he suggests, come at the end of a long lineage of normal generation and tradition; but their origin, back in time, is "fantastic." Even if we can trace back people like the "sons of the dead woman" for several respectable generations, this does not ultimately tell us anything about their real status.[104]

Ultimately, Walter refuses to sort out these confusing stories, as he says at the end of distinctio 2: he will assemble stories but not shape, order, or explain them. *Nostra modernitas* is a jumble of things, and the narrator of *De Nugis* does not recommend himself as the man to impose order on it. As a matter of fact, he feels similarly trapped in *modernitas* as he does in the court. This is the serious point to his repeated complaint that as a modern author, he will not be read: you must be dead to be an *auctoritas*, but, as Walter says, he does not intend to be dead just yet.[105] He blames this dilemma partly on the stupidity of the reading public, but it is also a problem of perspective, as his other musings on *modernitas* suggest: at one point, he offers the insight that as our past was once somebody's *modernitas*, our *modernitas* will have the status of *auctoritas* to another age.

Where the other writers are explorers and conquerors, Walter more or less passively waits for stories to come his way. To mix Walter's and William of Malmesbury's metaphors, Walter is inside the cave already; the hell around him is peopled with stories right from the start, which he presents in brief vignettes: "De Tantalo," "De Charo," "De Yxione."[106] What he lacks is a standpoint outside the stories from which to survey them. His advantage, and his problem, is his complete awareness of the situation: like his alter ego the paterfamilias, he is clear-sighted, sees through everybody's deception, but is powerless to do anything about it.

This turns Walter's persona into a cynic. He uses a guarded, modified Liar paradox throughout, which makes him out not only a liar, but also a thief, a credulous fool, and a violent man.[107] "Map," the name he uses for himself throughout the book, is a nickname for a Welshman; so every Welsh joke— of which there are many—is partly on him. Clearly this was Thomas Becket's point when he asked Walter whether a Welshman can be trusted[108] (although Walter, in his account of the episode, does not unequivocally identify himself as a Welshman, but as "marchio . . . Walensibus," i.e., a "Marcher," someone who dwells in the border region). On that occasion, Walter's reply, delivered as a story, is essentially that it depends on whether you are stronger than the Welshman; if you are armed and he is not, everything is fine; if he gets a chance to do harm ("potestatem nocendi"), he will do so. This fits the discussion of Welsh-English relations in the preceding chapter, but it also fits Walter, a man famous for clever put-downs; perhaps Becket was hoping to hear one. (Some of the unpleasant witticisms about Cistercian miracles, quoted above, are presented as parts of conversations Map recalls.) The conversation with Becket comes in the middle of a string of stories about Welsh thieves. In the previous chapter, there is a story of a Welsh custom that requires young men to go out and steal something on New Year's day as a sign of ingenuity and valor; stories, or information, are explicitly among the things one can "steal" on that occasion: young men go out "uel in predam, uel in furta, uel saltem in audicionem [to raid, to steal, or at least to listen]," and the young man in this particular anecdote chooses the last.[109] At the end of this *distinctio*, Walter describes himself as a hunter of stories; a thief of stories is not so far off: "audicio" is what he does—all his stories come from oral sources, as he frequently emphasizes; and for him, as for the young thief in this story, or for Cheueslin the Master Thief (a story told just after the conversation between Walter and Thomas Becket),[110] showing his skill and proving his superior wit is at least part of the point.

Paradoxically, although Walter attempts to raise his *nugae* to the authoritative status of a philosophy or history of the modern world, his whole scheme is always on the verge of imploding. While the writers with underground stories temporarily throw into question their ability to truly know and depict reality, Walter makes it clear from the outset that he has no authority: not the authority of texts, for despite his fondness for quotations and allusions, most of his material is oral, "not previously committed to writing";[111] not the authority of allegorizing religious truth, for he cuts off that connection by placing himself in hell and by constantly ironizing everything he touches; not even, in his case, the authority of the competent vernacular author, in the manner of Chrétien. The gestures toward the liar paradox are especially appropriate for Walter. The Liar is, after all, a paradox of inescapable self-inclusion and consequent dubious logical status of the statement. ("I, a Cretan — or Welsh-man — assert that all Cretans/Welshmen are liars. Being one myself, I have to include myself in that statement. But can I then meaningfully make such an assertion?") For Walter, the paradox takes the form "In tempore sum, et nescio quid sit tempus." There really is no "backing" to his stories, or the collection as a whole. He claims to have invented nothing, but he also makes it impossible for us to conceive of any standard by which we could verify this, or by which the claim would even make sense.[112]

Walter Map thus not only exemplifies but also reflects on the detached, ironic, disenchanted intellectual stance that he sees as characteristic of *modernitas*. One of his contributions to our understanding of this stance is that he ties it firmly to the milieu of the royal court. Walter is part of a relatively new phenomenon: a community of highly educated but mostly secular cleric-courtiers, some of noble origin, others not.[113] Under the Norman dukes and Anglo-Norman kings there emerged a class of educated royal chaplains and their staff; these officials, who were not necessarily in full orders and not generally of high birth but almost always highly educated, acted as scribes, administrators, and treasurers more than as priests. Especially in the expanding royal service of Norman England, such positions could serve as stepping stones for either an ecclesiastical or a secular career, often leading to a bishopric or the foundation of a wealthy aristocratic dynasty.[114] From about 1125 onward, as the Gregorian reforms took hold, strongly discouraging both clerical marriage and the appointment of bishops who were not priests, and as the kings began to look more widely for appointees to high offices, these career opportunities dried up somewhat. Educated clerics who were also *curiales* frequently found advancement difficult or impossible. (Walter Map became an archdeacon later in his career, a title he had in common with Geoffrey of Monmouth and Gerald of Wales; this was evidently the halfway position par excellence between clerical and secular status. On the other hand, advancement beyond such modest positions seems to have been difficult and fraught with political pitfalls. All three men were nominated or elected to bishoprics at some point, but in Walter's and Gerald's case, these ambitions came to nothing; Geoffrey, while nominally bishop of St. Asaph, does not seem to have exercised his office much, if at all.)[115] But semisecular clerks remained an important, hard-to-classify presence in England's cultural life. Walter Map and Gerald of Wales, as well as John of Salisbury, Peter of Blois, and other notable intellectuals in twelfth-century England, had studied in Paris and retained a certain nostalgic "francophilia."[116] Geoffrey of Monmouth, a full generation earlier, spent most of his life at Oxford, which, while not yet a "university," does seem to have been a center of higher learning and intellectual life of some sort.[117] The increasing formalization of higher education away from the cloister, in the half-ecclesiastical, half-secular institution of the university, combined with the continued need for professionally trained administrators in an increasingly central and bureaucratic government, consolidated the new class of courtier-"clerks."

These clerks found themselves from the start in an uncomfortably ambivalent position: clerics, not *milites*, highly educated yet inferior in formal status to most seculars, they were the victims of envy and sometimes of their own moral misgivings about their distinctly worldly occupations.[118] The new class of *curiales*, especially at the court of Henry II but also earlier in the century, attracted much attention and acerbic comment, especially from those of noble birth fearing that their status in the king's *familia* might be undermined by people of humbler birth rising to high office by virtue of their talent and training. Competition was evidently intense, as well as confusing: often the university-trained intellectuals, at least those from families of some standing, were among the most vocal advocates of aristocratic privilege and decriers of the "novi homines."[119] Even away from the royal court itself, many intellectuals occupied positions halfway between the priesthood and secular administration, and certainly much closer to the *vita activa* than to the contemplative life of the traditional monasticism that had produced most historical writing in earlier centuries. Even professionalized monks—writers, artists, and the like—such as William of Malmesbury and William of Newburgh, might find themselves in less contemplative surroundings than one might think; they certainly partook of the more secular spirit that was becoming the norm among their clerical counterparts outside the cloister.

The uncertainty of their professional lives seems to have kept these men on their toes and to predispose them to a certain irony, if not cynicism. They are extremely conscious of their hybrid status with its ethical contradictions on the one hand and uncertain prospects of advancement on the other.[120] Above all, they are conscious of the constant need for role play. The division of "outer" and "inner," the conscious manipulation of one's persona, becomes a commonplace both in court criticism and in advice literature. This is the advice of Alanus ab Insulis's allegorical *Honestas*:

Interius sibimet ut pauci vivat et extra
Ut plures, intus sibi vivens, pluribus extra;
Ut mundo natum se credat ut omnibus omnis
Pareat et sapiens sese cognoscat in illo.

to lead an inner life of his own such as few men lead and an exterior life such as many men lead, living for himself within and for the many outside; to acknowledge that he is sprung from the world, to show himself all things to all men, and to know himself wise in this.[121]

Abelard counsels his son:

Dissimulans simulat sapiens pro tempore multa,
Paucaque vi peragit, plurima consilio.
In cunctis sapiens tam tempora quam loca pensat,
Et facies multas sumit, ut ista decent.

The wise man will dissemble for a time and simulate many things; few things will he do by force, most by prudence. In all things the wise man considers the time and the place, and assumes many faces, as they fit the circumstances.[122]

The "wise man," in other words, shares with Walter the chief traits of alienation and of clever improvisation of his persona.

This is one of the characteristics that makes the loose-knit community of cleric-courtiers a fertile ground for the "emancipation of story" and the exploration of fictionality.[123] The court, as Walter shows, is both a distinctive social setting and a metaphor for a world that appears chaotic, self-enclosed, and unauthored; even though the ultimate assurance that it is held together by God is by no means lost, that assurance seems farther away and of less practical help (Walter thinks) than it used to be. The same loss of meaning and control that necessitates dissembling and intrigue and threatens the courtier's (or writer's) sense of self also permits considerable creative freedom for play and speculation, since the referential ties between the world and a higher reality are loosened, if not cut. The courtier and courtly writer, as a conscious manipulator of persona, implicitly acknowledges the "fictionality of the author."[124]

This freedom of persona gives each writer greater flexibility in positioning himself in relation to his "territory," stressing closeness or distance, strangeness or familiarity. In William of Malmesbury's stories, history is a separate place, literally "reified"[125] but dead—or ambiguously undead; it is untouchable, divided from the observer by various mechanical and magical barriers, and ultimately irretrievable. In William of Newburgh's series of marvels, and in Walter Map's *appariciones*, the past is also reified but less self-contained and less cut off. It tends to surface in small portions, unbidden, and intrude itself upon the present. These interlopers can be threatening or quite banal, or—perhaps the spookiest possibility—an uncertain combination of both.

While both Williams thus face the past as an independent reality and attempt to deal with its alterity, Walter positions himself right in the middle of a period, *nostra modernitas*, as both its prisoner and its mordant observer. *Nostra modernitas* is not yet history, but soon will be. It is both alien and familiar, too distant for Walter's alienated narrator to feel at home in, and too close for detached observation. In Walter's case, ironically, what makes history almost impossible to narrate is not its pastness but its presentness. Indeed, Walter sometimes longs for "pastness," suspecting that it would automatically convey a measure of order and *auctoritas*. William of Malmesbury and William of Newburgh have discovered, to their dismay, that this is not so. Once historiography, past or present, is thought of as textual, with its prime point of reference and its prime source of meaning located in the narrative itself, the security of unproblematic reference is lost.

To all three writers, the historian's position is troublesome, even frightening. The very status of the world they describe, the referentiality of their writing, and the possibility of truth-telling are at stake. The writers discussed in this chapter almost literally open up "spaces" in which issues of reference and truth-telling can be not so much "bracketed" as highlighted and discussed—in earnest or in play, or both.[126] In William of Malmesbury and William of Newburgh, these spaces are loci for probing the limits of truth-telling and threaten to shake up the narrative, yet are sufficiently contained to let the work proceed as "history." In Walter, the probing of reality becomes a poetic principle. In either case, invoking the possibility that the author may be a liar is not idle obfuscation but an important part of the exploration, since it confronts the accusation, always the crux of early discussions of fictionality, that fictional narratives are "lies." By playfully conceding that possibility, the writers implicitly recognize the "withdrawal of [the] referential function" that makes narrative self-referential—and inherently parodic.[127] In the next chapter, Gerald of Wales, who as a traveler is an expert at shifting his position vis-à-vis the land and vis-à-vis the reader, will allow us to explore further this play with fictionality and its narrative consequences.

⊁{ 4 }⊱

Quicksands

Gerald of Wales on Reading

The previous chapter took its point of departure from a motif that is surprisingly common in twelfth-century historiography: episodes that describe a descent into a cave, a journey to an underground world of amazing beauty and richness. The protagonist of the story attempts to take one of the objects with him; in some cases he is hindered, in others he succeeds, but it is always a forbidden act with uncertain consequences. In all cases, these stories draw attention to themselves and are given special status within the text. They are framed by auctorial musings on their authenticity, ending usually in a disclaimer of responsibility: marvels of this kind may or may not be true; the author will not decide for us. Although the story is not presented as the author's own adventure, it is usually at just one remove from his own biography: William of Malmesbury heard the story from an elderly monk when he was a boy; William of Newburgh reports that it happened to a peasant from his own native village, in a location with which he is very familiar. All these features lead me to conclude that the underground explorer is a stand-in for the author and the episode a reflection on the complexities of the historian's work.

All the cave stories deal with the retrieval, transmission, or preservation of objects from the "other world"—a world that, when it has a name, is often historicized as Roman antiquity. Removing the objects is forbidden, occasionally dangerous. It requires a bold, quick-witted act of theft, and even then it is frequently not successful. The protagonist may have special access to a special, extraordinarily rich world, either through his own ingenuity or through sheer luck, but he cannot necessarily capitalize on it. Although the problem is imaged quite differently in different versions, all versions signal a fundamental disjunction between the underground world and the everyday world the author returns to, between the "objects" found and their representation. The transfer, if it succeeds at all, is disruptive, and it often entails losses. The narrator's claim to a "special access" to the past—or whatever realm there is outside the text—is undermined at the same time that it is established. This raises fundamental doubts about the text's authenticity and its power to represent the past, about the author's authority and reliability.

The *Itinerarium Kambriae* by Gerald of Wales, a description of his journey through Wales in 1188 with Archbishop Baldwin, also contains an "underground" story that shares many features with the others.[1] What is distinctive about Gerald's use of the story is that he ties it much more firmly and explicitly into the context of his narrative—not only the immediate context, in which the episode is carefully introduced and framed, but the context of the entire work. The underground story resonates powerfully with the pervasive themes of knowledge (including special knowledge or special access to knowledge), of interpretation and its instability. Gerald thus strengthens and highlights some of the connections that are implied in other versions of the story. But the main reason why Gerald warrants a separate discussion is his awareness of—and teasing play with—the reader's role. While the descent to the underground world is, in Gerald as much as in the other sources, an emblem of the writer's activity, Gerald makes sure we understand that it concerns us as well. In a move characteristic of the entire work, Gerald turns the final responsibility for its interpretation, even its truthfulness, over to us: a playful *caveat emptor*, but also a serious insight into how texts are made and read.[2]

The *Itinerarium*'s constant attention to the processes of writing and reading, both serious and playful, is made possible in large part precisely by its travelogue format. The work's episodic structure gives it a deceptively casual, rambling tone and has generally led critics to underestimate its literary quality. The *Itinerarium* has been seen by most of its readers as a chatty, episodic travel narrative, a repository of historical anecdotes and folkloric information of great charm but little intellectual ambition. Gerald's text, of course, encourages such a disjointed reading, even in its organization. It is divided into brief chapters, each of which contains a leg of the journey. The chapter headings are uniform and neutral, promising no particular organization of the material beyond the diary division into travel days and places on the itinerary. The first chapter, for instance, is entitled, "De transitu per Herefordiam et Radenouram; cum notabilibus suis [The journey through Herefordshire and Radnor, with everything that is remarkable about them]."[3] The "notabilia," miscellaneous notes and anecdotes associated with each locality, are grouped in apparently random order within the chapter, with minimal attention to logical connections or transitions.

The lack of explicit logical, especially causal, connection has often been described as typical of early narrative.[4] Erich Auerbach links this "paratactic" style to typological thinking; he argues that the logical connections that should link episodes "horizontally" (especially causality) make way for "vertical" connections to different levels of meaning, such as the "moral" or "allegorical" level of theological interpretation. The paratactic mode therefore has not only a primitive dramatic force, but also explanatory possibilities of its own. Yet the interpretive possibilities offered by Auerbach's paratactic style do not reside in the text itself; they invite the reader to go beyond the text, to decode it by referring it comparatively to a different (higher) level of meaning that exists apart from and outside the text. In less sophisticated — or less theologically oriented — paratactic narrative (such as many chronicles of the more pedestrian variety), that outside reference may be weakened, and we may be left with a thinly connected, naively episodic narrative with little interpretive potential.[5] In either case, to the dismay of many modern readers, the paratactic narrative fails to be fully "textual," to resonate with itself and create its own universe of meaning in the way that we generally associate with literary sophistication.

But Gerald, in my view, is a good reminder that we should not too quickly dismiss such paratactic chronicling as unsophisticated. He displays considerable literary self-awareness and control; and what is instructive about him is that he achieves this not *despite* his paratactic technique but *because* of it. Gerald embraces, even emphasizes, the aesthetic and cognitive possibilities of parataxis to guide his readers and to accentuate playfully as well as seriously the textuality of his text.

One important strand of the *Itinerarium* is its commentary, overt and hidden, on the troubled political scene in Wales during and after the Anglo-Norman conquest — a conquest (if it can truly be called that) in which Gerald was deeply implicated throughout his varied political career.[6] Stephen Nichols observes that the itinerary format has meaning in and of itself: the *Itinerarium* chronicles a Crusade-preaching campaign, which is implicitly compared to the Crusade itself; it is, in fact, described as a kind of dry run for a Crusade.[7] This pervasive image permits oblique political commentary: Wales, like the Holy Land, is an occupied territory, being held by the English; while Gerald's loyalties in this conflict are complicated, he accentuates the ambivalence and turns it into a recurrent theme. Nichols invokes Bakhtin's concept of "polyphony": Wales, while subjugated both politically and culturally, is almost personified in Gerald's account; it has a voice of its own, which is heard, in various degrees of loudness, throughout the book.[8]

Over and above this topical commentary, Gerald uses the journey metaphor to address, self-reflexively, the complexities of navigating through a historical text — both for the writer and for the reader. The journey becomes our journey as well as his, with Gerald as a far from unproblematic and often downright unhelpful guide. The double function of the text's central metaphor — the journey, or conquest — is reminiscent of the *gaainable tere* motif discussed in chapter 2: as in Geoffrey, or in Cistercian foundation stories, political interests and self-aware poetological reflections not only coincide but blend into each other; in the discussion that follows, it will indeed be difficult, if not impossible, to look at them separately. While keeping an eye on Gerald's politics, I am primarily interested in the way Gerald exploits the itinerary form to create meaning and coherence — and the way in which he both signals and challenges this notion in the text.

The travelogue format in itself is a wonderful framework for establishing connections and creating echoes, for producing, in other words, larger frames of reference and meanings that go beyond the segments of individual episodes. Apart from its metaphoric possibilities, the journey image provides, and even accentuates, a mobile deictic center: while the personal point of reference remains stable, the temporal point of reference shifts, if only slightly and very predictably (a day at a time); the spatial coordinate, which in a travelogue is arguably the primary point of reference, must, by definition, be in motion. This device combines great flexibility with unity of perspective. For historians — and many travelogue writers see themselves as historians, or antiquaries — the form permits an interesting reshuffling of materials. Events can be taken out of their chronological context and combined around a new, usually spatial, point of reference, without necessarily losing their temporal orientation.[9] The technique Gerald uses (or, for that matter, Pausanias or Mandeville or writers of travel guides to the Holy Land) typically works something like this: as he describes a section of the journey he will pause at important landmarks to describe their *notabilia* — everything that is remarkable about them, such as miraculous properties or unusual natural phenomena, but also past events associated with the location.[10] The organization, then, is primarily spatial, but most events are also situated in time, with some adverbial phrase such as "diebus nostris," in our days. Typically, Gerald will move backward, from an event "diebus nostris" to one "tempore Henrici primi" or just "aliquando," sometime in the past. Over and above these spatial and temporal connections, however, Gerald uses a thematic, associative principle: often, after relating an event that happened "here and now" (or sometimes "here but earlier"), he will introduce a similar event that happened elsewhere. The thematic connection can be very straightforward (for instance, he reports that a Welsh lake broke its banks and overflowed at the moment Henry I died, and then follows this with a similar instance from Normandy),[11] or it can be tenuous, even whimsical. Often the more distant episodes are especially worth paying attention to. Frequently, though not always, they are Gerald's most outspoken episodes, with the clearest topical relevance and political bite. Their convenient placement "elsewhere" and/or "earlier" seems to allow more freedom of political expression, but their reference to "here and now" is perfectly clear, since they are thematically linked to the more harmless "here and now" stories that precede them.

Of course the two systems—spatial/temporal and thematic association— blend into each other. We may be told that something happened "non procul inde," not far from here, but understand at the same time that the proximity is thematic as well as spatial. Gerald's Latin can even semantically blend the two concepts when he tells us that a story he is about to tell is "haud longe dissimile [not far dissimilar]" from the previous episode.[12] Thus the *Itinerarium* sets up an ideal system for creating all kinds of multiple links and correspondences.

To see what this system of organization accomplishes, it is useful to compare the *Itinerarium* to the *Topographia Hibernica*, an earlier geographical work by Gerald. Gerald clearly regarded it as a predecessor to the Welsh books (the *Itinerarium* and its companion piece, the *Descriptio Kambriae*). He mentions it frequently in the *Itinerarium*, and he even tells us that Archbishop Baldwin read it, a chapter a day, on the journey through Wales.[13] One can therefore with some justification see the *Topographia* as an earlier stage in Gerald's geographical and narrative method. The *Topographia* is not a mere taxonomical description. As in other scientific works of the period (such as bestiaries), it is assumed that all facts have meanings and can be interpreted on different levels. In this work, in contrast to the Welsh books, the meanings are fairly mechanically found and explained. For instance, the osprey's remarkable vision and spectacular diving skills are compared to the devil's preying on human souls.[14] Each fact is allegorized separately; while connections may arise through the repetition of similar themes, the emphasis is, in Auerbach's terms, clearly "vertical" rather than "horizontal." The *Topographia*, in other words, is essentially a moralized geography.

In the *Itinerarium*, such overt interpretations are absent. This does not mean, however, that there is no interpretation. The process has only become subtler, and much of it happens through paratactic juxtaposition — horizontally through motif correspondences, not vertically through allegorization. After a while, one becomes sensitized to this technique and learns to read a chapter, and indeed larger sections, for such correspondences, which are often instructive, sometimes startling and/or amusing — once one begins to see them. In fact, as any attempt to analyze them systematically will reveal, the whole book is so overdetermined that the cataloguing effort will be frustrated, or lead to an ultimately redundant rewriting of the entire book. It is not much of an exaggeration to say that everything is connected to everything else, if not directly then through one or more intervening steps. This multiplicity of connections and interpretations, however, seems to be part of the point — a point that is subtly articulated in the book and closely related to Gerald's fears about the "many voices" described in the prologue.[15]

A few examples may serve to illustrate Gerald's technique. The first example is very straightforward: I.9 is a very short chapter, which consists of only two anecdotes.[16] After a brief account of the day's journey, Gerald discusses the region's *notabilia.* "In this region [in partibus istis]," Princess Gwenllian, wife of the Welsh prince Gruffydd ap Rhys, led an army against the local English governor, Maurice of London. Most of her troops were killed, including her young son, and she herself was captured and executed. There is not much commentary, except for a poetic epithet characterizing her as "Pentesilea secunda." This episode is followed by another story about the aforementioned Maurice of London — apparently a very simple kind of association principle, with no further logical connection. Maurice, who is a passionate hunter, is tricked by his wife into believing that the deer whom he keeps in his private forest are ferocious sheep-killers. She shows him stag intestines that she has stuffed with wool and urges him to take charge and do something. Maurice, a credulous and not very bright man, believes the story and has all the deer killed. No explicit connection is made between this comic anecdote and the story of Gwenllian, but it is hard not to infer a connection, especially in view of the speech addressed to Maurice by his wife:

"Mirum," inquit, "quod bestiarum dominator bestiis dominari jam desiisti, et cervis non utendo, cervis jam non imperas sed servis."

It seems very odd to me that you who own all these animals cannot control them better. Your deer do exactly as they wish. Instead of taking their orders from you, they seem to be telling you what to do![17]

The lady's pun on "cervis" (stags) and "servis" (servants) helps us make the connection: the last clause can be heard as "you don't command your stags but serve them," or "you don't command your servants but serve them." Her practical joke is aimed both at her husband's personal lack of authority and his precarious grip on power. Maurice's overreaction in killing the deer illustrates the kind of violence that is likely to result from such an unstable situation. If we relate this to the Gwenllian story, the implication is that Maurice was also excessively brutal in his suppression of Gwenllian's rebellion. In broader terms, it is suggested that English control in Wales is unstable and likely to breed the kinds of nervous overreactions and brutal crackdowns that come with political tension and fear. This fits in very well with several other comments concerning English and Welsh relations and with the constant harping on English fears when entering Wales or traveling through Wales.[18]

My next, more complex example is I.11.[19] It is, admittedly, gruesome and sensational, but it is also particularly valuable in illustrating Gerald's technique. For convenience's sake, I am not presenting this chapter in its precise order. This, of course, means that I am already interpreting the relationships and creating thematic centers of my own, but that is precisely the interpretive contribution required of the readers of this text. Here and in the following wanderings through Gerald's maze, my exposition will serve, among other things, as an illustration of our decoding techniques in reading Gerald.

The centerpiece of this chapter is a pair of anecdotes about prisoners and hostages. In the first—a local story—a "notorious freebooter" (latro famosus) is held prisoner by the earl of Haverfordwest. He makes friends with his captor's young son and two of his friends. One day he manages to lure the boys into his cell, and, threatening to kill them with an axe, forces the earl to free him.

The second story, which happened in France and is, as Gerald remarks, "haud dissimile," is far more dramatic. This time, the prisoner has been blinded by the lord of the castle—in fact, not only blinded, as we soon find out. But the prisoner, "ex diutina frequentia, vias castri cunctas, turriumque gradus et ascensus, cordis oculo jam tenuisset [From long use, he had all the passageways of the castle and the steps which led up to the tower in his mind's eye]."[20] In an unguarded moment, he grabs the knight's only son and takes him to the top of the tower, locking all doors behind him. Then, threatening to throw the child from the tower, he shouts out his demands: the father must castrate himself, immediately and in public, if he wants to save his son's life. Since the prisoner is blind, the knight naturally tries to deceive him: he only pretends to do what he is ordered to do, the second time even hurting, though not maiming, himself in order to make the noises more realistic. The prisoner, however, has his own way of verifying whether his demand has been fulfilled: after each pretended blow, he asks the knight where it hurts. The knight tries the obvious answer first, then a random guess. Finally, in his despair, he really castrates himself, and thus finds out the answer that the prisoner knows to be correct—and it is only now that we learn, or know for sure, that the prisoner himself had been castrated as well as blinded: the most acute pain is felt in the teeth. Having thus ensured that his captor will not be able to produce another heir, the prisoner reneges on his part of the deal and kills both himself and the child.[21]

These two stories have numerous echoes in this chapter and beyond. The chapter begins with a miracle report: Archbishop Baldwin, in whose retinue Gerald is traveling, heals a blind woman. Next there is a note on the Flemish knights who control this district: these settlers, says Gerald, are fine warriors and merchants, if only they would be less contemptuous and vindictive toward their Welsh subjects. That is, before the hostage story, the theme of blindness has been sounded already (but in this case, the blind woman is cured); we also have the theme of Welsh subjugation, but, in this case, with a conciliatory plea. Immediately after the French hostage drama, we return to Haverfordwest and another hostage story of sorts: Caradog, a saintly hermit, dies, and his dying wish is to be translated to the church of St. David's (a church, as it happens, with which Gerald's later career was intimately connected). Tancard, lord of Haverfordwest, tries to prevent the translation because he wants to keep the relics for himself. He immediately falls ill, but recovers when he promises to let the body go. He recants and falls ill again; this process is repeated several times. The episode is explicitly compared to pharaoh and the Children of Israel. Thus, in addition to the captive saint, we now have a captive nation—which ties in neatly, if quite indirectly, with the complaint about the Flemish landlords. Looking ahead to the next chapter, we find, with no explicit reference to the two hostage stories, or indeed any commentary at all, another tale of revenge and of children held hostage: a man finds a litter of baby weasels in his house and takes them away. He then watches as the mother returns and cannot find her babies, and he sees her spit her venom (weasels, apparently, are venomous) into a jug of milk that she seems to know is intended for the man's children. When the man returns the babies unharmed, she knocks over the jug to make sure that his children, too, will be safe. This is, essentially, a version of the hostage stories in chapter 8, but with a happy ending: both parties relent and abstain from revenge.[22]

To confirm these connections we could enlarge our scope and point to numerous other stories of revenge elsewhere in the book: stories of divine vengeance, of vengeful saints, vengeful animals, spirits, and people—as well as all the oblique comments on the Welsh and their plight. The motifs come together more and more toward the end. The apparently random references to revenge sort themselves out and result, at the end of book II, in a fairly clear plea for an end to mutual retribution, a plea for coexistence and moderation—the same point, it would seem, that is suggested in the weasel story. Chapter II.12 begins with a story about a young man who refuses to join the Crusade, wanting to avenge a slain friend instead. As he speaks, the spear he is brandishing to lend force to his words breaks in pieces. He interprets this as a divine warning and abstains from revenge. After a casual remark about the excellent horses that are bred in the district, there is another story about forgone revenge, but this time explicitly Welsh-English: King Henry II led a gratuitously violent (and ultimately unsuccessful) campaign into Wales, killing hostages and burning down churches. Owain Gwynedd talked his sons and followers out of retaliating, advising them to leave revenge to God. At the end of the chapter, Gerald explicitly singles out several Welsh princes for their moderation and their mediating role in the Welsh-English hostilities.[23]

In the *Itinerarium*, Gerald has created an effective way of "building" a point cumulatively, by indirection. The episodic itinerary format, with its potential for creating new and unexpected connections, clear or oblique, allows themes to develop slowly. It has stories echo each other in various ways, confirming or contradicting each other, in apparently random order. But meanings will crystallize, emerging from between the contradictions, the extraneous material. No firm guidance or conclusive interpretation is given, but readers have the impression that the apparently confused details sort themselves out in the course of the book. The farther we read, the richer the web of associations becomes. In the latter parts of the book, a brief mention of a theme or image is often sufficient to evoke an entire set of connotations that has been established earlier.

Indeed, many motifs that are given full play in book I recur in a compressed form in book II, with some of the details reshuffled; but we, more or less unconsciously, reconstitute the full picture. In II.11, for example, there is a reference to tame deer that reminds one of Maurice of London in I.9: although in this instance the deer are not killed but simply used for dairy farming, the remark is followed by reports of natural prodigies (which in turn refer us back to I.2), some of which are killed—gratuitously, as Gerald makes clear.[24] Thus, although the element of gratuitous violence and overly severe vengeance is displaced to the following anecdote, we are still likely to hear the resonances of "tame deer" and "unnecessary killings" together, simply because of their close proximity, and make the connection to Maurice and ultimately to Gwenllian and Welsh resistance. In the same chapter, there is a very brief passage on a river that moves its fords, a phenomenon that the local inhabitants use for prognostication. This echoes, among other episodes, the story of Rhydderch the Liar, who escorts a party of travelers across a river with moving fords,[25] and a story that precedes it, about Henry II crossing the ford at Rhyd Pencarn, consciously exploiting a local belief about a Merlin prophecy.[26] Since there is also a remark about the salmon that are found in the river but not in the lake that it springs from, we are also reminded of several *mirabilia* concerning fish and lakes—a traditional motif, it seems, that in both Gerald and Geoffrey of Monmouth tends to have political overtones.[27] That we are not far off in thinking of politics in this apparently innocuous three-sentence passage on geography is confirmed by what follows: first, we hear of the presumed burial places of Emperor Henry V and of Harold Godwinson; then, via the deer and natural prodigy stories, we pass on to the next chapter, which tells positive exempla about forgoing revenge and seeking ways of peaceful coexistence between the Welsh and the English.[28]

As these examples demonstrate, more or less hidden political allusions and comments are almost always present, even in superficially casual anecdotes. One can easily use the hints Gerald provides to trace a fairly coherent strand of political commentary in the book. Not that there is a conclusive political statement, but enough motifs point in similar directions to "add up to" a consistent picture of Gerald's political interest: he is troubled by the English occupation of Wales; while he will not come down clearly in favor of one side or the other, his allusive, elliptical technique allows him to explore many facets of the problem, while at the same time dissuading arrogance or violence on either side and advocating at least a truce and a minimum of mutual respect.[29] The book ultimately ends on an open note. The final impression we are left with is reminiscent of the strategy of the *Descriptio Kambriae*, where the ambivalence of the question is simply resolved (or, more precisely, not resolved) into an *in utramque partem*: one chapter makes recommendations on "Qualiter gens ista sit expugnanda [How the Welsh can be conquered]"; the next chapter suggests "Qualiter eadem resistere valeret, et rebellare [How the Welsh can best fight back and keep up their resistance]."[30] Gerald explains:

Sed quoniam pro Anglis hactenus diligenter admodum et exquisite disseruimus, sicut autem ex utraque gente originem duximus, sic aeque pro utraque disputandum ratio dictat, ad Kambros denuo, in calce libelli, stilum vertamus.

I have set out the case for the English with considerable care and in some detail. I myself am descended from both peoples, and it seems only fair that I should now at the end of the book put the opposite point of view.[31]

At the same time, his technique of repeated allusion, resonance, and selective highlighting and reshuffling of details allows Gerald to keep several layers of meaning in an even, unobtrusive balance. Indeed, for almost every episode for which I will suggest a poetological reading, there is another episode elsewhere in the book that echoes it at a political level. Bishop David's encounter with Rhydderch the Liar (I.8) corresponds, on the one hand, with another story about a false guide, a Welsh priest who deliberately misleads Henry II, and with another story about fords and risky crossings—the Rhyd Pencarn story I just mentioned, which again involves Henry II and his imperial ambitions. Similarly, the quicksand episode, also in I.8, is echoed later, in another reference to quicksand—again, in connection with a failed military campaign led by Henry II. It is not necessary, however, or even possible, to find a consistent relationship between the political level and the poetological level; thanks to the lightness and indirection of Gerald's connection building, various layers of significance chime with each other and occasionally come together for surprising local effects, but they do not in any consistent sense "stand for" each other; the relationship is best seen not as allegory but as a kind of interlacing.[32]

It is this intertwining and cumulative echoing that shifts the main locus of meaning from the "vertical" axis, from encouraging more or less unambiguous "translation" between more or less stable "levels," to the horizontal axis, that is, to encouraging the tracing of one or several motifs as they meander on a single level or at most unstable, ad hoc levels of text. We may recall the theory proposed by critics like Haidu and Bäuml (though they limit it to vernacular writing) that intellectual and aesthetic complications on the "horizontal" level will ensue almost automatically as soon as the strictly "vertical," allegorical, ecclesiastical associations of an older (Latin) textuality disappear.[33] This disappearance frees narrative from the need to refer "vertically," tropologically, to a higher reality, allows it to "bracket[ ] off . . . the question of importance . . . , and specifically the question of meaning";[34] it can therefore concentrate on its "horizontal" axis, become self-referential, ironic. Narrative "changes its communicative function from commenting on 'reality' to constituting a 'reality.'"[35] In other words, narrative can become self-consciously fictional.

As Gerald and the other Latin writers discussed in the previous chapter demonstrate, it is inaccurate to locate this development too specifically in the birth of vernacular writing.[36] It is helpful, though, to associate the beginning sense of fiction with a growing, and increasingly self-conscious, sense of secularity.[37] This was discussed more fully in chapter 3; suffice it here to recall Walter Map's basic conceit, half-funny, half-poignant, that he is writing from "hell" and his many direct statements to the effect that God is absent from the *modernitas* that both fascinates and frightens Walter. Gerald, who shares Walter's social status as a noble-born, university-trained courtier and ecclesiastic, and who was in friendly contact with Walter over many years,[38] articulates a similar anxiety in his prologue, when he laments the "centrifugality" (Nichols's term) of the modern world: while he asserts the need for a unifying voice, he also senses that such a voice is no longer available. Despite his longing for a single authority, his overarching sense of reality is diffuse, "polyphonic," and secular.[39] Although it is true that throughout the book he vigorously champions the great accomplishment of the Word, the preaching of the Crusade that will bring Christendom together, both the preaching tour and the Crusade are acknowledged, at the end of the book, to be less than an unqualified success.[40]

This diffuse sense of reality and meaning causes Gerald serious anxiety, but it also empowers him, not unlike Walter Map, to develop his own "diffuse," secular poetic. His web of stories, themes, and associations helps him create a self-contained, self-consciously textual, ironically distanced world that is quite different from the discrete units of tropological meaning in the *Topographia*. Obviously, to the extent that it is not merely subliminal, the process of association, cross-reference, and "sorting out" described above requires considerable reader participation. One of Gerald's distinctive achievements is that he is highly conscious of that point and alludes to it frequently.

In case readers doubt whether they are overinterpreting in making the connections they feel impelled to make throughout, Gerald drops strong hints by making interpretation a central concern in the entire book. Languages, secret knowledge, guessing right or wrong are key motifs, ranging from discussions of how dogs know where they are going to prophecy, prognostication, signs, dreams, and miracles. Secret knowledge, uncanny knowledge, special access to knowledge are an important strand in the gruesome French hostage story.

The blind man has, of necessity, memorized all the passageways in the castle; thus, it is implied, he knows the place more intimately that any seeing person could. He alone knows where it hurts when one is castrated, and he uses his knowledge against his captor—although, ironically, at the same time he forces the enemy to share his knowledge and thus gives up his "privileged" perspective.

An aspect of this theme resurfaces at the end of the same chapter, but in a much less serious version. We are told about the Flemish technique of prognostication from rams' shoulder blades, which enables the diviner, as Gerald stresses, to bridge both temporal and spatial distances. The matter starts quite straightforwardly. We are given a list of things the Flemings are able to predict: "pacis et guerrae signa, caedes et incendia, domestica adulteria, regis statum, vitam, et obitum [periods of peace and outbreaks of war, murders and conflagrations, the infidelities of married people and the welfare of the reigning king, especially his life and death]." But the examples degenerate quickly into the burlesque, going from politics via marital infidelity to flatulence. Gerald rings the changes on correct guesses, half-correct guesses, and ironically correct guesses, in which the diviner speaks the truth but lacks the appropriate context, thus being tricked into self-incrimination. In one of the brief anecdotes, a woman is handed a shoulder blade and correctly infers that the owner of this ram must have an unfaithful wife; what she does not realize is that the ram came from her own husband's herd. This, again, has points in common with the hostage story: guessing correctly is desperately important, and the person setting the "problem" wields considerable power over the guesser; but the Flemish divination story turns the whole issue into a farce.[41]

This rapid movement from the serious to the farcical is characteristic of Gerald's procedure. Prophecies and interpretations may be correct, incorrect, inconclusive, momentous, or trivial, and frequently two very different kinds are juxtaposed. In another instance, we are told of a miraculously prescient eagle who waits for corpses in a certain spot every Thursday, on the assumption that a battle will take place—the problem being, of course, that there is not a battle every Thursday.[42] We get little guidance on what to make of this or what is so remarkable about the bird's prophetic gift if it is wrong so often. It is hard to tell, even, whether the passage is meant to be humorous. Gerald does observe, with a straight face, that eagles know where, but not when, they will find their prey, as opposed to ravens, who know when they will find it but not where. At one extreme, then, the instances of prognostication collapse in comical self-reflexivity: the odd story about the prophetic eagle yields little more than a proverbial saying about prophetic birds. In the most inane of the Flemish examples, the inspection of a shoulder blade that was sent to an expert diviner reveals nothing except that the messenger who carried the bone farted on it. Nonetheless, the chapter ends on a note of awe and wonder on the remarkable "verisimilitude" of these Flemish conjurings, which can even involve several of the five senses—but at the same time, the practice is referred to as "illicita." [43] What we are to make of all this, or how seriously we are to take it, we are never told.

In another episode, one with multiple connections to numerous places in the book, Gerald is even more explicit in withdrawing his authorial guidance. A man repeatedly dreams that a treasure is hidden in a nearby well. When he finally acts on his dream and sticks his hand into the well, there is no treasure but a viper that bites and kills him. Gerald comments that, this story notwithstanding, there are many recorded instances where dreams did lead to the discovery of a treasure. Thus, he concludes, you cannot generalize about the credibility of dreams; just as with rumors, deciding whether or not to believe them is a matter of individual common sense and case-by-case judgment. [44] In a passage on dreams—a *locus classicus* for medieval comments on interpretation—we might have expected to get more reliable guidance, but we find ourselves on our own again.

The point of such remarks seems to be to invite interpretation but to keep it unstable—perhaps not even so much in its specific content as in its range of implications, its seriousness. Any kind of interpretation proposed in this work can range from the perfectly trivial and stupid to the serious. The questions, and the answers that are suggested or that we are left to infer ourselves, may be momentous and metaphysical; they may even be dangerous; but then again, they may not. We cannot tell, and the trouble is that we get little help in determining what needs to be taken seriously.

Although the travelogue format, in its leisurely regularity, discourages "central" episodes or significant ups and downs in the "plot," I.8, the chapter that contains Gerald's "underground world" story, can be said to be central to many of Gerald's thematic concerns, but above all to his narrative discourse, his ongoing "instruction manual" on how to read his text. [45] It is a point of intersection of many motif strands, including the ones just described; and, despite its apparent disjointedness, it is particularly carefully constructed. The underground world episode is neatly framed, contained, highlighted, in ways that both signal its importance and destabilize our reading of it.

It may be useful to begin with a brief overview, pointing out the connections as I see them. I.8 is titled, innocuously enough, "De Aveninae et Neth fluviis transcursis; de Abertawe quoque, et Goher; cum notabilibus suis

[Crossing the rivers Avon and Neath; traveling through Swansea and Gower; *cum notabilibus suis*]." It starts with an account of the dangerous territory on the River Neath, with its treacherous quicksands. Despite the services of a competent local guide, Gerald's party has considerable trouble with these quicksands. One packhorse almost drowns but is rescued; some of Gerald's books are damaged in the process. The reason for the trouble, says Gerald, is that the travelers are going too fast, trying to get this frightening stretch over with as quickly as possible, which is not a good idea:

> Per sabulum quippe absorbens, contra ducis monita, nos viae terror in-
> solitae festinare coegit, et
> > "Timor addidit alas";
> cum per hujuscemodi pericula, sicut ibi didicimus, sit potior incessus
> moderata maturatione temperatior.

> Against the advice of our leader, our fear of the unusual surface made us hurry across the quicksands, for "Terror gave us wings." As we came to realize before we won through, it is better to advance more slowly and with great circumspection over such dangerous terrain as this.[46]

Next the party crosses the river Neath, by boat, not by a ford; for the fords of this river are treacherous, since they change with the tide and are often hard to find.

Speaking of fords, Gerald recalls a story about another dangerous passage in the same location. David II, bishop of St. David's (incidentally, Gerald's uncle, whom he later attempted to succeed as bishop), was making the same trip with a local guide named Rederth Falsus, or Rhydderch the Liar, a chaplain who had been suspended from office for some transgression. Rhydderch was sent ahead, on the bishop's own horse, to locate a ford. This was obviously a dangerous task, but he crossed the river safely, only to gallop off into the woods, leaving the bishop's party stranded on the other side. He returned later and negotiated his reinstatement as chaplain, plus a monetary compensation.

Next we are told about a trick played on the archbishop by a penitent in Swansea, who by means of legalistic quibbles obtains permission to pay his way out of a pledge to join the Crusade.

If we have forgotten about the quicksands in the meantime, we are now reminded. Two monks of the archbishop's party chat about their eventful day and the dangers of the trip. One says, "provincia dura est ista." The other replies, "Quinimmo, nimis hesterna die mollis inventa est [Not at all, I found it too soft yesterday]." In case we didn't get the joke, Gerald explains that one was talking about the roughness of the territory, the other about the soft quicksands.[47]

Thus forewarned, we go on to the next story, which is situated somewhat vaguely as "parum ante haec nostra tempora," not too long ago, and "his in partibus," in this region. The protagonist is identified in a similarly vague manner: "quam sibi contigisse presbyter Eliodorus constantissime referebat [a story that the priest Elidyr always insisted had happened to him]."[48] A twelve-year-old boy runs away from his studies and is approached by two "pygmy-sized" people, who invite him to their subterranean kingdom. He finds an attractive miniature world, pleasant and fruitful, although a little dark; the people are beautiful, if undersized, and they live by perfect moral standards, although they are not Christians. Gold is abundant but not the object of greed. The boy stays there as a companion for the king's son, making frequent visits home to see his mother. This arrangement is satisfactory to all involved, until the boy's mother persuades him to bring her a golden ball from there. He is pursued by some of the fairies; after forcing him to return the ball, they leave, openly showing their disgust and contempt. After this, he spends about a year trying to find the entrance to the underground world again, but it is lost to him. Then, says Gerald, the boy's shame for his behavior and his nostalgia for the fairyland faded, "sibique restitutus" ("and he became himself again," in Thorpe's translation; more literally, "he was given back to himself"). He returned to school and eventually became a priest. Elidyr seems well adjusted to his ecclesiastical environment; he works for Bishop David (Gerald's uncle, whom we have encountered before). But whenever the bishop questions him about this story, he still bursts into tears. He also remembers snatches of the fairies' language, and we are treated to some samples, with a philological discussion. This discussion is remarkable, for it slowly and almost imperceptibly drifts away from Fairy language and begins to substitute the Welsh language for it. Some words in Fairy, says Gerald, closely resemble Greek. For instance, Fairy for "water" is *ydor*, almost like Greek *hydros*; Welsh *dufr* is clearly also a cognate. The word for "salt" is *halgein*, as in Greek *hals* and Welsh *halen*. This is not surprising, says Gerald, since the Britons, after all, came from Troy via Greece, so early Welsh is a lot like Greek. What has happened to the Fairy language, which started the whole discussion in the first place? As if to cover his tracks, Gerald adds more cognates of Greek *hals* from other European languages, and leaves it at that.[49]

The chapter ends with a reflection on the truth of the fairy story, with a waiver of responsibility that is similar to the one we have already seen, but even stronger:

> Sin autem interpositae relationis de veritate qui sentiam scrupulosus investigator inquiras, cum Augustino respondeo, admiranda fore divina miracula, non disputatione discutienda: nec ego negando divinae potentiae terminos pono, nec affirmando eam quae extendi non potest insolenter extendo. Sed illud Ieronymi semper in talibus ad animum revoco: "Multa," inquit, "incredibilia reperies, nec verisimilia, quae nihilominus tamen vera sunt. Nihil enim contra naturae Dominum praevalet natura." Haec igitur, et his similia, si quae contigerint, juxta Augustini sententiam inter illa locaverim, quae nec affirmanda plurimum, neque neganda decreverim.

> But if you, careful reader, should ask me what I think of the truth of this little digression, I answer with Augustine that divine miracles should be wondered at, not subjected to contentious dissection. So I will not, by denying the story, set limits to God's power, nor, by affirming it, rashly stretch the truth farther than it should be stretched. In such matters, I always call to mind this quotation from Jerome: "You will find much that is incredible or improbable, but nonetheless true. For Nature is powerless against the Lord of Nature." So, in accordance with Augustine's dictum, I put this story and similar ones (if there are similar ones) with those matters that should be neither affirmed nor denied.[50]

In discussing this chapter, one can, first of all, follow along the investigative lines suggested by Nichols and read it in terms of its political significance; in fact, it is hard not to. Quicksands, as I have already mentioned, recur later, in book II. This time they cause trouble for Henry II, who, in one of several botched raids into Wales, has made the mistake of not listening to his guide. (To be precise, the moment of "trouble" here is associated not with the quicksands themselves but the dense forest that surrounds them; but such displacement of significant details, as we have seen, is typical of Gerald's technique.) Wales, in this book, is continually both too hard and too soft for the English who travel in it;[51] stories of ambushes, killings, or the sheer impenetrability of the mountain landscape abound and must make any English reader at least a little uncomfortable.[52] That the archbishop's religious mission, unlike most military campaigns, overcomes all these difficulties, has to do with Gerald's ecclesiastical bias, his allegiance to his archbishop, and, as Nichols points out, his belief in the power of the Word. The archbishop proudly jokes, toward the end of the journey, that there are no nightingales in Wales because they are too smart to go to such an inhospitable place: "nos autem insipienti [freti sumus consilio], qui Kambriam et penetrauimus et circuiuimus [we, however, are acting foolishly: we both penetrated into Wales and traveled all through it]."[53]

The political implications also extend to Gerald's own biography. Such a reading is encouraged by the fact that this "otherworld" story employs much the same mechanisms for signaling a special closeness to the author as do the stories of William of Malmesbury and William of Newburgh: the story is an oral report by an older man, and it is further anchored in Gerald's personal history by Elidyr's association with Gerald's uncle. The point of the fairy-land story — to unravel the matter from here — seems fairly clear. It is a simple story about growing up and losing one's innocence, but it is coupled with a vernacular-Latin, as well as a Welsh-English theme. The boy is running away from school — and this obviously means Latin training, seeing that he ends up becoming a priest. He manages to withdraw to his mother's world (he does not appear to have a father) and beyond, to a place that even his mother cannot reach. It is a world of natural law, a strange counterpoint and mir-ror image of the ecclesiastical world that he is being trained to enter. It is a world whose language is not at all unlike Welsh. At the other end, there is a father figure, Latin, ecclesiastical: the bishop who wants to hear all about the adventure (and who is, coincidentally, also Gerald's uncle, one of the men re-sponsible for making him a churchman). Gerald, as he frequently stresses, is Welsh on his mother's side and Anglo-Norman on his father's. Being an am-bitious young man, he is naturally more attracted to the victor's side initially: after studying in Paris, he hopes for ecclesiastical preferment in England. It is only when he realizes that he is not making headway there that he rediscov-ers his Welshness, accepts a nomination to the bishopric of St. David's, which he had previously refused, and begins an energetic but quixotic campaign to have his see raised to the status of an archbishopric.[54] The *Itinerarium* is pre-served in three versions, which can be dated several years apart; it is therefore difficult to correlate precisely with any particular stage of Gerald's career. But in view of Gerald's situation, his ambivalence about English-Welsh relations is hardly surprising. Elidyr's story of the lost land of his Welsh childhood is quite conceivably Gerald's story; it is a story that must have been common in Wales at his time, and indeed in any occupied country at any time.

The suggested connection to Gerald's biography allows us to take our read-ing of the fairyland story even further: since his Welsh-English heritage, his family connections, and the vicissitudes of his ecclesiastical career are very much part of his narrative persona, the childhood story works as a bridge to a poetological layer of the book. Like William of Malmesbury in the guise of Gerbert or the Aquitanian monk, or William of Newburgh in the guise of his peasant, the historian Gerald here imagines a descent to a point of origin: the *real* source of his history, an innocent, oral, vernacular locus "where it all starts" (hence the insistence on the oral transmission of this type of story). He is, however, hopelessly and irrevocably exiled from there. His attempt to salvage something from the "point of origin" fails, as it does in the case of William of Malmesbury's Gerbert. The isolated Fairy words Elidyr remembers do not amount to a real language or a coherent account (just as, in William of Newburgh, the cup stolen from the fairies turns out to be a rather useless, "empty" item in the outside world: a "container without content").[55] The fact that he does salvage some snatches of the language suggests that there can be some form of tradition, a transfer of information from one realm to the other. But it is a broken tradition, one that, to Elidyr's distress, cannot be lived in any more; it can only be reconstructed in fragments, just as we can follow our language back to Greek and Trojan by the kind of philological ingenuity Gerald displays—but that is the only direct access to the world of our "Trojan ancestors" that we have. The historian's situation in this regard differs from ours only in degree. To be sure, the historian/Elidyr is "privileged" in that he once had privileged access to another realm, but that privileged access does not, in real terms, amount to much.

The story itself, moreover, is both confirmed and thrown into doubt by the material that frames it. It is bound into a symmetrical series of warnings and disclaimers: first the admonition that, in passing over quicksand, you should follow your guide and proceed slowly; then, as if to cancel this out, the story about the false guide, the liar, which would tend rather to shake one's faith in the guide; the little conundrum about the land that seems hard but is in fact treacherously soft; finally, Gerald's refusal to commit himself as to the truth of the fairyland story, hiding behind authorities and managing ultimately to say yes and no equally strongly.

The quicksand story is an almost overly transparent metaphor for "progress" through the book—both Gerald's and ours. It is Gerald, after all, who almost drowns in the sand. (More precisely, his books almost drown, but since he is a scholar and a writer, we readily accept the books as a metonymy for the author.) On the other hand, especially in view of the "moral" Gerald appends, and the "too hard—too soft" joke, the quicksands are also a patent warning to the reader: slow down here—things are getting "soft," and you do not want to rush. Thus, the quicksand story does something that is implicit in the entire book: it equates the journey with the book, the terrain with the material that both writer and reader have to cover. There is a telling wordplay at one point in the text that Thorpe's translation misses entirely. Gerald mentions that the archbishop had a copy of Gerald's earlier book, the *Topographia Hibernica*, with him in Wales and read a section of it every day, either by himself or with his attendants; "tandem in Anglia reversus, lectionem una cum legatione compleuit [when he finally returned to England, he completed his reading together with his mission]."[56] That is, the *lectio*, the reading, of the *Topography* coincides precisely, day by day, with the *legatio*, the journey through the real-life "topography"; and what book could be more fitting, on a trip to wild Wales, than a book that promises to unveil the "mysteries of the West."[57]

If, however, Gerald's *Itinerarium* is a writerly as well as a physical one, this opens up a whole new range of metaphoric overtones in the book.[58] For one thing, it takes us back to the *gaainable tere* motif discussed in connection with Geoffrey of Monmouth and Denis Piramus (chapter 2). The *Itinerarium* is, in more ways than one, a book about a conquest. The takeover of Wales by the Anglo-Normans is in the recent past and in some ways still in progress; it is frequently recalled in the book, and it is, at the time of Gerald's journey, still a constant source of conflict. Moreover, the journey itself constitutes a kind of ecclesiastical conquest, both in a relatively benign spiritual sense, of winning over people to join the Crusade, and in a more prosaic, and less pretty, political sense: it is hinted several times that the Welsh bishops were less than enthusiastic about the archbishop of Canterbury preaching in their sees, since this suggested a gesture of overlordship at a time when the Welsh church tried very hard to assert its independence from Canterbury.[59] Seen in this light, the archbishop's joke about the wise nightingale and the foolish churchmen who "penetrated into Wales and traveled all around it" takes on a different coloring. The forceful verb "penetrare" calls to mind the many military incursions described in the book ("[violenter] intrare" is Gerald's usual term for military incursions); "circuire" is a typical gesture of taking possession of a land: it is, for example, what Geoffrey's Brutus does on conquering England.[60]

Gerald himself is implicated both in the military conquest (through the Anglo-Norman side of his family) and, even more directly, in the ecclesiastical one. He is, after all, of the archbishop's party and very loyal to his lord; he even suggests that Baldwin is a saint.[61] Moreover, he frequently emphasizes that he himself is one of the most successful "conquerors of souls" for the Crusade.[62] The *gaainable tere* motif of the fruitful, beautiful, attractive, desirable land (which, as our study of Geoffrey of Monmouth and Denis Piramus has shown, is associated with conquests) is found very frequently.[63] Like his friend

Walter Map, Gerald also makes use of the Cistercian topos of going into the wilderness and cultivating and appropriating it.[64] He is speaking of real Cistercian houses, of course, and his praise of some and his criticism of others is quite specific (I.3).[65] The whole chapter speaks coherently and clearly to contemporary issues of church reform, a matter that interested Gerald throughout his career. But church reform in Wales was closely linked to the political subjugation of the country;[66] given all the other "conquests" described and more or less openly criticized in the book, this chapter has to be related to a larger theme in the book of "land appropriation" that is justifiable and even noble, but has perhaps gone too far and been tainted by greed and lust for power. The *Descriptio Kambriae* consists virtually in its entirety of the rhetorical gesture of *gaainable tere*: the first chapters describe the land—and it is certainly "gaainable," in all senses; the final chapters talk about its possible conquest and how it can resist being conquered.

It is characteristic of Gerald's procedure that the theme of conquest, like everything else, is insinuated by cumulative repetition; we have to let the web of associations grow (the ecclesiastical conquest, in which Gerald is involved; the military conquest, with which he is associated by his lineage; the various related themes that are more or less closely related to Gerald) before we see the notion of the writer's conquest emerge. Since, however, we are encouraged to see the physical journey through Wales as a metaphor for the writer's (and reader's) journey, we may also see the ecclesiastical conquest as a writerly "conquest." Elidyr's fairyland, too, is *gaainable*: he is lured there by a promise of a "terra ludis et deliciis plena [a land full of play and pleasures]"; and it is, in fact, a "terra[ ] pulcherrima[ ], fluviis et pratis, silvis et planis distinctissima[ ] [a most attractive country, where there were lovely rivers and meadows, and delightful woodlands and plains]."[67] But the conquest—real or metaphoric—in the *Itinerarium* is never an entirely happy or successful one. Elidyr's hold on his *gaainable tere* is temporary, and once he loses it, he cannot find it again. All that remains for him is an intense nostalgia that still makes him, a grown man, cry every time the land is mentioned.

In this work, the writer's appropriation of his *tere* is never quite complete—not anymore: in a mythical childhood past, he had it all at his disposal. Now, whatever successes he does have are ultimately futile. Gerald's physical *Itinerarium* comes full circle as the party returns to Hereford: "A puncto quo per Gualliam laboriosum hoc iter arripuimus, tanquam in circino circueundo, ad punctum denuo jam reversi [we thus described a full circle and returned once more to the place from which we had begun this rather exhausting journey through Wales]";[68] and it ends, at least as one possibility, in a "naufragium," a shipwreck. In a passage that strikingly contradicts his usual optimistic tone, Gerald all but admits the futility of the whole mission, quoting St. Gregory on St. Paul's shipwreck: substantial numbers of people, according to Gerald, committed themselves to the Crusade, but the enterprise is slow in getting off the ground because of the dilatory behavior of those in power.[69] The image of St. Paul's *naufragium*, of course, holds out the promise of future success; so, eventually, the success of the mission — the 1188 preaching campaign and the historian-writer's conquest — is open again. (As we know, and as Gerald knew by the time he wrote the later redactions of the *Itinerarium*, the real Crusade failed.)

In the sense discussed above, the metaphorical journey of this book is the writer's. But, as the quicksand passage strongly hints, it is the reader's, too. One reader's *lectio*, Archbishop Baldwin's, is equated with a *legatio*; so perhaps we, as *lectores*, are on a *legatio* too. Certainly this is true for the direct recipients of the *Itinerarium*: the remark about the archbishop's commendable reading habits is clearly related to Gerald's almost discourteous insistence, in the dedication, that the recipients *read* the book and his unfriendly comments about previous dedicatees who treated his works as mere coffee-table books.[70] One is reminded of the techniques used during the *legatio* for badgering people into joining the Crusade — something Gerald repeatedly stresses he is very good at: here readers are being coaxed to embark upon the journey through Gerald's book, together with the archbishop, for whom the *lectio* coincided with an actual journey.

The quicksands are a trap for us as much as for the archbishop's party: we are being told to slow down. The passage, together with the riddle about "hard" and "soft" and Gerald's refusal to decide for us whether we should believe Elidyr, becomes a paradoxical invitation to us to do our own interpreting. To elucidate this further, it is useful to return to the other quicksand passage in II.10.[71] This stretch of quicksand is next to the forest of Coleshille, which Gerald helpfully glosses for us as "hill of coal." The hill, one presumes, would be suitable for mining — if only because two sentences earlier, we have been told that they are now traveling "per divitem venam fructuosumque argenti scrutinium, ubi penitima scrutando, 'Itum est in viscera terra' [A district where there is a rich vein of silver and successful mining works, and where, by delving deep, they 'penetrate the bowels of the earth']." The words used for "delving" and "mining works," "scrutare" and "scrutinium," can mean scrutinize, examine as well as mine or dig.

Taken by itself, this chain of associations may not be particularly convincing. But this is another case where a very condensed remark in book II echoes a much more extensive passage in book I. I.5 is about archaeology. First, we hear of Caerleon and its archaeological remains: there are "aedificia subterranea, aquarum ductus, hypogeosque meatus," as well as above-ground "pristinae nobilitatis . . . vestigia [subterranean buildings, water pipes, subterranean passages . . . vestiges of its former splendor]."[72] Immediately after this, we hear of a rock called Goldcliff, from its remarkable sheen when the sun shines on it. Gerald adds:

> si foret, qui venas ibidem, et penitima terrae viscera, arte praevia transpenetraret; si foret, inquam, qui de petra mel eliceret, et oleum de saxo. Multa nimirum occulta latent naturae beneficia, quae, per incuriam hactenus incognita, posterorum educet cura propensior et diligentia. Nam sicut antiquos in humanae vitae commodis inveniendi viam ipsa necessitas urgens edocuit, sic junioribus industria sedula plurimum contulit, et ingenii perspicacioris acumen multa modernis aperuit. Quoniam, ut ait poeta, duas inventionum istarum causas assignans,
> "Labor omnia vincit
> Improbus, et duris urgens in rebus egestas."

> If someone who was skilled in such work would only dig down into the mineral deposits and penetrate the very entrails of the earth, he might extract sweet honey from the stone and oil from the rock. Indeed, many of nature's riches still lie hidden from us, undiscovered as yet because we have given no attention to them, but the diligence and careful inquiry of later generations will no doubt reveal them. Sheer urgent necessity set our ancestors on the way of inventing certain of the amenities of human existence. In the same way zeal and industry have brought advantages to those who have come after, while their superior intellectual powers have made many things available to our contemporaries. That is what the poet meant, when he said that there were two reasons for discoveries of this sort: "Hard work finds its reward, / Unwelcome though it be, and need when times are hard."[73]

The passage not only has striking verbal parallels to the mining and quicksands passage cited above ("venae," "penitissima terrae viscera"). Both passages also combine the reference to mining or digging with the theme of plenty: in one we have a rich silver mine, in the other a golden rock that may shelter enormous riches, next to a splendid old Roman city. One is again reminded of the original quicksand chapter and Elidyr's underground world: a world of great scenic beauty and fruitfulness and full of possibilities. Now we may consider the possibility that this *gaainable tere* is for us to conquer as well as for the author—although we will not have an easier time of it than the author does. The story is framed with various invitations for us to "interpret," but also with warnings that make the effort seem suspect again.

The Goldcliff passage encourages the metaphoric reading of "digging" since it is perfectly ambiguous as to what it is we are digging for: perhaps there is gold in the cliff; but "sweet honey from the stone and oil from the rock" sound like more intangible, intellectual treasures, especially if "opened up" to the "moderni" by means of "ingenii perspicacioris acumen [the keenness of a more discerning intelligence]." In fact, it is hard not to associate this passage with interpretation, since it is immediately followed by another story about interpretation: the story of Meilyr the Welshman, "futurorum pariter et occultorum scientiam habens [who could easily explain the occult and foretell the future]."[74] Needless to say, even this introductory remark evokes all the other stories about divination, prophecy, and true and false, serious and farcical interpretation. In many respects (even in his name) Meilyr resembles Merlin, who appears frequently in the book and was mentioned briefly just a few pages before. Like Merlin, Meilyr is associated with the devil and, like Merlin, he spends several years as a madman. Like Merlin, he uses his visionary gifts to make political prophecies. But, as by now we might have expected of Gerald, there are several twists to the story; it is designed to trip us up and ultimately to leave us confused about the nature and value of both prophecy and interpretation in general. Meilyr's prophecies, although true and often beneficial, are associated with unclean spirits[75] and with "the old enemy" himself.[76] To make matters worse, Gerald slips in his famous dig at Geoffrey of Monmouth: although he cannot read, Meilyr can tell whether a book is true or not. When he is tormented by his evil spirits and you touch him with a gospel book, he will immediately calm down; touch him with Geoffrey's *Historia Regum Britanniae*, and he goes completely wild.[77]

The precise nature of this joke is quite complicated. Many commentators have been puzzled to find that what appears like an outright rejection of Geoffrey's *Historia* does not appear to stop Gerald from freely using Geoffrey as a serious source.[78] In the *Descriptio*, Gerald at one point corrects an erroneous assumption popularized by "Geoffrey's fabulous history" ("sicut fabulosa Galfridi Arthuri mentitur historia"); but this bit of source criticism comes after a long passage that follows Geoffrey very closely, with no criticism or doubt, to the point of even copying an entire paragraph from him verbatim.[79] Similarly, in the *Itinerarium*, Gerald uses Geoffrey wherever it seems convenient—for instance, in bolstering his claim that St. David's should be considered the third metropolitan see of the British Isles, on a par with Canterbury and York.[80]

This might simply be medieval inconsistency about sources: a tendency to believe what is opportune and dispute what is harmful to one's own interests, with no clear sense of "source criticism" and no perceived need to be systematic in one's approach. But a closer look at the Meilyr story suggests that the matter is more complex. The story is, in a sense, a multilayered Liar joke: Geoffrey, a "guide" whom Gerald otherwise follows willingly, is termed a liar by Meilyr, a confirmed truth speaker (who, oddly, is also associated with one of Geoffrey's most famous characters); but Meilyr's truth is inspired by the devil and therefore made suspect again. In other words, Gerald is again refusing to commit himself as to the truth of his story. This brings us full circle, back to Rhydderch the Liar: Gerald, as our guide through his book, may know where the ford is, but he will not necessarily let us know.[81]

In a final twist, however, Meilyr himself, like Rhydderch, is another parodic alter ego of the historian. Prophecy, as Walter Map explains, is simply an extension of history in another temporal direction: if we know the past through *narracio* and the present through *manifesta memoria*, we know the future through *diuinacio*.[82] The prophet is, therefore, a natural image of the historian and his insight into historical reality, especially since the "future predictions" in the narrative, spoken in the past, have often "come true" already and are, therefore, from our point of view, "past" history expressed in a different mode. This is the technique of Merlin's prophecies in Geoffrey of Monmouth, which contain enough recognizable detail of "already fulfilled" history to engage readers and dispose them to accept the as yet "unfulfilled" rest. Hanning argues that "Merlin is Geoffrey's symbol for the artist-historian, whose insight into predetermined history gives him some control over the historical process."[83]

That Gerald's Merlin parody should serve a similar (though parodic) function is, if anything, even easier to see, since Gerald goes out of his way to undercut the supernaturalness of Meilyr's visions and bring his insights closer to normal common sense. For one thing, Meilyr's vision has both spatial and temporal limits: he can only see so far.[84] Furthermore, as he frequently does in similar contexts, Gerald attempts to elucidate the nature and source of Meilyr's special knowledge. He suggests, first of all, that the "old enemy" works by observation and induction — not unlike an intelligent human being:

longis rerum experientiis et subtilitate naturae, ex signis quibusdam conjecturalibus argumentando de praeteritis, argute futura conjectat, sic et, indiciis haud dissimilibus, hominibus insidiando, interiorem mentis conceptum per exteriora quandoque perpendit.

From his long experience of things and by natural intuition, drawing his conclusions from certain conjectural signs and from his knowledge of what has happened in the past, the Old Enemy can foretell the future with great skill. In the same way, and by taking note of the same revealing signs, he can insinuate himself into men's hearts, and sometimes discover the workings of their minds from exterior appearances.[85]

Meilyr's political prophecies are, indeed, rather like commonsense advice by a well-informed, shrewd observer. There is nothing particularly supernatural about his advice to Hywel, a local nobleman who has conducted private feuds and fears King Henry's revenge:

"Ne timeas," inquit, "Hoele, regis indignationem; quoniam ad alias eum partes intendere oportebit. Urbs enim melior, quam in transmarinis habet, jam a rege Francorum obsidetur. Unde ad partes illas, postpositis omnibus aliis, quanta poterit festinatione transibit." Cujus eventum rei, urbe Rothomagensi obsessa, infra triduum post certis rumoribus Hoelus accepit.

"Hywel," said he, "you need not fear the King's anger. In a short time he will have to turn his attention elsewhere. One of his cities, the noblest which he possesses across the Channel, is being besieged by the King of the French. He will be forced to put aside all other preoccupations and cross the sea without losing a moment." Three days later Hywel received the news that this had indeed come about.[86]

Seen in this light, the final reflection on Meilyr's ability "quod oculis carneis spiritus illos tam aperte videbat [to see these demons clearly with the eyes in his head]" becomes, rather, a reflection on everybody else's blindness: "ab aliis quoque praecipue praesentes et prope positi quomodo videri non poterant [How was it that they could not be seen by other individuals who were assuredly present and were standing quite near]?"[87] Although the issue is not resolved, it is possible to read the entire episode and conclude that Meilyr is no more prophetic than any other intelligent person, that he has no special insight at all; on the other hand, he is explicitly described as being possessed by demons and prophetically gifted.

The net effect of these ambiguities is to leave us unsure of the nature of what we are reading. The narrator undercuts himself by spinning off a series of self-parodies. As our "guide," he may or may not have privileged insight into the matters he professes to be leading us through; he appears, at least in his Meilyr guise, to be telling the truth, but to be diabolically inspired. If, on the other hand, he is calling Geoffrey of Monmouth a liar although he makes open and liberal use of him as a source, he is also calling himself a liar. As Elidyr, he is innocent but has nothing to show us: he has lost his special access. As Rhydderch, "Liar" is his name, and although he could show us the ford, he may leave us stranded at any moment.

Bäuml singles out "an awareness of the inevitable fictionality of the narrator" as the essential ingredient of fictional narrative.[88] Gerald, although a Latin writer, and a historian rather than a writer of romances, continually parodies the narrator, undermining his authority and the truth claim that is, after all, the defining element of historiography. As our sense of the referential relationship, the "vertical" connection, between the text and the world is shaken, and as the narrator's guidance is frequently withdrawn unexpectedly, we are thrown back on the narrative itself, its horizontal dimension. Whatever sense we make of this book grows on us slowly, incrementally, through the innumerable echoes and connections. In other words, the "paratactic" itinerary format with its potential for recombining materials, creating echoes and connections, serves to build and strengthen the "horizontal," to emphasize the textuality, the littérarité of the text. Surprisingly, then, what superficially looks like an archaic, primitive, less "textual" approach to narrative here becomes a means for weaving a self-contained, highly sophisticated, ironic textuality.

There is something frustrating as well as exhilarating in reading Gerald in this way. Everything is connected in this book; one can start in any one place and go on unraveling the connections forever; one will always find oneself going in circles. Gerald plays the role of the unreliable guide. He invites us to "dig" *and* confuses us about the validity, even the morality, of doing so; he hints that there may be "sweet honey in the rock," but we cannot be sure, and he will not tell us if we have found it. We may sense that there is a treasure buried at any point in the book, and there may be—but we dig at our own risk: like the man who dreamed of the treasure, we might be bitten in the attempt.

✦ Conclusion ✦

A t the end of the fourteenth century, long after the twelfth-century heyday of *inventiones*, the magnificent alliterative poem *St. Erkenwald* uses the conventions of the genre, transforming them in an imaginative way.[1]

The poem's plot is close to that of the *inventiones* described in chapter 1.[2] As Bishop Erkenwald's workers tear down the old heathen temple at London to build the "New Werke" of St. Paul's cathedral, they unearth a perfectly preserved, lavishly decorated tomb; the description is reminiscent of a late-Gothic chantry chapel. Its gold inscription is clearly preserved but indecipherable. The tomb turns out to contain the incorrupt corpse of a man in full regalia: ermine cloak, crown, and scepter. There is much puzzlement over the discovery: no one remembers the dead man, and a search of old books turns up nothing, although the rich tomb and regal clothing clearly indicate that the man must have been a person of some consequence. If the perfect preservation of the body and the textiles suggests that he cannot have been buried long, the depth at which he was found would seem to indicate the opposite. The excitement and tension almost lead to civil unrest, but the arrival of Bishop Erkenwald, who was away on pastoral visitations, saves the day. Erkenwald spends the night praying for guidance; then, in the presence of a spellbound crowd of clerics and laypeople, he interrogates the corpse, who readily provides all the information sought. In life, centuries ago, under King Belinus, he was a judge well known for his integrity and wisdom. But despite his perfect adherence to "paynymes laghe,"[3] the only law he knew, he cannot be saved, being a pagan. He mourns his banishment from eternal joy in a moving speech. Erkenwald, weeping with compassion, wishes he could help: if only the judge could come back to life long enough for the bishop to say, "I folwe þe in þe Fader nome and His fre Childes, / And of þe gracious Holy Goste [I baptize you in the name of the Father and of His merciful son, and of the merciful Holy Spirit]."[4] This baptismal formula, though spoken in the conditional, together with the water of Erkenwald's tears, is enough to save the pagan judge. He announces that his soul has just been admitted to the heavenly banquet. After that he speaks no more, and his body decays instantly.

This text is particularly suitable as both a chronological and a logical end point to my discussion of *inventiones* because it shows the range of metaphoric possibilities of the *inventio* narrative. Despite its title, *St. Erkenwald* is not, strictly speaking, a hagiographical poem. The body unearthed is not that of a saint, and the association with St. Erkenwald seems casual. Although Gordon Whatley shows points of contact between the poem and Erkenwald's *Vita*, points that may well have suggested the choice of Erkenwald as the protagonist of the poem, the incident described was at no time part of Erkenwald's legend, either before or after *St. Erkenwald*.[5] *St. Erkenwald* is, if not a poem *à thèse*, a poem that addresses itself to a specific intellectual controversy of its period: the status of the righteous pagan who did not have the benefit of Christian revelation.[6] The *inventio* plot is merely a vehicle for this debate.

It is not hard to see why it might be a particularly apt vehicle. The "righteous heathen" controversy is a question about time and eternity: Can divine grace overcome the inherent unfairness of linear time, which damns some individuals simply because they were born at the wrong time? But it is also a question about the relationship of the past to the present, and *St. Erkenwald* stresses this latter point.

The poem begins with an elaborate historical introduction. It emphasizes continuity and transformation: the miracle occurs as St. Paul's is built to replace—both continue and supersede—a pagan sanctuary; the pagan's salvation clinches the conversion of the English people and sanctions the beginning of Erkenwald's "new werke."[7]

Most important, however, the unknown poet is concerned with the hermeneutical problems of the present confronting the past.[8] The first half of the poem is devoted almost entirely to the attempts of the moderns to decipher what is left of the past. We see clerics, the mayor, and the entire London population trying to interpret the discovery. Books are consulted; old people are questioned. People try to reason logically from the archaeological evidence, remarking on the depth of the body's burial and the state of his clothes.[9] In other words, we see the same images, the same issues at work that we saw in the straightforward hagiographic *inventiones*; but here one senses much more conscious control, much more sophisticated play with the archaeological imagery the *inventio* has to offer.

Even to ask the question "Can a pre-Christian pagan be saved?" presupposes a certain historical imagination, an ability to abstract from one's own time and acknowledge historical difference.[10] The question implicitly recognizes an epoch different from one's own, with its own conditions, *laghes*, and beliefs; it recognizes that individuals in that epoch will have moral responsibilities, choices, desires, and aspirations not radically different from those of the present, but governed by the *laghe* of their time.

The chantrylike tomb, an accomplished, complex, and self-enclosed work of art appearing unexpectedly from the ground, is a perfect "poetic emblem" for this historical imagination. It is a solid artifact, evidence of the skill, taste, and ingenuity of an earlier age, although by virtue of its providential preservation it also transcends time. The tomb is familiar in shape—the poet simply described a tomb of his own era, with "gargoyles"—yet it is enigmatic. It carries its own explanation, in the form of an inscription, but the inscription is "roynish," a word explained by the editor as meaning either "mysterious" or "savage," but also "written in runes," so that the outlandishness is directly associated with the age and cultural provenance of the writing.[11] In order to make sense within a present-day context, the archaeological find must be interrogated in the right way: only St. Erkenwald is able to communicate with the dead man.

Once the communication is established, the discovery can be made to work for the people of the present, depicting, reflecting, and highlighting their own endeavor and providing moral instruction. But at the same time part of the point of the poem is the paradoxical wish to give something back to the past, to reach back through history and put right what went wrong there. The St. Albans *passio* of Saints Alban and Amphibalus—of the twelfth-century texts I have analyzed perhaps the closest to *St. Erkenwald* in its sensibility—suggests that the present-day historian can help his hapless dark-age predecessor by completing his work, by making known to the world what he kept hidden for fear of persecution.[12] Here, the contribution of the moderns to the past is to sanctify it retroactively. Not only is Erkenwald, somewhat to his own surprise, able to perform this service for the pagan judge; it is also the essence of his "New Werke," which consists in converting the old pagan temples to Christian observance. If Gollancz is right in surmising that *St. Erkenwald* is an occasional poem, written for some celebration at St. Paul's, that adds another layer to the symbolism: Erkenwald's "New Werke" matches the new work of fourteenth-century St. Paul's.[13] By celebrating and describing their tradition, fourteenth-century Englishmen both find their *fundement* and retroactively "baptize" their past. Since the poem is obviously part of that process, it also mirrors itself.

On a sliding scale from "referential" to "metaphoric," as proposed in the introduction, *St. Erkenwald* is clearly quite far on the metaphoric side — perhaps, as far as *inventiones* are concerned, at the outer limit. Unlike the older *inventiones*, this poem is not designed primarily to promote a particular religious house. Although it is associated with St. Paul's and has numerous local allusions, its ultimate purpose is not tied to that locale. It no longer matters much that the incident narrated was never before or after associated with the historical title figure of the poem, St. Erkenwald; nor does it matter that the "New Werke" of St. Paul's, a thirteenth-century structure, is anachronistically assigned to the seventh century.[14] The poem's "contract" with its readers stipulates that, in Stierle's definition of narrative fiction, "fictive statements are possible, and that in that case a better knowledge of the 'true facts' will be beside the point."[15] The specific local reference is reduced to the point where it does little more than provide local color; in its place, there is metaphoric reference: reference to theological concepts, to an important intellectual debate of the day, to other texts, and to the kind of historical commemoration that the poem itself performs. This kind of reference is, as we have seen, not entirely absent from the twelfth-century *inventiones*; but they retain their outside reference, their obligations to historical chronology and local topography, to a much larger degree than does *St. Erkenwald*.

The aim of this study has been to complicate our reading of twelfth-century English historiography. I have argued that many twelfth-century historians are much more aware of referential complexities, of the narrative possibilities offered by narrator roles and metaphor, than has been recognized. At the same time, I have suggested that it may be helpful, for the fact-bound genre of historiography, to see outside reference and fictionality not as mutually exclusive, but as two poles of a spectrum of gradations and intermixtures. Spatial reference has proved to be a useful category in reading historical texts along these lines, since it is, on the one hand, a particularly strong marker of the referentiality of historical writing and, on the other hand, particularly susceptible to metaphorical and self-referential transformations.

Thus I have argued that the local *inventio* narratives, although rather far toward the referential end of my scale, do exploit their inherent metaphorical possibilities; in narratives like Goscelin's "Vita S. Yvonis" or the *passio* of Alban and Amphibalus, reference and self-reference are so intimately connected that it is neither possible nor useful to disentangle them. Of the more ambitious literary historians, some are more adventurous than others in disturbing the referentiality of their narratives and making their spatial imagery self-referential. Writers like William of Malmesbury and William of Newburgh offer individual episodes, teasing glimpses of the complexities of historical reference, which leave the surrounding narrative largely intact but certainly color a reader's attitude toward the entire historical account. At the far end of the scale are ironists like Geoffrey of Monmouth (although he is notoriously difficult to classify), Walter Map, and Gerald of Wales. Many of these writers, but especially Walter and Gerald, who were active at the very end of the twelfth century and into the thirteenth, can be compared in their literary self-awareness to contemporary vernacular authors like Chrétien de Troyes, Marie de France, or Wolfram von Eschenbach. Their literary achievement has been underrated, partly because they worked in genres not usually associated with narrative complexity, partly because they wrote in Latin: a long-standing critical tradition has it that the "birth of the author" and the beginnings of literary fiction are the exclusive property of vernacular literature. To include these Latin writers in the canon of literary masters of the late twelfth century would correct and round out our picture of the cultural context that gave rise to literary narrative as an independent and dignified intellectual endeavor.

⊰ Notes ⊱

ABBREVIATIONS

AASS = *Acta Sanctorum quotquot toto orbe coluntur.* New ed. Paris: Palme, 1863– .

BHL = *Bibliotheca Hagiographica Latina Antiquae et Mediae Aetatis.* Brussels: Bollandists, 1898–99. With *Novum Supplementum.* Ed. Henryk Foos. Subsidia Hagiographica 70. Brussels: Bollandists, 1986.

BL = British Library.

MGH SS = *Monumenta Germaniae Historica . . . Scriptorum* t. 1–32. Gen. ed. Georg Heinrich Pertz. Hanover: Hahnsche Buchhandlung, 1826–1934. Reprint, Stuttgart: Hiersemann, 1963.

PL = *Patrologiae cursus completus, Series Latina.* Ed. J.-P. Migne. Paris, 1844–64.

INTRODUCTION

1. Haidu, "Repetition"; Bäuml, "Varieties and Consequences." For a classic statement of this idea, see Bezzola, *Les origines et la formation*, 2:241–43.

2. The hagiography discussed in this book is closely tied to local history, usually concerning the founding saint of the monastery that also possessed that saint's relics. The less localized cults of major international saints (such as St. Margaret or the Apostles) present different historiographical problems that exceed the scope of this study.

3. Southern, "Aspects of the European Tradition of Historical Writing: 4. The Sense of the Past"; quotation on p. 256. See also Gransden, "Realistic Observation," and *Historical Writing*, 265–95.

4. A quick, though impressionistic, way of assessing the place of world history in the overall historiographic output of medieval England is to look at Gransden's "Chronological Index of the Principal Literary Sources for English History to c. 1307" in *Historical Writing*, 524–29, which indicates what period is covered by each of the works listed.

5. See Classen, "*Res Gestae*, Universal History, Apocalypse," for a brief discussion of Otto and other twelfth-century theoreticians; but, although he makes no attempt to assess the relative frequency or importance of the different forms of historiography, Classen does suggest that Otto's work is somewhat exceptional. M.-D. Chenu, in his important essay "Theology and the New Awareness of History," discusses the interplay of theology and his-

toriography in the twelfth century. See also Vaughan, "The Past in the Middle Ages," who strongly argues against the generalization that medieval history was "providential, if not apocalyptic, universalizing, [and] Christocentric"; instead, he suggests that the Roman empire and its historiography was the predominant model. But this is hardly an either-or proposition, and Vaughan's discussion is necessarily rather general, since it ranges over six centuries and three countries. Some useful distinctions between world history, universal history, and salvation history are made in a skeptical brief statement by Borst, "Weltgeschichten im Mittelalter?"

6. Orderic Vitalis, *The Ecclesiastical History*. Although Orderic spent most of his life in Normandy, his links to England and his interests in English affairs remained strong enough to justify an occasional look at his work in connection with English historiography. The early books are compilations; the narrative voice does not fully awaken until the history reaches the writer's environment and recent past. Ralph of Diceto's *Abbreviatio Chronicorum* is a partial exception. But even though Ralph shows his "universal" ambitions by prefacing the work with an orientation to general chronology, and with extensive excerpts of prologues and theoretical statements from other major historians, the *Abbreviatio* is not so much a narrative history, let alone a "Geschichtstheologie," as a reference work, with a remarkably inventive and advanced indexing system to facilitate quick orientation. *Abbreviatio Chronicorum*, 1:3-4. See also Gransden, *Historical Writing*, 234-35 and plate 7; and Clanchy, *From Memory to Written Record*, 175-77.

7. See chap. 1 at n. 9.

8. William of Malmesbury, *Gesta Pontificum Anglorum*; Gerald of Wales, *Itinerarium Kambriae et Descriptio Kambriae*; Geoffrey of Monmouth, *Historia Regum Britanniae*.

9. Auerbach, *Mimesis*, 128-31. For elaborations and further developments of this brief assessment, see, for instance, Ollier, "Utopie et roman arthurien"; Schenck, "Vues sur le temps et l'espace chez Chrétien de Troyes"; Ribard, "Espace romanesque et symbolisme"; and Vermette, "Terrae Incantatae."

10. Bakhtin, "Forms of Time and of the Chronotope in the Novel," 84-85. Bakhtin's term, "chronotope," and his basic observations on its generic significance are helpful, although the specific classification into which he develops the concept is of limited relevance to my argument.

11. Spiegel, "Genealogy," 44. Implicitly, this is also the view taken by scholars like Gransden, who rarely touches on questions of epistemology or reference in her descriptive survey of medieval historiographical method.

12. Hanning, "Poetic Emblems"; Dällenbach, *The Mirror in the Text*.

13. In addition to the vast literature on history and narrative (some of which I will refer to later in this introduction), there have been some critical studies of medieval historiography as literature. I am obviously much indebted to Robert W. Hanning's pioneering study, *The Vision of History in Early Britain*, and to Nancy F. Partner, *Serious Entertainments: The Writing of History in Twelfth-Century England*. Medieval historiography is discussed in a larger context in Breisach, *Historiography: Ancient, Medieval, and Modern*. The four essays by Partner, John O. Ward, Roger Ray, and Donald J. Wilcox in Ernst Breisach, *Classical Rhetoric and Medieval Historiography*, are also very important, as is Southern's series of essays, "Aspects of the European Tradition of Historical Writing." Recent book-

length studies include Blacker-Knight, "From *Historia* to Estoire," and Lettinck, *Geschied-beschouwing*; also, the series of articles by Oldoni (see chap. 3, n. 18). An important recent contribution to the study of historiography from a literary point of view is Spiegel, *Romancing the Past*.

14. Coleman, *Ancient and Medieval Memories*, 281–82, 318; see also Stephen Bann's discussion of Ranke and nineteenth-century historicism in *The Clothing of Clio*, 8–31.

15. Here, perhaps, is the place to emphasize that my aim in this study is not source criticism; the factual accuracy of the texts I discuss is not at issue. I am not so much discussing their factual truth as the nature of their truth claim or, which amounts to almost the same thing, their assumptions about referentiality.

16. Bäuml, "Varieties and Consequences."

17. This is a charge that has been leveled, reasonably, against Hayden White; see esp. Weimar, "Der Text, den (Literar-) Historiker schreiben."

18. For example, Danto, "Some Reflections on Literature and Life," and Partner, "Making Up Lost Time." See also Partner, "Notes on the Margins."

19. Searle, "Logical Status," 67. For a further discussion of this view, see Gale, "The Fictive Use of Language." Gale is unhappy with Searle's notion that fictional assertion is the same illocutionary act as nonfictional assertion, but performed "non-seriously"; he prefers to consider this "nonserious assertion" a separate kind of speech act ("I hereby ask you to imagine that . . ."). But for our purposes, the modification is minor.

20. Searle, "Logical Status," 65. On play and fiction, see Warning, "Staged Discourse," 42–43.

21. ". . . daß mit der Möglichkeit von Fiktivität zu rechnen ist, und daß dann ein besseres Wissen des 'wahren Sachverhalts' nichts ausrichten kann" (Stierle, "Erfahrung und narrative Form," 97).

22. Bäuml, "Varieties and Consequences"; Nykrog, "The Rise of Literary Fiction," 594.

23. Early discussions of fiction, of course, often circle around the notion of lying—a notion that, as we shall see, some writers playfully exploit (chaps. 3 and 4). Sidney, in his *Defense*, was still seriously battling that charge, and Peter McCormick observes that the entire pragmatic definition of fiction as outlined above is essentially a modern reformulation of Sidney's argument that the poet does not lie because he "nothing affirms" (McCormick, *Fictions, Philosophies, and the Problem of Poetics*, 39). See also Nelson, *Fact or Fiction*, 1–9. This is why I am largely ignoring one set of medieval technical terms that touches on fictionality, which comes from the classical division of *narrationum genera* into *historia*, *argumentum*, and *fabula*: this terminology precisely does *not* bracket the truth issue, but rather attempts to define and defend fiction with reference to truth. This conception of fiction is therefore very different from the modern one, and the medieval one we are concerned with here. Although definitions vary greatly, most often *historia* is described as true, *argumentum* as not true but verisimilar, and *fabula* as neither true nor verisimilar. Recently, literary historians have become interested in this tripartite division as a factor in the early development of fictionality—not so much *fabula*, which was often treated dismissively, but *argumentum*, which is verisimilar and therefore a tertium quid between truth and falsehood and, being a hypothetical narrative used to illustrate a truth, morally acceptable. In the guise of the medieval *exemplum*, it can develop into a small and controlled space

within "serious" discourse (legal, historical, homiletic), in which narrative experimentation is possible. Important discussions of this subject include Trimpi, "The Quality of Fiction"; Knapp, "Historische Wahrheit und poetische Lüge"; and the very rich and thorough study by Peter von Moos, *Geschichte als Topik*. A related approach is taken by Eugene Vance, *From Topic to Tale*. Given the nature of my material, this approach is only marginally relevant to this study; but Moos, in an important digression, sketches a theory of play and *argumentum* that indicates points of contact between my material and the "rhetorical school" of fictionality (276–85). On *narrationum genera*, see Moos, *Geschichte als Topik*, 406–12, 52 n. 125, and 60–61 n. 147. See also Lausberg, *Handbuch der literarischen Rhetorik*, 1:165–67 (§§ 290–92). For an objection against using the category of hypothetical narrative to explain literary fiction, see Manfred Fuhrmann, "Die Fiktion im römischen Recht."

24. Searle, "Logical Status," 71–72. I am not concerned here with the semiotic problems of fictional reference; for my purposes, it is enough to consider the pragmatic understanding shared by readers and author as to what kind of reference is intended, and possible.

25. Ibid., 72.

26. Ibid., 73.

27. Auerbach, *Mimesis*, 129.

28. Cf. Wetzel, "Reconstructing Carthage."

29. Searle, "Logical Status," 73; see Wetzel, "Reconstructing Carthage," 20–22.

30. Ollier, "Utopie et roman arthurien," 226–27.

31. Coleman, *Ancient and Medieval Memories*, 281–82.

32. Quoted in Melville, "Wozu Geschichte schreiben?," 89. See Coleman, *Ancient and Medieval Memories*; see also Guenée, *Histoire et culture historique*, 18–19.

33. Walter Map, *De Nugis Curialium*, 128–29. For the "historia"-"fabula" distinction, see Lausberg, *Handbuch der literarischen Rhetorik*, 1:165–67, and Moos, *Geschichte als Topik*, 52 n. 125 and 60–61 n. 147.

34. Walter Map, *De Nugis Curialium*, 122–25. On Walter's definition of "modernitas," see Guenée, "Temps de l'histoire," and *Histoire et culture historique*, 82.

35. Stock, *Listening for the Text*, 80.

36. See Ray, "Bede's *Vera Lex Historiae*," 15–16.

37. For the "moderate" view on textuality, see, among others, Stock, *Listening for the Text*, 80–88; Koselleck, *Futures Past*, 112; and, with an urgent warning against "postmodern" flipness, Partner, "History without Empiricism." Where people express resistance to the entire thesis, it seems most often a panic reaction at the mere possibility of the extreme view. This, in an oddly indirect way, seems to be the subtext of Ginzburg's stimulating essay, "Veranschaulichung und Zitat." For another angry (and useful) reaction, see Tallis, " 'As If There Could Be Such Things as True Stories.' " See also the exchange between Perez Zagorin and F. R. Ankersmit in *History and Theory* 29 (1990): 263–96.

38. White, *Metahistory*, 7–11. See also White, "The Value of Narrativity," 7–15; in a passage that has become famous, White uses the example of the St. Gall Annals, a mere listing of dates and events, to show that there is no such thing as history without a "plot" (11–13). See also, among others, Mink, "Narrative Form as a Cognitive Instrument," 133.

39. Stierle, "Erfahrung und narrative Form," 107.

40. "Zweite historiographie-spezifische Erwartung im kommunikativen Alltagswissen: Historiographische Texte haben in allen Einzelteilen und im Hinblick auf alle Konsti-

tutionsebenen Wirklichkeitsreferenz" (Gumbrecht, "'Das in vergangenen Zeiten Gewesene,'" 485).

41. Mink, "Narrative Form as a Cognitive Instrument," 147.

42. Ibid., 143–45. See also Ankersmit, "Reply to Professor Zagorin," 277–78.

43. Gale, "The Fictive Use of Language," 325. Gale himself does not draw this conclusion, and I am not sure he would support it, but I am taking the liberty of borrowing his suggestive image.

44. Ricoeur, *The Rule of Metaphor*, 224, 247.

45. William of Malmesbury, *Gesta Regum Anglorum*, 2. This textile metaphor is discussed in John O. Ward, "Some Principles of Rhetorical Historiography," 103; Demandt, *Metaphern für Geschichte*, 311–19. It is hardly necessary to point out how "textual" the textile metaphor is.

46. To explain the process completely, one would of course have to describe the selection of common features that make the transfer possible—and to address the question whether the primary referent is in fact completely eliminated, or to what extent it remains present as a visual image.

47. Ricoeur, *The Rule of Metaphor*, 221.

48. Ibid., 256.

49. Ricoeur, *Interpretation Theory*, 36–37.

50. Ibid., 35.

51. Riffaterre, *Fictional Truth*, 84–111.

52. Dällenbach strongly discourages the extension of his term "mise-en-abyme" to all texts indiscriminately, as a kind of generalized text theory: "Although all literary works can be defined as structures that resonate and develop cross-correspondences, reflexion can only come into play through the presence of additional elements. This conclusion seems to call into question the validity of certain retrospective readings of texts. Although not necessarily invalid, this practice becomes so, in my view, when the decoding it involves is entirely unconnected with the encoding, for instance when the notion that all fictions are mere allegories of their own production is applied to texts that do not subscribe to this view" (*The Mirror in the Text*, 49).

53. For instance, Galfridus de Fontibus writes a "prequel" ("Liber de Infantia Sancti Edmundi") to Abbo's *Vita* of St. Edmund (ca. 1150), adapting and combining romance motifs (voyages, rings as signs of recognition, etc.). This is the source for Denis Piramus's full treatment of the Edmund story in French. Matthew Paris's ostensibly historical *Vitae Duorum Offarum* is unmistakably a romance, complete with sea voyages, lost queens, and hermit confessors in the woods. For a (dated) attempt to come to terms with the boundaries between fiction and history in hagiography by distinguishing between learned (or factual) and popular (legendary) elements, see Delehaye, *The Legends of the Saints*, 3–9 and 12–85 passim. A more recent discussion of the same topic is Sigal, "Histoire et hagiographie." For a good summary statement of the issues involved, see Fleischman, "On the Representation of History and Fiction."

54. Several essays appeared in the late 1970s and early 1980s that, largely independently of each other, made quite similar arguments: Bäuml, "Varieties and Consequences"; Haidu, "Repetition"; Nykrog, "The Rise of Literary Fiction"; Ollier, "Utopie"; Warning, "Formen narrativer Identitätskonstitution"; Zink, "Mutation de la conscience." An important new

study is Bruckner, *Shaping Romance*; on fiction and fictionality, see esp. pp. 104–8, 113–17. Bruckner's argument, though concerned exclusively with vernacular romance, intersects with mine in many important ways.

55. "Le moment où la littérature reconnaît que sa matière est fictive est aussi . . . celui où l'auteur entre en scène. C'est par excellence le moment du roman" (Zink, "Mutation de la conscience," 5; my translation).

56. Marichal, "Naissance du roman," 458, quoted in Zink, "Mutation de la conscience," 8; my translation.

57. The argument is somewhat reminiscent of Ricoeur's in *Interpretation Theory*, 25–44 and passim. See also Ricoeur, "The Hermeneutical Function of Distanciation."

58. Bäuml, "Varieties and Consequences," 249–50.

59. Ibid., 262, 256.

60. Haug, *Literaturtheorie im deutschen Mittelalter*, 104; my translation.

61. Warning, "Staged Discourse."

62. Haidu, "Repetition," 883, 885.

CHAPTER ONE

1. Parts of this chapter have appeared previously in my essay "New Werke" and are reprinted here with the kind permission of Duke University Press.

2. Heinzelmann, *Translationsberichte*, devotes a brief but informative section to *inventiones* (77–80). See also Aigrain, *L'hagiographie*, 186–92, and Leclercq's articles on "Translations" and "Reliques et reliquaires" in the *Dictionnaire d'archéologie chrétienne et de liturgie*, the latter article primarily on the early Christian centuries. A case study of a mid-eleventh-century example from Flanders, van Houts, "Historiography and Hagiography at Saint-Wandrille," contains a short description of the genre, p. 239 and passim.

3. Some examples, all of which will be discussed later in this chapter, are St. Albans, Bury St. Edmund, and Waltham. The *inventio* of the Black Cross at Abingdon is not the occasion of the monastery's foundation but is closely connected with it in the narrative, both by proximity and by several thematic connections. See *Chronicon Monasterii de Abingdon*, 1:2–8 (in *Historia Monasterii de Abingdon*), and 2:268–70 (in *De Abbatibus Abbendoniae*).

4. On the western European relic cult during that period, see Geary, *Furta Sacra*. Important regional studies include Head, *Hagiography and the Cult of the Saints*; Holzfurtner, *Gründung und Gründungsüberlieferung*; Patze, "Klostergründung und Klosterchronik"; Kastner, *Historiae fundationum monasteriorum*; and Töpfer, "Reliquienkult und Pilgerbewegung." A convenient collection of *inventiones, translationes*, and foundation narratives from Continental sources is the Monumenta Germaniae Historica volume *Vitae aliaeque historiae minores* (Scriptorum Tomus XV [= MGH SS XV], in two parts). Sources can also be found in a number of well-documented collections of excerpts on the history of art and architecture: for France, Mortet, *Recueil de textes relatifs à l'histoire de l'architecture . . . XIe–XIIe siècles*; Mortet and Deschamps, *Recueil de textes relatifs à l'histoire de l'architecture . . . XIIe–XIIIe siècles*; for Germany and Italy, Lehmann-Brockhaus, *Schriftquellen zur Kunstgeschichte*; for Great Britain, Lehmann-Brockhaus, *Lateinische Schriftquellen zur Kunst in England, Wales und Schottland*.

5. Some partial exceptions: Lantfred's *translatio* of St. Swithun, which has *inventio* elements (see Lapidge and Winterbottom, introduction to Wulfstan of Winchester, *The Life of St. Æthelwold*, cvi–vii and passim); and Abbo of Fleury's "Life of St. Edmund," which contains a kind of modified *inventio*.

6. Gransden, *Historical Writing*, 63–66, 107–11.

7. See, for instance, Southern, "Aspects of the European Tradition of Historical Writing: 4. The Sense of the Past," 246–56, and "The Place of England in the Twelfth-Century Renaissance," 208–9; James Campbell, "Some Twelfth-Century Views of the Anglo-Saxon Past." William of Malmesbury praises Goscelin's hagiographic work: "Denique innumeras sanctorum vitas recentium stylo extulit; veterum vel hostilitate amissas, vel informiter editas, comptius renovavit" (*Gesta Regum Anglorum*, 2:389; in J. A. Giles's translation, 355).

8. Platt, *The Abbeys and Priories of Medieval England*, 5–69.

9. Examples: *Liber Eliensis*; *Chronicon Monasterii de Abingdon*. Genet, "Cartulaires, registres et histoire," offers a table of all known English cartularies; although his chief interest is in later examples, he does include twelfth-century cartularies.

10. Ridyard, "*Condigna Veneratio*." On Norman hostility and Anglo-Saxon defensiveness, see, among many others, Knowles, *The Monastic Order in England*, 117–19; Bethell, "The Miracles of St. Ithamar," 422–23; Barlow, "The Effects of the Norman Conquest," 153–57; for Wales, see Walker, "Cultural Survival in an Age of Conquest." A judicious recent synthesis of available evidence and of the differing scholarly opinions, with many important examples, is Townsend, "Anglo-Latin Hagiography and the Norman Transition." Important local studies of pre- and post-Conquest hagiography include Rollason, *The Mildrith Legend*; Dominic of Evesham, "Vita S. Ecgwini episcopi et confessoris"; and Lapidge, "The Medieval Hagiography of St. Ecgwine."

11. London BL Cotton Vespasian B.xx. See Ker, *English Manuscripts in the Century after the Norman Conquest*, 27, 29, and plate 11. See also Clark, "People and Languages in Post-Conquest Canterbury."

12. Barlow, "Effects of the Norman Conquest," 153.

13. William of Malmesbury, *The Early History of Glastonbury*; also a long excerpt from this in *Gesta Regum Anglorum*, 2:24–29. See also Gransden, "The Growth of the Glastonbury Tradition."

14. Eadmer, "De reliquiis sancti Audoeni," and "Epistola Eadmeri ad Glastonienses."

15. On Goscelin, see Gransden, *Historical Writing*, 64–65 and 107–11; and appendix C, *The Life of King Edward*, 133–49. For his work in defense of St. Augustine's, see Goscelin, "Libellus contra inanes s. uirginis Mildrethae usurpatores," and "Historia translationis S. Augustini." On some of Goscelin's lives of female saints (though not the texts discussed here), see Millinger, "Humility and Power."

16. Gransden's phrase in *Historical Writing*, 174. William of Malmesbury, *Gesta Pontificum Anglorum*.

17. William of Malmesbury, *Gesta Regum Anglorum*, 1:1–2 and 2:518; in the translation by Giles, *Chronicle of the Kings of England*, 3–4 and 477.

18. Leckie, *The Passage of Dominion*, 21–22.

19. Jocelin of Brakelond, *Chronica Jocelini*, 62–64.

20. Abou-El-Haj, "Bury St. Edmunds Abbey between 1070 and 1124." See also Gransden, "Baldwin, Abbot of Bury St. Edmunds," and "The Legends and Traditions."

21. Platt, *The Abbeys and Priories of Medieval England*, 65–92; Gransden's chapter, "Local History from the Reign of King Stephen to John," in *Historical Writing*, 265–95; *Chronicon Abbatiae Rameseiensis*; *Chronicon Monasterii de Abingdon*; *The Waltham Chronicle*; Raine, *The Priory of Hexham*.

22. Sayers, "Papal Privileges for St. Albans Abbey." The best recent survey of St. Albans history (though focused primarily on manuscript production) is in Thomson, *Manuscripts from St Albans Abbey*, 1:1–78.

23. William's *passio* of Saints Alban and Amphibalus is printed in *AASS* under June 22. Ralph's verse life and many of the related treatises have not been printed. On these texts and surviving mss., see Thomson, "Two Twelfth Century Poems on the 'Regnum-Sacerdotium' Problem in England," 319, and *Manuscripts from St. Albans Abbey*, 57 and n. 52; 141 and n. 51. On the Ely-St. Albans controversy, see Vaughan, *Matthew Paris*, 198–204, and the sources listed there.

24. On *libelli*, see Wormald, "Some Illustrated Manuscripts of the Lives of the Saints." In its strict sense, the term refers to a collection of materials on a saint for liturgical use. In Wormald's definition, Matthew Paris's manuscript on the two saints, Trinity College Dublin Ms. 177 (see below), is not strictly speaking a *libellus* since its main text is in French; it would therefore seem to be intended for edifying reading rather than for liturgical purposes (263–64).

25. In Matthew Paris, *Chronica Majora*, 1:356–58 and 2:301–8, and *Gesta Abbatum Monasterii Sancti Albani*, 4, 192. On Roger and Matthew, see Galbraith, "Roger Wendover and Matthew Paris." Matthew says that the *Gesta Abbatum* goes back in part to a "rotulus" on local history compiled by "Bartholomew the clerk." See Vaughan, *Matthew Paris*, 182–84. Galbraith thinks it possible that there were in the twelfth century some simple annalistic notes at St. Albans on which Roger Wendover could have drawn, but almost certainly no more than that ("Roger Wendover and Matthew Paris," X15–X16).

26. The text is published in Matthew Paris, *La Vie de Seint Auban*; the cycle of illustrations is reproduced in Matthew Paris, *Illustrations to the Life of St. Alban in Trinity College Dublin ms. E.i.40* [now Trinity College Dublin Ms. 177].

27. On Matthew Paris's famous chronicle illustrations and their originality, see Lewis, *The Art of Matthew Paris*, esp. 32–52. The *inventio* is rare as an iconographic subject. There are a handful of examples in the Princeton Index of Christian Art, very different from each other in medium, dating, and provenance; none is from England, and only one is from an illustrated saint's life (St. Liudger discovers the body of the Anglo-Saxon saint Liafwin [*Vita Ludgeri*, Berlin, Staatsbibl. theol. lat. fol. 323; late eleventh century]). See Schrade, *Die Vita des heiligen Liudger*, fig. 4 and pp. 14–16; and Abou-El-Haj, *The Medieval Cult of Saints*, fig. 100. The eleventh-century illustrated lives of St. Cuthbert also contain a "discovery" scene, where Cuthbert's body is found to be incorrupt; but this is not strictly speaking an *inventio*, since the whereabouts of the body had been known all along (Abou-El-Haj, *The Medieval Cult of Saints*, figs. 101 and 105). As Abou-El-Haj's series of examples shows (figs. 91–106) all these scenes employ the iconography of entombment scenes; indeed, without captions or clarifying text, they are indistinguishable from entombments. Matthew Paris, to my knowledge, is unique in attempting to convey the specific circumstances of an *inventio*.

28. Matthew Paris, *La Vie de Seint Auban*, 63, lines 385–96 of the rubrics, which Harden prints as continuous text in an appendix; my translation.

29. On the close connection between *inventiones*, or the relic cult in general, and church building, see Cheney, "Church Building in the Middle Ages," and Platt, *The Abbeys and Priories of Medieval England*, 64–91.

30. Matthew Paris, *Illustrations to the Life of St. Alban*, plates 41–54. The *inventio* picture is plate 46. On Matthew Paris's drawings, see M. R. James, "The Drawings of Matthew Paris," and Lewis, *The Art of Matthew Paris* (on the *Vie de Seint Auban*, pp. 381-89 and passim; figs. 7, 58, 61, 67, 70, 225–28).

31. Another widely known text is Ambrose's letter on the *inventio* of Saints Protasius and Gervasius ("Epistola XXII"). But the narrative component of this letter is very brief; the letter consists chiefly of Ambrose's sermon on the *inventio* and on *inventiones* in general. See Heinzelmann, *Translationsberichte*, 27, 31, 78–79, and Dassman, "Ambrosius und die Märtyrer."

32. Abingdon and Waltham (see n. 21 above). At Waltham, there is no explicit mention of St. Helen. At Abingdon, the old foundation was dedicated to St. Helen. See Biddle, Lambrick, and Myers, "The Early History of Abingdon," and Stenton, *The Early History of the Abbey of Abingdon*, 3–4.

33. Vanderlinden, "Revelatio Sancti Stephani." The text is also printed in *PL* 41, 805–18, where it is followed by several other accounts of further translations and miracles associated with the relics.

34. St. Augustine, *De Civitate Dei*, XXII.8; Sermons 314–24, *PL* 38, cols. 425–47.

35. Bede, *De temporum ratione*, *PL* 90, cols. 559–60.

36. On text and manuscripts, see Vanderlinden, "Revelatio Sancti Stephani," 180–87, and Martin, "Die Revelatio S. Stephani und Verwandtes."

37. Vanderlinden, "Revelatio Sancti Stephani," 194. All translations from the *Revelatio* are my own.

38. Ibid., 213.

39. Ibid., 215.

40. See Heinzelmann, *Translationsberichte*, 79–80.

41. On the "odor of sanctity," see Finucane, *Miracles and Pilgrims*, 22–23, and Heinzelmann, *Translationsberichte*, 79 n. 147.

42. On Bede, see n. 35 above, and the bibliographical note in *PL* 41:807–8. *Liber Eliensis*, 230; Thomas of Monmouth, *The Life and Miracles of St. William of Norwich*, 118.

43. On Goscelin and Folcart, see nn. 6 and 15 above. On Abbo of Fleury's visit to England, see Gransden, *Historical Writing*, 78–79; Mostert, "Le séjour"; and Cousin, *Abbon de Fleury-sur-Loire*, 60–74. On the flourishing historiographical and hagiographical tradition of Fleury, see Head, *Hagiography and the Cult of the Saints*, 235–81 and passim. Much has been written about English-Continental ecclesiastical relations in the two centuries prior to the Conquest; see, for instance, Musset, "Les contacts entre l'église normande et l'église d'Angleterre."

44. Usually, the connection with the Norman Conquest is not explicitly made; more often, the overt association is with Viking raids and the disruption to monastic establishments that they caused (see n. 140 below). In the case of Tynemouth, a cell of St. Albans,

the conquest does become an overt issue. The *inventio* of St. Oswin, which motivated the refoundation of Tynemouth, is dated 1065, a date whose ominous significance is explicitly recognized; perhaps it had to be, since Tynemouth had some reason to be defensive about its founder, Earl Tostig, who was King Harold's brother. Tostig's failure to give the *inventio* his immediate and full attention, it is hinted, was one of the causes of the debacle of 1066 ("Vita Oswini Regis Deirorum," 14).

45. Goscelin, "Vita S. Yvonis."

46. Mostert, "Le séjour," 199–200, and *The Political Theory of Abbo of Fleury*, 40.

47. In Version B. Vanderlinden, "Revelatio Sancti Stephani," 209.

48. The *miracula* are omitted from the *AASS* edition, but are printed in *Chronicon Abbatiae Rameseiensis*, lix–lxxxiv.

49. Clearly the intention in Matthew Paris's autograph (Trinity College Dublin Ms. 177). The arrangement of the diverse St. Albans materials in London BL Cotton Faustina B.iv (early thirteenth century) and the later London BL Cotton Claudius E.iv (fourteenth century) is somewhat confusing, but the compilers and rubricists clearly attempted to establish at least one complete *vita-inventio-miracula* sequence. For other instances, see St. Nectanus in "Vie de S. Rumon"; "Inventio reliquiarum Sancti Eligii"; "Vita et miracula S. Bege Virginis"; the story of St. Judoc in book 3 of Orderic Vitalis's *Ecclesiastical History*, 2:156–69. Ms. Oxford Corpus Christi College F. 134, the earlier (ca. 1160) Tynemouth manuscript on St. Oswin, does not have the *inventio* account in the usual place, proceeding right from the *vita* to the *miracula*; it does have ample materials on the *inventio* at the end of the volume (fol. 93 ff.; ends imperfectly). In the later ms., London BL Cotton Julius A.x., also from Tynemouth (early thirteenth century), this irregularity has been remedied: the tract on the *inventio* is now incorporated into the main narrative, between *vita* and *miracula*. (This is the text printed as "Vita Oswini Regis Deirorum" in J. Raine's *Miscellanea Biographica*; the *inventio* is chap. 4, pp. 11–17.) See Thomson, *Manuscripts from St. Albans*, nos. 67 and 71, 1:117, 118. In collections of hagiographic materials, such as the Codex Gothanus, texts from different sources are sometimes combined to produce the *vita-inventio* or *translatio-miracula* sequence. See the annotated table of contents in Paul Grosjean, "De Codice Hagiographico Gothano."

50. Cf. Geary, *Furta Sacra*, 125–30 and passim.

51. Cf. ibid., 131.

52. *Bede's Ecclesiastical History*, 34–35, and Levison, "St. Alban and St. Albans."

53. Abbo, "Life of St. Edmund," 81; my translation. The question "Ubi es?" is rendered with (presumably unintended) humor in French, two centuries later, by Denis Piramus: "U est tun chief, martir seint rei / La plus principal part de tei? [Where is your head, holy king and martyr, / The most important part of you?]" (*La Vie Seint Edmund Le Rei*, 105, lines 2715–16).

54. *Liber Eliensis*, 43–44; my translation. Cf. *Bede's Ecclesiastical History*, 392–95.

55. *Liber Eliensis*, 229–30.

56. Ibid., 29–30. Cf. "Vita, Inventio et Miracula Sanctae Enimiae." As I shall show in chapter 2, the motif of perambulation in search of a spot to found a monastery or town is also very common and not unrelated to *inventio*.

57. *Liber Eliensis*, 53 n. This precisely parallels the case of Much Wenlock, where St. Mil-

burga is "invented" as the defunct monastery is being refounded. See Edwards, "An Early Twelfth Century Account," and William of Malmesbury, *Gesta Pontificum*, 305–6.

58. *Liber Eliensis*, 120.

59. Ailred of Rievaulx, "De sanctis Ecclesiae Haugustaldensis," 190; my translation.

60. Goscelin, "Historia translationis S. Augustini."

61. Gervase of Canterbury, *The Historical Works*, 1:3–29.

62. On the separate but related issue of physical continuity and individual identity, see Bynum, "Material Continuity."

63. Simeon of Durham, *Historia Dunelmensis Ecclesiae*, in *Symeonis monachi opera omnia*, 1:50–81, and the eleventh-century "Historia de Sancto Cuthberto," ibid., 2:207–8.

64. Simeon, *Historia Dunelmensis Ecclesiae*, 1:36.

65. First in Abbo, "Life of St. Edmund," 82–87 (on the growing hair and nails: 82–83); repeated and expanded upon in Denis Piramus, *La Vie Seint Edmund le Rei* (grooming of the corpse: 117–19, lines 3035–70; protection miracles: 120–55). The first volume of the Rolls Series *Memorials of St. Edmunds Abbey* contains two further miracle collections: by Herman the Archdeacon (ca. 1100), 26–92, and by Abbot Samson (begun shortly before 1180), 105–208. Both show the same interest in miracles concerning the property and the safety of the monastic community.

66. Abou-El-Haj, "Bury St. Edmunds Abbey," and *The Medieval Cult of Saints*, 33–60 and passim. The *libellus* is New York, Pierpont Morgan MS 736.

67. Jocelin, *Chronica*, 114. See also Finucane, *Miracles and Pilgrims*, 27–28.

68. *Liber Eliensis*, 45; adapted from *Bede's Ecclesiastical History*, 394–97.

69. This motif may have been suggested by Bede's remark that the lid fit precisely, and that the sarcophagus turned out to be perfect in size, as if made for Æthelthryth.

70. Due to the composite nature of the *Liber*, a slightly different, less compelling version of the same story is also told at the end of book 1, pp. 60–61.

71. *Liber Eliensis*, 229–30.

72. See my forthcoming essay, "The Temptation of St. Æthelthryth."

73. For a typical case of editorial apologetics see, for instance, "Vie de S. Rumon," 385. On truth and relics, see Schreiner, " 'Discrimen veri ac falsi,' " and "Zum Wahrheits-verständnis im Heiligen- und Reliquienwesen des Mittelalters." Closely related is the debate on medieval document forgery, which also elicits widely divergent judgments and responses. See Horst Fuhrmann, "Die Fälschungen im Mittelalter," with discussion by Karl Bosl, Hans Patze, and August Nitschke; the monumental conference proceedings, *Fälschungen im Mittelalter*; and Constable, "Forgery and Plagiarism in the Middle Ages."

74. One is reminded of Gregory of Tours's much quoted dictum that, instead of *vitae sanctorum*, it is more appropriate to speak of a singular *Vita Sanctorum*: an ideal type to which all individual saints' lives strive to conform (e.g., Heffernan, *Sacred Biography*, 6–7). It will become clear from my discussion that I find this aphorism only partially helpful in understanding the historicity of saints' lives.

75. On the early history and the connotations of that term, see Gagov, "Il culto delle reliquie nell'antichità.' "

76. Herrmann-Mascard, *Les reliques des saints*, 243–53, and Heinzelmann, *Translations-berichte*, 80.

77. Wilson, *The Bayeux Tapestry*, plate 26, and pp. 180–81.

78. Herrmann-Mascard, *Les reliques des saints*, 242.

79. Ibid., 74–105. Specifically on England, see Foreville, "Canterbury et la canonisation des saints au XIIe siècle."

80. Matthew Paris, *Gesta Abbatum*, 12–19. See also Horst Fuhrmann, "Fälschungen," 543–44. Eadmer's letter to Glastonbury, on the other hand, relies on a careful, point-by-point refutation of Glastonbury's claim to St. Dunstan's relics ("Epistola Eadmeri"); so does Goscelin's "Libellus contra inanes s. uirginis Mildrethae usurpatores."

81. Guth, *Guibert von Nogent.*

82. The truth of this assertion has been in dispute from the earliest documents onward. The "Vita Haroldi," found in one ms. side by side with "De Inventione" (Ms. BL Harley 3776), makes the fantastic claim that Harold survived Hastings and was seen alive in Chester as late as the late twelfth century (see also Michel's preface, *Chroniques Anglo-Normandes*, 2:xxiv); see Schmidt, "*Veritas naufragatur.*" A more plausible rival tradition has it that Harold was buried on the seashore at William the Conqueror's command. Modern historians have no additional evidence to offer either for this tradition or for the Waltham claims. For an overview of contemporary opinion, see the introduction to *The Waltham Chronicle*, xliii–xlvi; and Freeman, *The History of the Norman Conquest*, 3:510–20 and 781–90. Freeman proposes that both traditions could be true: Harold might have been buried on the shore first and then transferred to his church at his family's insistence. For a short overview of the abbey's history, see Ransford, *The Early Charters*, xviii–xxvi, and *The Waltham Chronicle*, xiii–xxix.

83. The "Vita Haroldi" does indeed treat Harold as a saint: he spends the end of his life as a hermit, and at one point is referred to as "Vir Dei Haroldus" (194–206). In the *Gesta Pontificum*, William of Malmesbury makes no mention of Harold's burial place, but his brief note on Battle Abbey turns Harold into a kind of national saint: "Altare ecclesiae est in loco ubi Haroldi pro patriae caritate occisi cadaver exanime inventum est [the church's altar is in the place where the corpse of Harold, killed for love of his country, was found]" (209).

84. *The Waltham Chronicle*, 50–57. Freeman, *The History of the Norman Conquest*, suggests that the presence of Edith is one argument in favor of the Waltham story: surely the canons would not go out of their way to introduce the king's mistress if this were a fabricated story (3:784–85).

85. *The Waltham Chronicle*, 1–19. On Tovi, see the introduction to this edition, xvi–xviii.

86. *The Waltham Chronicle*, 46–47.

87. Langmuir, "Thomas of Monmouth"; Jessopp and James, introduction to Thomas of Monmouth, *Life and Miracles of St. William of Norwich*, lxiv–llix; James Campbell, "Some Twelfth-Century Views of the Anglo-Saxon Past," 147–48; Benedicta Ward, *Miracles and the Medieval Mind*, 68–76; and Finucane, *Miracles and Pilgrims*, 118–21.

88. Thomas of Monmouth, *The Life and Miracles of St William of Norwich*, 53.

89. Ibid., 18.

90. A very common defense of fictional narrative; see Moos, "*Poeta* und *Historicus* im Mittelalter."

91. Edwards, "An Early Twelfth Century Account," discusses the plausibility of this attribution, but seems to lean toward accepting it (136–37).

92. I am quoting from the translation by A. J. M. Edwards, in "An Early Twelfth Century Account." Unfortunately, I have not had access to the Latin original of this very interesting text, which has never been published. See also Finberg, "St Mildburg's Testament," 197–98.

93. *The Life of King Edward*, 94–95.

94. Edwards, "An Early Twelfth Century Account," 150.

95. Goscelin, "Historia translationis S. Augustini," cols. 21–22.

96. Langmuir, "Thomas of Monmouth."

97. Hanning, "Poetic Emblems."

98. Denis Piramus, *La Vie Seint Edmund le Rei*, 6–19, lines 95–432.

99. *Chronicon Monasterii de Abingdon*, 1:2–5.

100. Bovo of St. Bertin, "Bovonis Abbatis relatio de inventione et elevatione S. Bertini."

101. Again, it may be the *Revelatio S. Stephani* that suggested this topographical precision: Yvo's instructions are not unlike the painstaking directions provided by Gamaliel. The problems in finding the right location at Much Wenlock also seem at least in part inspired by the *Revelatio*, despite Edwards's detective work showing that it might very well have happened that way.

102. Brown, *The Cult of the Saints*, 86–87. See also Delehaye, "Loca Sanctorum."

103. Matthew Paris, *Chronica Majora*, 1:360. See also William of Malmesbury, *Gesta Regum Anglorum*, 1:85, and *Gesta Pontificum*, 316–17.

104. *The Waltham Chronicle*, 16–17. The Waltham *inventio* has an interesting variation on the motif of the oxen, or horses, indicating where the relic must be taken: here, this traditional expedient is not an unexpected miracle but a deliberate test.

105. *The Chronicle of Battle Abbey*, 44–45.

106. Rollason, "Lists of Saints' Resting Places"; Liebermann, *Die Heiligen Englands*. Rollason notes that there are medieval lists of resting places of the apostles, evangelists, and other major saints, but there are no other national lists (74–75). See also James Campbell, "Some Twelfth-Century Views," 137. The Anglo-Saxon lists may be influenced by Celtic memorial practices, of which traces survive, for instance, in the Welsh, "stanzas of the graves" (englynion y beddau), a mnemonic listing of burial places of warrior heroes (Jones, "The Black Book of Carmarthen 'Stanzas of the Graves' ").

107. An analogous development is described in Halbwachs, *La topographie légendaire*.

108. ". . . quatinus in hujus oratorii pavimento *glebam coporis mei* quaerat [that he is to look for the dust of my body in the pavement of that church]" ("Vita Oswini," 12); "Locum autem in quo *corporis proprii cadaver* reconditum est, te nosse ammoneo. . . . Vult namque Dei Filius Dominus Noster, quo tuae allocutionis revelatione *meum corpus* debeat inveniri [I urge you to find the place where my dead body is hidden. . . . For the son of God, our Lord, wants my body to be found, revealed through your testimony]" ("Corporis Sancti Fidelis . . . inventio," 356). Translations and emphases mine.

109. Vanderlinden, "Revelatio Sancti Stephani," 194–95.

110. Edwards, "An Early Twelfth Century Account," 146, 160.

111. Jocelin of Brakelond, *Chronica*, 111–16.

112. Brown, *The Cult of the Saints*, 89–91. On the pagan use of reliclike "pignora" that "hold together the Roman Empire [pignora quae imperium romanum tenent]" (Virgil, *Aeneid*, VII.138), see Gagov, "Il culto delle reliquie nell'antichità," 498–99.

113. See Deluz, "Indifférence au temps." Stock makes a similar observation about a more

secular *inventio*, that of Charlemagne by his successor Otto III: "Otto . . . was sensitized in his dream to the fact that Charlemagne belonged to a distinctive cultural period in the past. He himself therefore represented modernity. The hiatus was symbolized by the need to dig up the body and to verify its physical existence. Yet, in distancing himself from his illustrious predecessor Otto nonetheless interrelated the past and the present in a new way" (*Implications of Literacy*, 512). The text referred to is Ademar of Chabannes's *Chronicon*. On the same episode, see also Nichols, *Romanesque Signs*, 66–94. His argument is almost the opposite of mine: he traces the typological associations of the episode, arguing that it turns "from history into *historia*." For a fuller discussion of Stock's and Nichols's arguments, see my article "New Werke."

114. "Alia Acta SS Albani, Amphibali et sociorum. . . ." For a summary account of the St. Albans texts regarding the *inventiones*, see above at nn. 23–26.

115. Gildas, *The Ruin of Britain*, 28–29. See also Meyer, "Die Legende des h. Albanus."

116. Geoffrey of Monmouth, *Historia Regum Britanniae*, 316, 512. The name appears to be the result of a misreading—accidental or deliberate—of the noun "amphibalus," cloak, as a proper name. See Tatlock, "St. Amphibalus," and Levison, "St. Alban and St. Albans," 353–56.

117. Matthew Paris describes the *inventio* in *Chronica Majora*, 2:301–8; the *libellus* on the event is mentioned on p. 308. See also McCulloch, "Saints Alban and Amphibalus in the Works of Matthew Paris," and Levison, "St. Alban and St. Albans."

118. *AASS* Junii Tomus V, 137. All translations from this text are my own. See also McCulloch, "Saints Alban and Amphibalus," 768, and Levison, "St. Alban and St. Albans," 356.

119. While even the Bollandist editors express doubts about William's implication that the source dates from the sixth century (*AASS* Junii Tomus V 127B), some modern critics have seriously considered William's claim that he is translating from the Old English and that there could be an intervening source between Bede and William (e.g., Harden in the introduction to Matthew Paris, *Vie de Seint Auban*, x–xi; G[aston] P[aris], "Review of *Vie de Seint Auban*, ed. Robert Atkinson, 1876"). While this is not impossible, there is no need to assume a source apart from Bede, other than Geoffrey's brief note, which William acknowledges; and since there were no relics, and therefore no cult, of St. Amphibalus at St. Albans before 1178, it is unlikely that anyone would have elaborated Bede's story in this way prior to that date.

120. *AASS* Junii Tomus V, 129.

121. On "realistic" description of ruins and old buildings in other twelfth-century sources, see Gransden, "Realistic Observation," and *Historical Writing* (index s.v. "description"). Her characterization of such descriptions as "antiquarianism," however, seems to me to fall short of an adequate explanation.

122. "quendam britannici sermonis librum uetustissimum" (Geoffrey of Monmouth, *Historia Regum Britanniae*, 219). There are, of course, other precedents; see Wilhelm, "Ueber fabulistische Quellenangaben." But given the mention of Geoffrey in the prologue, one is surely justified in assuming that Geoffrey is the source here.

123. In Matthew Paris's Anglo-Norman verse adaptation of William's story, the narrator is an eyewitness, presumably for these reasons; this is clearest in the rubric section title before line 1812: "Ci parole cist Sarrazins cunvers ki estoit presenc a tutes cestes aventures e tut mist en escrit, ke puis fu translaté en latin [Here speaks that converted Saracen (i.e.,

pagan) who was present at all those events and put them all in writing, which was then translated into Latin]" (Matthew Paris, *Vie de Seint Auban*, 50; my translation).

124. For example, Alban's executioner is struck blind on the spot, his eyes popping out of his head. This becomes part of the standard iconography of Alban's martyrdom (see Lewis, *The Art of Matthew Paris*, figs. 5, 58, 60). Alban is converted after seeing Christ's passion and resurrection in a dream, and he enthusiastically reports to Amphibalus the next morning: "Mira res! Cadaver extinctum remeavit ad vitam; resumptisque viribus clauso prodiit monumento: qui qualiter a mortuis resurrexit, propriis oculis ipse conspexi [An amazing thing! A lifeless cadaver came back to life; it regained all its strength and came forth from a closed tomb: and I myself saw with my own eyes how he rose from the dead]" (*AASS* Junii Tomus V, 130).

125. Alban is converted by Amphibalus; one of Alban's executioners is converted on witnessing the miracles that accompany Alban's death; thousands of witnesses willingly follow Amphibalus into martyrdom.

126. *AASS* Junii Tomus V, 138.

127. Matthew Paris, *Chronica Majora*, 2:302–3. Luard's edition conveniently shows Matthew's additions to Roger's text in a different typeface.

128. Summarized and discussed by Stock, *The Implications of Literacy*, 513–17.

129. Matthew Paris, *Chronica Majora*, 2:302–3; my translation. This brief passage contains references both to local landmarks and to incidents in the familiar account of Alban's martyrdom. In Alban's *passio*, the Ver is a very dangerous river to cross; Alban, on the way to his martyrdom, miraculously shrinks the river and resuscitates several Roman soldiers who had drowned in it. The road is clearly Watling Street, one of the main geographic features anyone would have associated with St. Albans.

130. This is also a beautiful example of the loss of the numinous commented on before: St. Alban does have supernatural attributes, but that does not keep the visionary from treating him like an old friend. As they return to St. Albans, "sanctus suam intravit ecclesiam, et homo ille domum suam ingressus, proprio sese lecto recepit [the saint entered his church, and that man, entering his house, went back to bed]" (Matthew Paris, *Chronica Majora*, 2:304; my translation). The parallelism and the casual mention of Robert's going back to bed almost comically domesticate Alban's "residence" in the church.

131. "Finding of writings," a term used by Wilhelm, "Über fabulistische Quellenangaben"; it is particularly evocative because "Auffindung" is also the term used for relic *inventiones*.

132. *AASS* Junii Tomus V, 137.

133. Hanning, "Poetic Emblem"; Dällenbach, *The Mirror in the Text*. See introduction above.

134. Dällenbach, *The Mirror in the Text*, 90–93 and 181–83.

135. Ibid., 182, 92.

136. Ibid., 92.

137. Haidu, "Repetition," 885. Cf. Ricoeur, *The Rule of Metaphor*; see introduction at n. 47.

138. Partner, "Making Up Lost Time," 106; see also Wetzel, "Reconstructing Carthage," 15–18.

139. For the preponderance of partial relics, see any relic list, many of which are printed

in Lehmann-Brockhaus, *Lateinische Schriftquellen zur Kunst in England, Wales und Schott-land*; also Bethell, "The Making of a Twelfth-Century Relic Collection." All *inventiones* of body parts, rather than whole bodies, that I am aware of, concern heads: as Denis Piramus observed, "la plus principal part" of a body (see above, n. 53). There is a twelfth-century French *inventio* of the head of St. Margaret, but as an "international," nonlocal saint, her case is a bit different anyway. In the case of St. Edmund, the search is for a head, but the goal is to reassemble the entire body.

140. For example, "Corporis Sancti Fidelis . . . inventio et prima translatio, auctore coaevo," and the example of Bovo, mentioned above at n. 100. See Aigrain, *L'hagiographie*, 190–91, and Heinzelmann, *Translationsberichte*, 59. Felice Lifshitz argues that the disruption of religious life due to Viking attacks was overstated, that it is, in effect, an early historiographical cliché that has been perpetuated by modern historians ("The 'Exodus of Holy Bodies' Reconsidered").

141. "Vita, Inventio et Miracula Sanctae Enimiae," 278–79.

142. *AASS* Junii Tomus II, 286–87; my translation.

143. In his discussion of the *inventio* of Charlemagne (see above, n. 113), Nichols suggests that such allegorizing is indeed the central function of an *inventio*: Otto III's discovery of his predecessor is a symbolic enactment of the semiosis (as theorized by Charles Sanders Peirce, but also quite similarly by John Scot Eriugena) that makes him, Otto, stand for the great emperor, who in turn stands for Christ (*Romanesque Signs*, 66–94). The argument is part of the larger thesis of Nichols's book, that the task of historiography in the high Middle Ages was to uncover the semiotic relations that bind human history to Christ and therefore give it meaning; or, in Nichols's terminology, the medieval historian turns human history (lowercase "h"), which is multifarious, chaotic, and in itself meaningless, into Historia (capital "H"), through an interpretive process Nichols calls "theosis." Nichols's reading does, I believe, address one important facet of *inventio*, but it is incomplete and even misleading unless the other crucial aspects, the sense of discontinuity, loss, and distance from the past, are also taken into account. See Stock, *Implications of Literacy*, 512.

144. *Chronicon Monasterii de Abingdon*, 1:7.

145. Matthew Paris, *Gesta Abbatum*, 26–27; my translation. The episode is strongly reminiscent of the Middle English *Saint Erkenwald*, where the miraculously preserved body of the pagan judge disintegrates as soon as the purpose of the *inventio* — the corpse's testimony and his posthumous baptism — is completed. See conclusion below.

146. Matthew Paris, *Gesta Abbatum*, 25; my translation. Cf. "Vita Sancti Rumwoldi," 113 and n. 6.

147. Matthew Paris, *Gesta Abbatum*, 85–86. In the *Chronica Majora*, Matthew adds the detail of the gold circlet to Roger of Wendover's account of Alban's *inventio* in 792 (1:357).

148. See n. 73 above.

149. In the "Inventio reliquiarum Sancti Eligii" — a misleading title, since it is not in fact St. Eligius who is found, but relics that he collected when alive — it is made quite clear that the *inventio* responded to popular demand for relic "ostensiones": "Confluente igitur ex more multitudine male se habentium ex adjacentibus longe lateque regionibus ad beati Eligii patrocinium, saepe et multum plures ex illis non parvis obsecrationibus insistebant quatinus de praefati sancti pigneribus aliqua solito digniora eis ostenderentur, sive de corpore ipsius seu quae ipsi specialius atque vicinius adhaesissent [A multitude of sick people,

from far and wide, from all the adjoining regions, converged on St. Eligius's shrine; many of these frequently requested, with considerable insistence, that some of the aforementioned saint's relics be shown to them in a more solemn manner, be it relics from his body or else objects that had come into close and special contact with it"; my translation].

150. On the controversy, see Vaughan, *Matthew Paris*, 198–204.

151. See n. 74 above.

152. This case has been forcefully restated recently by Morse, *Truth and Convention in the Middle Ages*.

CHAPTER TWO

1. Parts of this chapter have previously appeared as "*Gaainable Tere.*" I am grateful to Garland Press for permission to reprint.

2. *Tobler-Lommatzsch Altfranzösisches Wörterbuch*, s.v. "gaaignable"; *Anglo-Norman Dictionary*, s.v. "gainable."

3. Denis Piramus, *La Vie Seint Edmund le Rei*, lines 219–20 and 403–4.

4. For examples and discussions of early modern explorers' narratives, see Mary B. Campbell, *The Witness and the Other World*, esp. chap. 5, "'The End of the East': Columbus Discovers Paradise"; and Kolodny, *The Lay of the Land*, esp. chap. 2, "Surveying the Virgin Land."

5. R. R. Davies, *Domination and Conquest*, 1–24 and passim.

6. On the literary motifs of monastic foundation stories, see Kastner, *Historiae fundationum monasteriorum*, esp. the section on hunting legends (104–16). See also Rollason, *The Mildrith Legend*.

7. *The Chronicle of Battle Abbey*, 44–45.

8. Bouton and Van Damme, *Les plus anciens textes de Cîteaux*, 59–60; my translation.

9. Quoted by Berman, *Medieval Agriculture*, 6 n. 18; similar quotations from several other Cistercian texts, ibid.

10. Stock, *Implications of Literacy*, 90.

11. Gransden, *Historical Writing*, 286–95.

12. "The Foundation of Kirkstall Abbey." The work is preserved only as part of a longer chronicle in a fifteenth-century manuscript, but the editor believes that the early part was written in the early years of the thirteenth century, possibly by Hugh (171). Hugh is the author of the much better known "Narratio de fundatione Fontanis Monasterii"; on St. Mary and its lively foundation narrative, see also Bethell, "The Foundation of Fountains Abbey," and Baker, "The Foundation of Fountains Abbey." On Kirkstall, see also Barnes, *Kirkstall Abbey*, 4–11.

13. "Foundation of Kirkstall Abbey," 175.

14. Ibid., 176–77. For the last sentence, cf. Diana's prophecy to Brutus in Geoffrey of Monmouth's *Historia Regum Britanniae*: "Illa [insula] tibi fietque tuis locus aptus in aeuum. / Hec erit et natis altera troia tuis. [That island will be for you and for yours a suitable place forever. / For your children, too, it shall be another Troy]." See below at n. 43. On Virgilian borrowings in Geoffrey, see Pähler, *Strukturuntersuchungen*, 64–70, and Patterson, *Negotiating the Past*, 200–202.

15. "Foundation of Kirkstall Abbey," 177.

16. Ibid., 178.

17. Ibid., 179.

18. "Historia Selebiensis Monasterii." This text gives the date of its composition as 1174 (54). For the history of the monastery, see Fowler's introduction to *Coucher Book of Selby*, v–xx.

19. Fowler, introduction to *Coucher Book of Selby*, v.

20. "Historia Selebiensis Monasterii," 11. Cf. 2 Corinthians 12:3. All translations from the "Historia Selebiensis Monasterii" are my own.

21. "Historia Selebiensis Monasterii," 12–13.

22. Ibid., 2.

23. On Cistercian foundations, settlement and agriculture, see Knowles, *The Monastic Order in England*, 119–23; Lekai, *The Cistercians*, 33–51 (38–41 on the British Isles) and 284–86; Dronkin, *The Cistercians*, 39–51 and 103–20; Hill, *English Cistercian Monasteries*, 27–52; Williams, *The Welsh Cistercians*, 1:1–31; Berman, *Medieval Agriculture*; and McCrank, "The Cistercians of Poblet."

24. Of the studies cited in n. 23, see esp. Dronkin; Berman, 11–30; and McCrank.

25. Walter Map, *De Nugis Curialium*, 84–113.

26. Ibid., 92–93.

27. Ibid., 104–5.

28. Ibid., 106–7.

29. Ibid., 52–53.

30. Ibid.

31. Ibid., 130–31.

32. Geoffrey of Monmouth, *Historia Regum Britanniae*, 253–54. The translation used is Geoffrey of Monmouth, *The History of the Kings of Britain*, trans. Lewis Thorpe; here, p. 75. Hereafter, citations will include the original *Historia*, edited by Griscom, and the Thorpe translation.

33. Griscom, 270; Thorpe, 86.

34. Griscom, 261–62; Thorpe, 81. On Geoffrey's use of monuments, see Flint, "The *Historia Regum Britanniae* of Geoffrey of Monmouth," 453. This may be one of the instances where Geoffrey is harking back to Celtic traditions, such as the Stanzas of the Graves. See Jones, "The Black Book of Carmarthen," and Roberts, "Geoffrey of Monmouth," 30.

35. Griscom 383; Thorpe, 161.

36. Gildas, *The Ruin of Britain*, 89–90; *Bede's Ecclesiastical History*, 14–21; *Nennii Historia Britonum*, 6–7; Henry of Huntingdon, *The History of the English*, 5–13; *Pauli Orosii Historiarum Adversum Paganos Libri VII*, 28–30.

37. Griscom, 221; Thorpe, 53.

38. Griscom, 221–22; Thorpe, 54. I have slightly adapted Thorpe's translation here, which seems to contain a distorting typographical error.

39. Griscom, 222; Thorpe, 54.

40. *Bede's Ecclesiastical History*, 16–17.

41. Griscom, 237–40; Thorpe, 64–66.

42. For example, the rededication of the British temple by Faganus and Duvianus

(Griscom, 328–30; Thorpe, 124–25); Aurelius's pledge, during his campaign against Hengist, to rebuild the destroyed temples as soon as he is victorious (Griscom, 401–2; Thorpe, 189).

43. Griscom, 239; Thorpe, 65. On the ancient Greek tradition of such "colonization oracles" and their cultural function, see Dougherty, "When Rain Falls."

44. Griscom, 249–53; Thorpe, 72–74.

45. Griscom, 249; Thorpe, 72.

46. Griscom, 249; my translation; Thorpe's translation, "with the approval of their leader they divided the land among themselves" (72), does not quite capture the force of the Latin "donante duce," which implies that Brutus grants the land, rather than merely sanctioning his followers' choices.

47. Griscom, 251–52; Thorpe, 73–74.

48. Griscom, 251, emphasis added; my translation (cf. Thorpe, 73).

49. Griscom, 249; Thorpe, 72. Cf. William the Conqueror's supply of building stones, which had also been there "ab euo" (above, at n. 7). Cf. also R. R. Davies, *Domination and Conquest*, 20–22. See also Dougherty, "When Rain Falls," 32.

50. On Virgil's use of *patria*, see Patterson, *Negotiating the Past*, 173.

51. On the colonialist or "imperialist" overtones in Geoffrey's *Historia*, see Tatlock, *The Legendary History of Britain*, 305–20, and Waswo, "The History That Literature Makes." See also Mary B. Campbell, *The Witness and the Other World*, and Annette Kolodny, *The Lay of the Land* (as in n. 4 above). Many historians have also seen parallels between American "frontier" imagery and frontier theories, and medieval, esp. Cistercian, settlement. See Berman, *Medieval Agriculture*, 8 and n. 26 for bibliography; and McCrank, "The Cistercians of Poblet," for a detailed elaboration of the parallel as well as a discussion of its appropriateness.

52. See Pähler, *Strukturuntersuchungen*, 148–49.

53. Both Pähler, *Strukturuntersuchungen*, 127 and 159–60, and Schirmer, *Die frühen Darstellungen des Arthurstoffes*, 13, describe the prophecies as the work's "structural center," set against the rise and fall of Arthur's reign, the "climax of the action" to produce a meaningful tension.

54. Gillingham, "The Context and Purposes of Geoffrey of Monmouth's *History*," and Roberts, "Geoffrey of Monmouth."

55. Hanning, *The Vision of History*, 140–41 and passim. See also Schirmer, *Die frühen Darstellungen des Arthurstoffes*, 24–32.

56. At the same time, as Tatlock (*The Legendary History of Britain*, 427) and Schirmer (*Die frühen Darstellungen des Arthurstoffes*, 27) point out, the Mordred episode would probably have reminded Geoffrey's contemporaries of Stephen's usurpation of the throne.

57. Hanning, *Vision of History*, 164. I am not in a position to judge how partisan the Welsh reception of the *Historia* is, though, interestingly, R. R. Davies sees the Welsh reception of the *Historia* not so much as a reinforcement of native historical tradition but as an embracing of Continental literary tastes (*Domination and Conquest*, 19). But see Gillingham, "Context and Purposes," 110.

58. Tatlock comments: "Most of the present book is in vain if it does not show the *Historia* as planned to seem as lifelike as William of Malmesbury or Henry of Huntingdon; as

reflecting contemporary conditions rather than remote traditions" (*The Legendary History of Britain*, 425). Schirmer sees the *Historia* as a "political treatise addressed to [Geoffrey's] contemporaries," specifically about the civil wars, originally on the side of Mathilda (*Die frühen Darstellungen des Arthurstoffes*, 23, 28). That is almost certainly too specific a reading, but Schirmer's analysis of contemporary allusions is useful.

59. Hanning, *Vision of History*, 128–29; Schirmer, *Die frühen Darstellungen des Arthurstoffes*, 31; Bartlett, *Gerald of Wales*, 11–12.

60. Griscom, 536; Thorpe, 284 n. 1; translation slightly adapted. Leckie thinks that Geoffrey "intended his account as a counterbalance to the meagre, often unflattering data available on the Britons in earlier sources" and had a markedly "pro-British bias" which was not lost on contemporaries (*The Passage of Dominion*, 27); to Gillingham, this is the main purpose of the text.

61. On the dedications, see Tatlock, *The Legendary History of Britain*, 436–37; Schirmer, *Die frühen Darstellungen des Arthurstoffes*, 38. For a different view, esp. on the political role of Robert of Gloucester and its implications for the *Historia*, see Gillingham, "Context and Purposes."

62. Wace, *Le Roman de Brut*, vol. 1, line 2.

63. Geffrei Gaimar, *L'Estoire des Engleis*, lines 6429–526, notes pp. 277–78, introduction ix–xii; Leckie, *The Passage of Dominion*, 78–79; Short, "Gaimar's Epilogue and Geoffrey of Monmouth's *Liber vetustissimus*."

64. Both Robert's prologue and Henry's letter are inserted into Robert of Torigni's *Chronicle*, 60–75. See Leckie, *The Passage of Dominion*, 76–78. Leckie argues that while Robert of Torigni and Henry of Huntington do not reject the *Historia*, they treat it with "reserve," ultimately leaving it out of their own historiographical work. But in his view this has more to do with inconsistencies of dating than with ethnic partisanship.

65. See Gillingham, "Context and Purposes," 103.

66. Ibid., 117–18; Leckie, *The Passage of Dominion*, 102–9.

67. For biographical sketches of Geoffrey, see Tatlock, *The Legendary History of Britain*, 438–48; Schirmer, *Die frühen Darstellungen des Arthurstoffes*, 21–23; Rigg, *History of Anglo-Latin Literature*, 41–46. Geoffrey may have been born in Monmouth, but it has often been suggested, and is sometimes presented as a proven fact, that he was of Breton extraction, perhaps born in Brittany or else born in Wales of Breton parents.

68. Brooke, "The Archbishops."

69. Ibid.; Hughes, "British Museum Ms. Cotton Vespasian A.XIV ('Vitae Sanctorum Wallensium')," 184.

70. R. R. Davies, *Domination and Conquest*; cf. also Bartlett, *Gerald of Wales*, 13–15, and Roberts, "Geoffrey of Monmouth," 40.

71. R. R. Davies, *Conquest, Coexistence, and Change*, 179–94.

72. Brooke, "The Archbishops." After its first printing (in *Studies in the Early British Church*, ed. Nora K. Chadwick), Brooke's article drew furious reactions from some Welsh historians (e.g., J. W. James, "The Book of Llandav"). But their objections, as Brooke points out in the extraordinarily apologetic preface to the 1986 reprinting, are mostly to the tone, not the substance, of his argument. For a less heated reassessment of the *Book of Llandaff*'s seriousness, see Wendy Davies, "Liber Landavensis: Its Construction and Credibility."

73. Brooke, "The Archbishops," and "Geoffrey of Monmouth as a Historian"; Flint,

"The *Historia Regum Britanniae* of Geoffrey of Monmouth." For a survey and discussion of critical opinion on the subject, see Partner, "Notes on the Margins," 10–14.

74. Haidu, "Repetition" (even though Haidu himself might hesitate to apply this argument to a Latin text). See also Hutcheon, *A Theory of Parody*, esp. 50–68, where she insists on the possibility of "serious" parody and draws important distinctions between parody, satire, and irony.

75. For example, Pähler, *Strukturuntersuchungen*, 53–60; Hanning, *Vision of History*, 126–37.

76. Hanning, *Vision of History*, 121, 141, 143.

77. Ibid., 135–36.

78. Brooke, "Archbishops," 18, 20.

79. Eadmer, *Historia Novorum in Anglia*, 1; William of Malmesbury, *Gesta Regum Anglorum*, 1:1–2. On Geoffrey's "parody," see Hanning, *Vision of History*, 123–36, and Flint, "The *Historia Regum Britanniae* of Geoffrey of Monmouth."

80. William of Malmesbury, *Gesta Regum Anglorum*, 1:1.

81. Patterson shows how Virgil and the whole *translatio imperii* idea supplied a linear model of history, if a problematic one, to the twelfth century (*Negotiating the Past*, 160–61, 201–2). On genealogy and linear history, see Spiegel, "Genealogy."

82. William of Malmesbury, *Gesta Regum Anglorum*, 1:2.

83. Griscom, 219; Thorpe, 51.

84. For contemporary critics of Geoffrey, see Gransden, *Historical Writing*, 212–13, 246, 264–65; and Schirmer, *Die frühen Darstellungen des Arthurstoffes*, 82–83.

85. Griscom, 219; Thorpe, 51. See Short, "Gaimar's Epilogue."

86. Pähler suggests that the language and narrative style of the *Historia* are similarly "antiqued," made to sound like "the translation of an old book"; the first variant's "smoothing" of such archaisms would seem to confirm that suspicion (Pähler, *Strukturuntersuchungen*, 37); for a similar argument concerning Laȝamon, cf. Stanley, "Laȝamon's Antiquarian Sentiments."

87. Griscom, 261, 534; Thorpe, 80, 283.

88. On the Eagle of Shaftesbury, see Tatlock, *The Legendary History of Britain*, 44. Wace admits that he knows nothing about the bird or the content of its prophecies (*Le Roman de Brut*, lines 1616–18); Laȝamon makes a feeble attempt to invent a plausible "prophecy" (Laȝamon, *Brut*, vol. 1, lines 1412–16; *Layamon's Brut*, trans. Bzdyl, 57). For further near-contemporary solutions to the Eagle problem (equally clueless) in John of Cornwall and the Welsh *Brut y Brenhinedd*, see Rigg, *A History of Anglo-Latin Literature*, 47. For possible further instances of Geoffrey's "bravado" see Brooke, "Geoffrey of Monmouth as a Historian."

89. *Chronicon Monasterii de Abingdon*, 1:6–7

90. "Alia Acta SS Albani," 129; Matthew Paris, *Gesta Abbatum*, 26–17. (See above, chap. 1.) This may be inspired in part by the well-known source fictions of the Latin histoires of the Trojan War, Dares and Dictys. See Wilhelm, "Über fabulistische Quellenangaben," 294–300.

91. See above at n. 14 and also nn. 18–22 above; further examples are in Rigg, *A History of Anglo-Latin Literature*, 47–51 and 295–96. Ullmann's article on Geoffrey as "applied history"—attempts by later kings and politicians to base legal or political arguments on the

Historia—would seem to suggest a similar conclusion: Geoffrey apparently inspired such behavior in a way other historians did not ("On the Influence of Geoffrey of Monmouth in English History").

92. Griscom, 238; Thorpe, 64.

93. Griscom, 249; Thorpe, 72. The dragons underneath Vortigern's tower immediately come to mind (Griscom, 382-83; Thorpe, 169-72; see also Patterson, *Negotiating the Past*, 202). Closer in time to the Brutus story is Locrinus's attempt to keep his adultery hidden, and harmless, by banishing his mistress underground (Griscom, 255-56; Thorpe, 76-78).

94. Griscom, 241-42 and 250; Thorpe, 67-68 and 71-72. There are similar accents in the story of Belinus and Brennius: "Brennius stayed on in Italy, where he treated the local people with unheard-of savagery" (Griscom, 290; Thorpe, 99).

95. Leckie, *The Passage of Dominion*, 20 and passim.

96. Cf. Patterson, *Negotiating the Past*, 162, on Virgil's "literary exorcism."

97. O'Gorman's reflections on "discovery" and "invention" are interesting in this context: *The Invention of America*, 9-13 and 9 n.

98. For full and illuminating accounts of the political contexts of Bury hagiography prior to Denis, see Gransden, "Baldwin, Abbot of Bury," and Abou-el-Haj, "Bury St. Edmunds."

99. Abbo, "Life of St. Edmund," 69-70.

100. Denis Piramus, *La Vie Seint Edmund le Rei*, lines 219-20. All translations from the *Vie Seint Edmund* are my own.

101. Denis Piramus, lines 259 and 278.

102. Lines 279-84.

103. Lines 403-4.

104. Lines 1503-4.

105. Lines 1515-16.

106. Lines 1541-50.

107. Lines 1589-1756.

108. Lines 1949-92.

109. Lines 3338-42.

110. Lines 2665-744.

111. Lines 2819-26.

112. Lines 2997-3005.

113. Lines 2828-30.

114. Lines 2895-99.

115. Line 3024.

116. Although the only extant text of this romance is a fourteenth-century prose "re-maniement," we can be fairly certain that the passage under discussion here was in the thirteenth-century French verse romance seen and described by John Leland in the sixteenth century: a sizable part of it (the ghost's prophecy) is in verse and can be shown to be a remnant of the old text; the editors also point out several rhymes in the prose text that point to the underlying verse model (*Fouke*, 67; see also the editors' introduction, xix-xvi).

117. On "ancestral romance," see Legge, *Anglo-Norman and Its Backgrounds*, 139-75 (on *Fouke*, 171-74), and Crane, *Insular Romance*, 53-91 (on *Fouke*, 16-18 and 57-58).

118. *Fouke*, 3-4.

119. Ibid., 64 (note for p. 3, line 17). Cf. the comment on the Norman settlement of Wales in the *Gesta Stephani*, quoted in R. R. Davies, *Domination and Conquest*, 23.

120. *Fouke*, 4–7.

121. Crane, *Insular Romance*, challenges the widespread notion that ancestral romances — and *Fouke* in particular — served as propaganda for specific noble families; she instead ties them to the political interests of the entire baronial class (see n. 117 above). For other views on *Fouke*'s political context, see the introduction to the edition by Hathaway et al., ix–xv and xxvii–xxxii; Brandin, "Nouvelles recherches sur *Fouke FitzWarin*"; and Francis, "The Background to 'Fulk FitzWarin.'"

122. *Fouke*, 5–6.

123. Le Goff, "Melusina: Mother and Pioneer." See also Perret, "L'invraisemblable vérité."

124. The most recent edition (still unfinished) is Laȝamon, *Brut*, ed. G. L. Brook and R. F. Leslie, 2 vols., E.E.T.S. o.s. 250, 277. In subsequent quotations, line numbers refer to the "Caligula" text, on the lefthand side of Brook's and Leslie's parallel text edition. The translation I have used is Laȝamon, *Layamon's Brut: A History of the Britons*, trans. Donald G. Bzdyl. Criticism on the *Brut* and its literary and social context is summarized and discussed in a recent book by Le Saux, *Laȝamon's Brut*. She makes many plausible suggestions on Laȝamon's sources and political outlook (summarized on 228–30), but does not address the question of possible patronage or audience. She also attempts to narrow down the dating of the poem to the earlier part of the range proposed by earlier critics: 1185–1216 (1–10). For a recent discussion of Laȝamon's political position, see Donoghue, "Laȝamon's Ambivalence."

125. Lines 1002–9; Bdzyl, 50.

126. Lines 14–15, 24–26; Bdzyl, 33.

127. See n. 22 above.

128. Stanley, "Laȝamon's Antiquarian Sentiments"; Donoghue, "Laȝamon's Ambivalence."

129. Lines 16–23; Bdzyl, 33.

130. Chrétien de Troyes, *Erec et Enide*, lines 1–25; Thomas, *Le Roman de Tristan*, 1:lines 2107–56.

131. Chrétien, *Erec et Enide*, line 22; my translation.

132. Lines 11492–99, 9410–12; Bdzyl, 215, 184.

133. Lines 36–37. I have here substituted my own very literal translation, since Bzdyl's (35) is too free to capture the tone of this poetic opening and to reproduce the subtle play of the oral term "seið," "songe," and "speked" against the source reference, "þe boc.'"

134. See introduction, esp. nn. 54–58.

CHAPTER THREE

1. Auerbach, *Mimesis*, 90. Also quoted in Hanning, *Vision of History*, 69.

2. See introduction.

3. John O. Ward, "Some Principles of Rhetorical Historiography," 147–48; see also Coleman, *Ancient and Medieval Memories*, 276 and passim; Goetz, "Von der *res gesta* zur *narratio rerum gestarum*," 711–12.

4. Haidu, "Repetition," 882–83.

5. William of Newburgh, *The History of English Affairs, Book I*, 32–33. All quotations from book 1 will be from this edition, and the translations will be Walsh's and Kennedy's, hereafter cited as Walsh and Kennedy. References to later books will be to William of Newburgh, "*Historia Regum Anglicarum*," in the Rolls Series volume *Chronicles of the Reigns of Stephen, Henry II, and Richard I*, ed. Richard Howlett, hereafter cited as Howlett.

6. Walsh and Kennedy, 34–35.

7. Schapiro, "On the Aesthetic Attitude in Romanesque Art," 8–9. The reference is to Bernard's "Apologia ad Guillelemum Sancti-Theoderici Abbatem," *PL* 182:915–16.

8. Walsh and Kennedy, 36–37.

9. William of Malmesbury, *Gesta Regum Anglorum*, 1:2.

10. On fiction made possible by literacy, see Bäuml, "Varieties and Consequences," 247–59; on reference reading and libraries, Clanchy, *From Memory to Written Record*, 154–84, and Saenger, "Silent Reading," 385–86.

11. Goody and Watt, "The Consequences of Literacy," 48 and passim.

12. Mink, "Narrative Form as a Cognitive Instrument," uses a version of it as a starting point for one of his explorations into the "fictionality" of history.

13. Ibid., 142–43; White, *Metahistory*, 7–11; Stierle, "Erfahrung und narrative Form," 92–99. See also Goetz, "Von der *res gesta* zur *narratio rerum gestarum*."

14. Gransden devotes an entire chapter to William (*Historical Writing*, 166–85). Thomson, *William of Malmesbury*, discusses William's career, intellectual background, and historical method, 1–38; on source criticism, 16–18. See also Galbraith, "Historical Research in Medieval England," and Blacker-Knight, "From *Historia* to *Estoire*," 15–16. For a dissenting view, see Coleman, *Ancient and Medieval Memories*, 298.

15. Spiegel, "Genealogy," 45; see also Gransden, *Historical Writing*, 175.

16. Thomson, *William of Malmesbury*, 22.

17. Spiegel, "Genealogy," 45–46; see also Partner, *Serious Entertainments*, 183–93, on evidence in historical writing.

18. I am indebted to Massimo Oldoni's extensive work on the Gerbert legend, which includes a substantial discussion of William's version of it, and of Walter Map's rather different Gerbert story: "Gerberto e la sua storia" (cited as "Oldoni 1"); " 'A fantasia dicitur fantasma.' Gerberto e la sua storia, II. Prima parte" (Oldoni 2); and " 'A fantasia dicitur fantasma.' Gerberto e la sua storia, II. Fine" (Oldoni 3). The findings of this thorough study are summarized in a more accessible form in Oldoni, "*Imago e fantasma*." Since these rich and important essays have received less attention than they deserve, and since, being in Italian, they may not be readily accessible to all scholars interested in the subject, I shall document and paraphrase Oldoni's argument rather extensively in the notes. Oldoni's approach is chiefly thematic, and his primary interest is in the way the legend exemplifies twelfth-century *mentalité*. Gerbert, "the pope of the year 1000," stands for a major shift in Western intellectual history. He "is the symbol of the great movement of the Middle Ages towards *curiositas* as the dominant ethical theme from the end of the first millennium" (3:245). I will make use of Oldoni's conclusions and occasionally disagree with them; but I am interested primarily in the poetological consequences of including Gerbert's remarkable story in a history. On Gerbert, see also Graf, "La leggenda di un pontefice." A wonderful dis-

cussion of magic in William of Malmesbury is David Rollo's "William of Malmesbury: Literacy and Necromancy" (unpublished), which he has kindly let me see in typescript.

19. John O. Ward, who declares the long "digression" on the Crusade the hidden thematic and ideological center of the work, is nonetheless willing to dismiss the Gerbert material as "a loss of narrative control" ("Some Principles of Rhetorical Historiography," 120–21). I think these stories are equally important and, in fact, form an indispensable counterweight to the Crusade narrative.

20. William of Malmesbury, *Gesta Regum Anglorum*, 1:197 (henceforth cited as Stubbs); William of Malmesbury, *Chronicle of the Kings of England*, 176 (henceforth cited as Giles).

21. Stubbs, 1:198; Giles, 177–78.

22. Stubbs, 1:198; Giles, 178. For analogues of this not uncommon story, see Oldoni 2. See also Graf, *Roma nella memoria*, 119–42. The motif is also common in folklore. There are numerous analogues to the stories discussed here, as well as to individual submotifs, in the chapter on fairies in Briggs, *A Dictionary of British Folk-Tales*, esp. 182–84, 199–204, 214–17, 225–27. See also Menefee, "Circling as Entrance to the Otherworld," and *Handwörterbuch des deutschen Aberglaubens*, s.v. "Schatz," and s.v. "Berg" and "bergentrückt."

23. Cf. Oldoni 2:568–69; Graf, *Roma*, 135–58.

24. Stubbs, 1:200; Giles, 179.

25. Stubbs, 1:201; Giles, 179.

26. Oldoni suggests that this emphasizes the underground world's pagan nature: the rules of "Christian" magic, as opposed to the Jewish magic tried later, do not obtain here. This seems a little forced; the narrative is too vague on this point to support such a far-reaching interpretation, and at any rate the devils do "envy the name of God" sufficiently to make a major defensive effort. But perhaps there is simply a problem of translation here: maybe "obstipatus" means "obstructed," for instance with rocks or earthwork, rather than "beset" by the demons themselves. This would largely dispose of the problem.

27. Stubbs, 1:201–2; Giles, 179–80.

28. Stubbs, 1:202–3; Giles, 180–81.

29. To Oldoni, William's Gerbert is a figure of *curiositas*, a kind of premodern Faust. Armed with (half-forbidden) scientific expertise and *ingenium*, he penetrates to another level of reality—in this case, the Roman past; the buried "treasures of Octavian" stand for the classical foundations of medieval Christian civilization: "*ingenium*, not faith, is the passepartout of the journey. . . . All this describes the history of a reality without God, on which then grows the true, good, just, humane and merciful history of faith and of the faithful" ("Imago e fantasma," 760–61). He is, in other words, a figure of twelfth-century modernity—an evocation of the increasingly thinkable option of secular scholarship, but banished, as it were, underground, and denounced as diabolical. Rome, in Oldoni's reading, is the key to this ambivalence: it is the city of Western Christianity, but also the city of a pagan past, and of all kinds of magic, trickery, and both sexual and political corruption. The Gerbert story is, then, the dark underside of William's more sober, positive section on Rome, chiefly derived from Hildebert of Lavardin, whose mixed Christian and humanistic-classicizing tone he adopts (Stubbs, 404–8; Giles, 367–71).

While Oldoni is right in stressing the concepts of *ingenium* and *curiositas*, I see no reason for reading William's treatment of the Gerbert story principally as a Christian condemnation of these "modern" secular qualities. I am not convinced that we are faced here with a reaffirmation of an orthodox Christian world picture in the face of increasing secularity. While it is true that Rome and the Crusade form important structural centers in the work, William is not the kind of writer to erect doctrinal edifices; indeed, most readers have felt that the Christian element is rather understated in William and that his interest in classical antiquity is humanistic rather than theological (see, for instance, Blacker-Knight, "From *Historia* to *Estoire*," 17, and Thomson, *William of Malmesbury*, 7). The primary issue in William's Gerbert stories appears to be epistemology, not morality. I find it most fruitful to examine *ingenium* and *curiositas* as elements of William's poetics, and to see how the underground treasure episodes inform the narrative itself.

30. Dällenbach, *The Mirror in the Text*, 53. Dällenbach's examples are taken primarily from eighteenth- to twentieth-century fiction.

31. Oldoni 2:604.

32. On the condemnation of all magical arts, including "varias species mathematicae," and for a fascinating list of all sorts of conjurers, soothsayers, and illusionists, see John of Salisbury's *Policraticus*, 49–54.

33. Walsh and Kennedy, 114–15.

34. Partner, *Serious Entertainments*, 115.

35. Howlett, 489–90; Partner, *Serious Entertainments*, 140.

36. Howlett, 474–82. Discussed in Partner, *Serious Entertainments*, 134–40.

37. Howlett, 471–73.

38. Walsh and Kennedy, 122.

39. The editors note that the story does not correspond to anything in Aarne and Thompson's motif index (185–86). It is, however, reminiscent of much later stories about "wolf children"; interestingly, the ditch they come from is called "Wlfpittes, id est luporum fossa."

40. Walsh and Kennedy, 116–17.

41. Cf. Partner, *Serious Entertainments*, 121.

42. Walsh and Kennedy, 118–19.

43. I am also intrigued by the motif of the airtight cavity that preserves the prodigies, which echoes miraculously sealed graves such as Æthelhtryth's and William of Norwich's.

44. Walsh and Kennedy, 120–21.

45. Oldoni 2:357–59.

46. See below, chap. 4.

47. The word "ratio" is difficult here. William first defines "mirum": "mira vero huiusmodi dicimus, non tantum propter raritatem, sed etiam quia occultam habent rationem." Walsh and Kennedy as well as Partner translate "occultam habent rationem" as "they have a hidden significance" (sense 5 of "ratio" in the *Oxford Latin Dictionary*); if that is the sense here, then there is an implicit assurance of a "meaning," even though it is never revealed in the narrative. But the phrase could also mean, "because their ruling principle/essential constitution / rationale / *ratio* (order of existence) is obscure" (senses 12, 13, or 15); that is what ratio clearly suggests on p. 114, where Walsh and Kennedy translate it as "rational basis." In that case, no promise of interpretation would be implied.

48. Walsh and Kennedy, 120–21. On William's Augustinian argument, see Partner, *Serious Entertainments*, 123–29.

49. Walsh and Kennedy, 120–21. The apt image of "unearthing" is, alas, not William's but the translators'; "indagare" means, more precisely, "to hunt down."

50. In this section of direct comparison between William of Malmesbury and William of Newburgh, I resort — reluctantly — to the clumsy expedient of identifying each writer by his cognomen as though it were a modern surname. Of course "Malmesbury" and "Newburgh" are not these authors' names but rather their hometowns. But the reiteration of "William of Malmesbury" and "William of Newburgh" in close proximity would make the section too confusing.

51. Stubbs, 520; Giles, 476–77.

52. See introduction at n. 32. Specifically with regard to medieval historiography, see also John O. Ward, "Some Principles of Rhetorical Historiography," 104–6.

53. Oldoni argues that the ban on taking objects from the underground treasure stands for the dangers of refusing to believe without seeing. He extrapolates this from the *Gesta Romanorum* version of the story, where it is thus allegorized. But it does not follow that it therefore means the same thing in William of Malmesbury. In fact, given Oldoni's insistence elsewhere that the entire story has to do with *curiositas*, with the pursuit of secular history and secular knowledge in general, the explanation is not very satisfactory. Surely the requirements of Christian faith do not extend to pagan antiquity.

54. Oldoni 2:604.

55. See Hanning on magicians as author figures in vernacular narrative: "Poetic Emblems," 13–24.

56. Stubbs, 1:203; Giles, 182.

57. Goody and Watt, "The Consequences of Literacy," 44–49, 67. See also Constable, "Forgery," 20–23, and Stock, *Implications of Literacy*, 456.

58. Oldoni 2:604.

59. Graf, "La leggenda di un pontefice," 29–30.

60. "Quia enim is Silvester non per ostium intrasse dicitur; — quippe qui a quibusdam etiam nichormantiae arguitur; de morte quoque ejus non recte tractatur; a diabolo enim percussus dicitur obisse; quam res nos in medio relinquimus; — a numero paparum exclusus videtur. Unde lector quaeso, ut et hic et alibi, si qua dissonantia te offenderit de nominibus vel annis vel temporis paparum, non mihi imputes, qui non visa, sed audita vel lecta scribo [Because this Silvester is said not to have entered through the door — or, for that matter, is accused by some of necromancy; and also there was something amiss with his death, for he is said to have died from a blow by the devil; but we shall leave these things undecided — he is apparently excluded from the series of popes. Therefore I ask you, reader, if here or elsewhere you are struck by any inconsistency of names or years or dates of popes, do not blame it on me, for I am recording things I have not seen but merely heard or read]" (Sigebert of Gembloux, quoted in Graf, "La leggenda di un pontefice," 52; my translation). William of Malmesbury ends his first Gerbert chapter with the reflection that if God gave Solomon special powers: "Credo, inquam, quod et isti hanc scientiam dare potuerit, nec tamen affirmo quod dederit [I am saying he could have conferred such knowledge on (Gerbert) also; but I do not therefore assert that he did confer it]" (Stubbs,

198, quoted in Graf, "La leggenda di un pontefice," 57; my translation). William Godell ends his brief note on Gerbert: "Hec de prefato Gerberto papa ab aliis audivi; utrum vero sint subnixa veritate, lectoris arbitrio inquirenda derelinquo [This is what I have heard from others about the aforementioned pope Gerbert; whether, however, it is in accordance with the truth, I leave it to my reader's judgment to figure out]" (quoted in Graf, "La leggenda di un pontefice," 59; my translation).

61. Oldoni 1:652 n. 88; my translation.

62. On the Liar in the twelfth and early thirteenth centuries, see De Rijk, "Some Notes on the Medieval Tract De insolubilibus," and Spade, "The Origins of the Medieval *Insolubilia*-Literature." Of the vast general literature on the subject—most of which is far too technical for what is needed here—I have found useful Rüstow, *Der Lügner*; Anderson, "St. Paul's Epistle to Titus"; and Barwise and Etchemendy, *The Liar*, 1–25.

63. De Rijk, "Some Notes on the Medieval Tract De insolubilibus," 83. "The Mediaeval variant of the Liar had this basic form: *'what I am saying is false'* (*'ego dico falsum'*), provided I do not utter any proposition other than *'what I am saying is false'*" (86).

64. Ibid., 95 and 104–5. It appears that in the earliest discussions of the Liar and other circular paradoxes, the condition of self-reference was not fully understood, and logicians were willing to accept "difficult-to-solve" (difficile solubilis) propositions as equivalent of the true paradox.

65. On Walter and his work, see Rigg, *A History of Anglo-Latin Literature*, 88–93.

66. Cf. Oldoni 3:194: "Il De Nugis oltre a storie ed irregolari segmentari novellistici, riesce a costruire una sua logica anche storiografica, nata proprio dalla somma di quest'universo così polivalente e multiespressivo: finché tutto si pone come una globale interpretazione della realtà, delle cose e della storia."

67. Hinton, "Walter Map's *De Nugis Curialium*." See also Seibt, "Über den Plan der Schrift *De Nugis Curialium*."

68. Introduction to *De Nugis Curialium*, xxxii.

69. Ibid., xxx.

70. *De Nugis Curialium*, 6–7.

71. Ibid., 132–33.

72. Shepherd, "The Emancipation of Story," 53.

73. *De Nugis Curialium*, 208–9.

74. Hinton speculates that distinction 1, chapters 1–12, constitute one "fragment" ("Walter Map's *De Nugis Curialium*," 94–99).

75. *De Nugis Curialium*, 8–9.

76. Ibid., 14–17.

77. For example, ibid., 127–29.

78. Ibid., 132–33.

79. Ibid., 48–49.

80. Ibid., 80–81.

81. Ibid.

82. Walter's satiric discussion of the new orders is especially interesting in light of Bynum's essay, "Did the Twelfth Century Discover the Individual?" Walter is mocking both the idea of a "corporate identity," the search for a "life" or "order" rather than individualism, and the notion of modeling oneself on Christ, both of which Bynum isolates

as essential ingredients in the twelfth-century sense of self. On both subjects, sometimes with close parallels to Walter, see also Walter's contemporary and fellow satirist Nigellus Wireker, in his *Speculum Stultorum*.

83. *De Nugis Curialium*, 68–69.

84. Ibid., 116–17.

85. Cf. Gerald of Wales's introduction to his *Itinerarium Kambriae* (see chap. 4 below).

86. Cf. Coleman, *Ancient and Medieval Memories*, 314–15, on John of Salisbury's scepticism.

87. *De Nugis Curialium*, 2–3.

88. An approximate quotation — presumably from memory — of *Confessiones* XI.14.

89. *De Nugis Curialium*, 24–25. Cf. Peter of Blois, *The Later Letters*, 31.

90. *De Nugis Curialium*, 36–37.

91. Ibid.

92. Ibid., 16–25.

93. Ibid., 24–25.

94. Ibid., 116–17.

95. Ibid., 26–31. On time and the Herla story, see also Schmitt, "Temps, folklore et politique."

96. *De Nugis Curialium*, 35–36.

97. Oldoni 3:223: "Walter Map, accettando di non normalizzare la storia, persuaso che serva più accettare mille verità caduche e parziali piuttosto che predicare una sola verità che non si manifesta mai . . ."

98. *De Nugis Curialium*, 17–25 — under the heading "De germinibus noctis" (Of the Creatures of the Night).

99. Ibid., 158–59.

100. Ibid.

101. Ibid.

102. Ibid., 160–61.

103. In Oldoni's reading, this is what Walter's version of Gerbert stands for. Walter's Gerbert story (350–63) has no underground adventures; it has nothing in common with William of Malmesbury's version except for the ending, Gerbert's death in "Jerusalem." The main story, in Walter, is an analogue of Marie de France's "Lanval": Gerbert, a brilliant but poor student, enters into a pact with an endlessly munificent and generous fairy named Meridiana, receiving from her not only sexual favors and money, but also learning and success. His relationship with her remains his guilty secret while he becomes bishop, then pope; he repents just in time to escape a terrible punishment. This story helps Oldoni to link the theme of "fantasticae appariciones" with other antifeminist passages in *De Nugis Curialium* (notably the long misogynist tract "Dissuasio Valerii ad Rufinum"): "fantasmata," like women, tempt, emasculate, and sometimes kill men. On the other hand, the name of Gerbert's devil, "Meridiana," ties her to the notion of the "meridianum daemonem," which is associated with "acedia," the sin and spiritual malaise to which intellectuals are most susceptible. Finally, we can make the equation "sapere-Diavolo," knowledge and Devil. This is the notion that, according to Oldoni, all versions of the Gerbert legend grapple with in one way or another (Oldoni 3:200–241).

104. This is in striking contrast with the Melusina legend, with which Walter's stories

have rightly been compared: tracing the family's genealogy back to the fairy Melusina seems to enhance its prestige, rather than inspire uneasiness. See Le Goff, "Melusina: Mother and Pioneer"; Lecouteux, *Mélusine et le chevalier au cygne,* 24–25 and 28; Lundt, *Melusine und Merlin im Mittelalter,* 71–83.

105. *De Nugis Curialium,* 36–37.

106. Ibid., 8–11. Some of these chapters are missing at the beginning but supplied in the final *recapitulacio,* 498–513.

107. That the Welsh had a reputation for lying is also suggested by several of Gerald of Wales's anecdotes, discussed in the next chapter. See also the advice given to Peter of Leia, a Norman bishop of St. David's, by one of his advisers: "Sire, ne creez vus unques un sul de cel pais ne clerc ne lai [Sir, don't you ever believe anyone from that country, cleric or layman]" (Gerald of Wales, *Opera Omnia* 1:223; quoted in Richter, *Giraldus Cambrensis,* 90; my translation). On Gerald of Wales's opinion that the Welsh are naturally mendacious, see Bartlett, *Gerald of Wales,* 35–36.

108. *De Nugis Curialium,* 194–95.

109. Ibid., 188–89.

110. Ibid., 199–200.

111. Ibid., 36–37.

112. There are many striking similarities between Walter's work and certain Elizabethan satirists, especially Thomas Nashe, writing at what is perhaps a rather similar historical moment. See Crewe, *Unredeemed Rhetoric,* esp. 45–54, 65, 74. I am grateful to Jonathan Crewe for drawing my attention to this parallel.

113. Much has been written about the "curiales" at the court of Henry II and in the earlier parts of the twelfth century. See, for instance, Baldwin, *Masters, Princes and Merchants,* 1:175–204; Stollberg, *Die soziale Stellung,* who devotes a section to Walter Map and also discusses John of Salisbury, Gilbert Foliot, and others; Clanchy, "*Moderni* in Education and Government"; Turner, "Changing Perceptions of the New Administrative Class," "The *Miles Literatus,*" and his book, *Men Raised from the Dust,* which offers case studies of some less well known figures at Henry's court. A more general discussion of twelfth-century courts, courtliness, and the clergy, centered primarily on the emperor's court but also touching on French and English figures, is Jaeger, *The Origins of Courtliness.* On the literary scene associated with Henry and Eleanor, see Dronke, "Peter of Blois," and (though with an assessment of its characteristics that differs considerably from Dronke's and mine), Bate, "La littérature latine d'imagination."

114. Musset, "La formation d'un milieu social original"; Brett, *The English Church under Henry I,* 106–12; Köhn, "Militia curialis," 234–35.

115. On Walter's career, see Stollberg, *Die soziale Stellung,* 71–81. On the office of archdeacon, Brooke, "The Archdeacon and the Norman Conquest."

116. Bartlett, *Gerald of Wales,* 94; Baldwin, *Masters, Princes and Merchants,* 1:17–18.

117. Schirmer, *Die frühen Darstellungen des Arthurstoffes,* 21; Salter, "Geoffrey of Monmouth and Oxford."

118. Turner, *Men Raised from the Dust,* 27; Jaeger, *Origins of Courtliness,* 54–66. A *locus classicus* for such criticism is Peter of Blois's "Epistola XIV"; see also Köhn, "Militia curialis."

119. Turner, "Changing Perceptions," 106–8; Clanchy, "*Moderni* in Education and Government," 680–86.

120. Bartlett, *Gerald of Wales*, 58–69.

121. Quoted in Jaeger, *Medieval Humanism*, 94.

122. Jaeger, *Medieval Humanism*, 94; my translation.

123. Shepherd, "The Emancipation of Story." Despite the intense competition and general distrust of courtly life, there seems to have been some opportunity for intellectual friendships and community between these displaced clerics. Geoffrey of Monmouth's dedications and allusions reveal a "circle" of educated Norman laypeople, ecclesiastics, and fellow archdeacons such as Walter of Oxford, who gave him the "ancient book," and Henry of Huntington (Tatlock, *The Legendary History of Britain*, 18, 208, 422–24, 443–44, and nn. 34–37). Walter Map, Gerald of Wales, and other contemporaries were certainly very aware of each other's work and sometimes in friendly correspondence with each other.

124. See introduction at nn. 54–56.

125. Cf. Goody and Watt, "The Consequences of Literacy," 66.

126. Cf. Haidu, "Repetition," 883.

127. Ibid., 884–85.

CHAPTER FOUR

1. Gerald of Wales, *Itinerarium Kambriae et Descriptio Kambriae*, ed. Dimock, 75–78; the translation used is Gerald of Wales, *The Journey through Wales and the Description of Wales*, trans. Lewis Thorpe; here 133–36. I have occasionally adapted Thorpe's translation or substituted my own where a more literal rendition was needed. I will indicate when I have done so, but still give the page number in Thorpe for easier reference. On Gerald's life and work, see Rigg, *A History of Anglo-Latin Literature*, 93–96, and Bartlett, *Gerald of Wales*.

2. One may compare to this Walter Map's conclusion to the second distinctio of *De Nugis Curialium*: "I set before you here a whole forest and timberyard, I will not say of stories but of jottings. . . . I am but your huntsman. I bring you the game, it is for you to make dainty dishes out of it" (209).

3. Dimock, 13; Thorpe, 74; my translation.

4. Auerbach, *Mimesis*, 70–76 and passim; Partner, *Serious Entertainments*, 197–211.

5. Such is Nancy F. Partner's disillusioned complaint in "The New Cornificius": rejecting her own earlier analysis of the paratactic style of medieval historiography, she concludes, "Frankly, the texts in question seem to sink beneath the weight of such critical complication. Medieval history is not great history measured against the Greek and Roman past, or against the future; it is not great literature measured against the literature of its own age. It is merely very, very interesting. It is 'wonderful' in the Jamesian tone of combined respect and amusement" (18). She exempts only a handful of medieval histories from this verdict.

6. Bartlett, *Gerald of Wales*, 13–16, 47–49.

7. Nichols, "Fission and Fusion." See Dimock, 148; Thorpe, 205.

8. Gerald, in fact, all but suggests the notion of polyphony himself in his prologue, where he describes with both admiration and alarm the multiplicity of interests, profes-

sional pursuits, intellectual disciplines, and voices in his society; he expresses the hope that by joining the ranks of the "divini poetae" he can work toward reinstating the unified standard, the authoritative voice society has lost but needs to regain if it is not to disintegrate (Dimock, 2–7; Thorpe, 63–67).

9. For instance, as will be shown below, the *Itinerarium* does not narrate the history of Henry II's military campaigns into Wales in a coherent, chronological fashion, but dissolves it into separate anecdotes, which are inserted into different, often surprising, contexts.

10. Cf. Jacob, "The Greek Traveler's Areas of Knowledge"; Mary B. Campbell, *The Witness and the Other World.*

11. Dimock, 19; Thorpe, 78–80.

12. Dimock, 24; Thorpe, 84.

13. Dimock, 20; Thorpe, 80. David Rollo offers a very stimulating close reading of the *Topographia* and its modes of signification in his forthcoming "Gerald of Wales's *Topographia Hibernica.*"

14. Gerald of Wales, *The History and Topography of Ireland,* 42–43.

15. The technique brings to mind Gerald's contemporary Wolfram von Eschenbach. I should like to acknowledge that some of the very stimulating, lively scholarship on Wolfram's poetics has helped shape my thinking on Gerald's, esp. Brall, "Diz vliegende Bîspel"; Curschmann, "Das Abenteuer des Erzählens"; Haug, "Die Symbolstruktur des höfischen Epos"; and Schweikle, "Stiure und lere." For an entertaining demonstration of the redundant interconnectedness of anything and everything in Wolfram's *Parzival,* see Johnson, "Lähelin and the Grail Horses."

16. Dimock, 78–80; Thorpe, 136–38. For brevity's sake, when I am discussing an entire chapter of the *Itinerarium* I will refer to it by book (Roman numeral) and chapter number (Arabic numeral).

17. Dimock, 79; Thorpe, 137–38.

18. Nichols, "Fission and Fusion," 38.

19. Dimock, 82–89; Thorpe, 141–47.

20. Dimock, 84; my translation (cf. Thorpe, 142–43).

21. Castration and blinding was a common punishment for sedition or treason; Orderic Vitalis has several examples (Chibnall, *The World of Orderic Vitalis,* 126). It might thus have had a special resonance in occupied Wales with its sporadic episodes of resistance.

22. Dimock, 91; Thorpe, 149.

23. Dimock, 142–45; Thorpe, 200–203.

24. Dimock, 141; Thorpe, 199.

25. Dimock, 73; Thorpe, 131–32; discussed below.

26. Dimock, 62–63; Thorpe, 121–22.

27. Other miraculous fish in Gerald: Dimock, 19/Thorpe, 79–80; Dimock, 33/Thorpe, 93; Dimock, 135/Thorpe, 195. The motif, which goes back to the section on "mirabilia" in the *Historia Britonum* (*Nennii Historia Britonum,* 59–60), is also prominent in Geoffrey of Monmouth (*Historia Regum Britanniae,* 447). See also Pähler, *Strukturuntersuchungen,* 79–82.

28. Dimock, 142–45; Thorpe, 200–203.

29. On Gerald's ambivalence in Welsh-English affairs, see Richter, *Giraldus Cambrensis,* 61–82, and Bartlett, *Gerald of Wales,* 9–57.

30. Dimock, 160; Thorpe, 219.

31. Dimock, 226; Thorpe, 273. (More literally, "that I should turn my pen to the cause of the Welsh at the end of the book.") Peter von Moos comments on *disputacio in utramque partem* as an important intellectual tool that allows thinkers to reach serious insights by playfully freeing themselves from received truths (*Geschichte als Topik,* 254–85). Both he and Wesley Trimpi ("The Quality of Fiction," 75–97) stress the importance of this concept for an early sense of fiction as a serious, though playful, mode of narration and thought, as a tertium quid between lie and truth. See also Ginsberg, *The Cast of Character,* 98–100.

32. I do not mean to suggest that the terms "interlacing" and "allegory" are strictly anti-thetical, but they do seem to denote two opposite preferences. In that sense, my use of the term "interlace" is different from Eugene Vinaver's, one of the critics who helped coin the term: to him, it bears no particular relation to Auerbach's "vertical" or "horizontal" options, but is contrasted with Aristotelian "unity of action." Allegory, in his book, is loosely associated with a general interpretive turn of mind, and its relationship to "interlace" is not at issue (*The Rise of Romance,* 68–98 and 13–32). Partner, in *Serious Entertainments,* uses "interlace" similarly, as a way of explaining what to the modern reader appears like rambling digressions and lack of explicit connections in medieval historiography; but she comes closer to suggesting that allegory and interlace are alternatives: having just skepti-cally declined Auerbach's offer of "allegory" to explain the paratactic mode, she proposes "interlace" as a less metaphysically charged, more down-to-earth (if also less satisfying) alternative (see n. 4).

33. See introduction at n. 62.

34. Haidu, "Repetition," 883.

35. Bäuml, "Varieties and Consequences," 265. See also Spiegel, *Romancing the Past,* 222–24, who makes a parallel argument about thirteenth-century French prose chronicles.

36. In an influential article, Walter Haug shows precisely the same process, of strength-ening the "horizontal" connections at the expense of the "vertical," at work in Wolfram von Eschenbach's adaptation of Chrétien's *Perceval* ("Die Symbolstruktur des höfischen Epos"). That the move here is not from Latin to vernacular, but from one vernacular to another, suggests that the phenomenon may have as much to do with the process of writ-ing from written sources, which makes the author a reader as well as a writer, as with Latin versus vernacular: what Wolfram does, among other things, is to make the connections and inferences a reader of a "paratactic" text automatically supplies. This observation, of course, is close to Haidu's notion of "repetition."

37. On secularity in twelfth-century historical writing, see Hanning, *The Vision of His-tory,* 123, 108–13, and Partner, *Serious Entertainments,* 212–30. The key to Partner's dis-agreement with Auerbach and Alter, it seems to me, lies precisely in the question of whether twelfth-century historians can be seen as predominantly "Christian" or "ecclesi-astical" in their outlook — something Partner denies.

38. On Walter Map and Gerald, see Bartlett, *Gerald of Wales,* 4–6 and 147–48, and Thorpe, "Walter Map and Gerald of Wales."

39. Nichols, "Fission and Fusion," 24 and passim. My argument differs from Nichols's

chiefly in emphasis—though the difference is major: Nichols sees the voice of authority as Gerald's primary reality, with the "polyphony" of the modern world intruding as a subversive element; my analysis of Gerald's narrative leads me to reverse the priorities.

40. See below.

41. Dimock, 87–89; Thorpe, 145–47.

42. Dimock, 136; Thorpe, 195. Thorpe's translation here ("every fifth feast day") is incorrect, I believe: "quinta feria," in liturgical usage, is Thursday. The story almost reads like a parody of Geoffrey of Monmouth's prophetic eagles that convene on Loch Lomond every year to predict with their shrill cries "prodigium quod in regno venturum esset" (Griscom, 441). The difficulty—although it is not at all acknowledged here—is the same as in Gerald: the cyclical regularity of the meeting is hard to reconcile with the notion that the eagles' cries predict specific "prodigia." On Geoffrey's eagles, fish, and possible connections between them, see Pähler, *Stukturuntersuchungen*, 78–82.

43. Dimock, 89; Thorpe's translation of this word, "occult" (147), does not seem adequate.

44. Dimock, 111; Thorpe, 170.

45. Dimock, 72–78; Thorpe, 130–36.

46. Dimock, 72; Thorpe, 131.

47. Dimock, 74–75; Thorpe, 133.

48. Dimock, 75; Thorpe, 133; my translation.

49. Dimock, 77; Thorpe, 135–36.

50. Dimock, 78; Thorpe, 136; my translation.

51. One is reminded of one of the thieves/eavesdropping anecdotes in Walter Map, where the "thief," trying to interpret the chance conversation he has overheard, decides that "the sea," mentioned in passing, must stand for Wales: "a mari, id est Wallia, que semper in motu est [from the sea, that is, Wales, which is always in motion]" (*De Nugis Curialium*, 188–90).

52. See, for instance, the stories about anti-English violence in I.4; or the strange mishaps that befall Hugh of Shrewsbury on Anglesey: "From that moment onwards the English lost their control of Anglesey" (Dimock, 128–29; Thorpe, 187–88). A little subtler is the passage in II.5 that describes the roughness of the mountain landscape in Merioneth and the isolation this causes, after which Gerald adds, somewhat unnervingly, that "they use very long spears in this area" (Dimock, 122–23; Thorpe, 182).

53. Dimock, 125; Thorpe, 185; my translation.

54. Richter, *Giraldus Cambrensis*, 83–127; Bartlett, *Gerald of Wales*, 45–57.

55. Walsh and Kennedy, 120. (See chap. 3 at n. 44.)

56. Dimock, 20; Thorpe, 80; my translation.

57. For the "prodigies of the West," see Gerald of Wales, *The History and Topography of Ireland*, 31. The equation of book and journey is well captured in the "D" manuscript's colophon, which reads "Explicit Itinerarium Giraldi [Here ends Gerald's Journey]" (Dimock, 152; Thorpe, 209). Obviously, too much weight cannot be attached to a colophon, since it is usually scribal and more or less random in its precise wording; besides, "Itinerarium Giraldi" makes a perfectly straightforward title for the book. But the metaphoric reading here is very attractive, especially because at the end of the book, just preceding the colophon, there are also unmistakable overtones of the "end of one's life's journey":

in the last chapter, we hear of Archbishop Richard's deathbed vision and of Archbishop Baldwin's death during the siege of Acra. The book ends with a final prayer that makes substantial use of the journey metaphor: "May He who is alone 'the way, the truth, and the life,' the way without offence, the truth without shadow of doubt, the life without end, teach their 'hands to war and their fingers to fight'; and direct their journeyings, their lives and every act in the way of truth, together with the whole body of God's elect, to the glory of His name and the palm of faith which He Himself planted. Amen" (Thorpe, 209).

58. Michel Butor, "Travel and Writing," offers a stimulating, informal catalogue of possible variants and ramifications of the "travel"/"writing" metaphor.

59. Richter, *Giraldus Cambrensis*, 52–56 and passim.

60. See above at n. 53. Griscom, 251.

61. Not so much in the formal portrait at the end, where Gerald's admiration for Baldwin is overshadowed by criticism of his political leadership, but most clearly in the miracles ascribed to Baldwin: Dimock, 113/Thorpe, 172; Dimock, 83/Thorpe, 141.

62. For example, Dimock, 83; Thorpe, 141.

63. Most notably in the long passage on Llanthony Abbey (Dimock, 37–41; Thorpe, 96–101). Other instances include the description of Gerald's birthplace, Manorbier (Dimock, 92–93; Thorpe, 150–51). The description of Anglesey (Dimock, 127; Thorpe, 187) is a variation of the theme: the island is described as "arida tellus et saxosa, deformis aspectu et inamoena," yet it is exceptionally fruitful. After reading Geoffrey of Monmouth and Denis Piramus, one will not be surprised to find that this passage is immediately followed by an account of the conquest of the island. (See chap. 2 above.)

64. See chap. 2 above.

65. See Stollberg, "Die soziale Stellung," 152–54, on anti-Cistercian feelings among Gerald's and Walter Map's circle.

66. Bartlett, *Gerald of Wales*, 49 and passim.

67. Dimock, 75; Thorpe, 133–34; translation adapted.

68. Dimock, 146; Thorpe, 204.

69. Dimock, 147; Thorpe, 204–5.

70. Dimock, 7–8; Thorpe, 67–68.

71. Dimock, 136–39; Thorpe, 195–98.

72. Dimock, 55; Thorpe, 114; my translation.

73. Dimock, 56–57; Thorpe, 116.

74. Dimock, 57; Thorpe, 116.

75. Dimock, 57; Thorpe, 117.

76. Dimock, 59; Thorpe, 119.

77. Dimock, 58; Thorpe, 117–18.

78. Gransden, *Historical Writing*, 246; Schirmer, *Die frühen Darstellungen des Arthurstoffes*, 37.

79. Dimock, 179; Thorpe, 232.

80. See Thorpe, 159 n. 255, and the quotation of Merlin's prophecy regarding St. David's (Dimock, 56; Thorpe, 115).

81. If one may be permitted to speculate about the meaning of Rhydderch's eventually providing the information after all, but only for money, one might be reminded of Wolfram von Eschenbach's similar games of evasion and misleading, and Schweikle's attractive

glossing of "stiure" in the *Parzival* prologue as "tax, contribution" rather than "guidance." The sentence in Wolfram would then read something like: "Readers surely want to know what 'tax/contribution' this narrative requires, and what good instruction it offers." Wolfram then goes on to say that readers must be versatile in following his "crooked" and unpredictable story; their "witze" (wit, ingenuity) would then be the "contribution" required by the story (Schweikle, "Stiure und lere").

82. Walter Map, *De Nugis Curialium*, 122–23 (see introduction at n. 34). See also Southern, "Aspects of the European Tradition of Historical Writing: 3. History as Prophecy."

83. Hanning, *The Vision of History*, 154, 237 n. 141.

84. Dimock, 57–58; Thorpe, 117.

85. Dimock, 59–60; Thorpe, 119.

86. Dimock, 60; Thorpe, 120.

87. Dimock, 61; Thorpe, 120. I am cheating here by leaving out important parts of the sentence. Gerald is considering different options: If the spirits are incorporeal, how can Meilyr see them? If they are corporeal, why can't the rest of us? But I want to highlight the subtext of this little exercise in logical reasoning.

88. Bäuml, "Varieties and Consequences," 252.

CONCLUSION

1. The edition referred to is *St. Erkenwald*, ed. Clifford Peterson (cited as Peterson). For a fuller discussion of *St. Erkenwald*'s sense of the past, see my essay "New Werke." Parts of that essay are reprinted here with the permission of Duke University Press.

2. The poem's more direct models are versions of the widespread legend of St. Gregory praying for the pagan emperor Trajan. Gordon Whatley suggests that the immediate source might have been Jacopo della Lana's commentary on Dante's *Commedia* ("Heathens and Saints," 334–36). Gollancz prints the passage in question, as well as other versions of the Trajan legend, in an appendix to his edition of the poem (*St. Erkenwald [Bishop of London 675–93]*, 51–52). But the Trajan model is clearly mixed with motifs from indigenous *inventiones*. See Peterson, 39–44 and 91 n. 52, and Morse's introduction to her edition of *St. Erkenwald*, 19–31.

3. Line 203.

4. Lines 318–19.

5. Siegfried Wenzel, "St. Erkenwald and the Uncorrupted Body," notes a fifteenth-century allusion to an *inventio* at St. Paul's that may well be the incident the poet had in mind; but that *inventio* does not appear to be at all connected with Bishop Erkenwald. For the hagiography of St. Erkenwald, see Whatley, "Heathens and Saints," 353–63. On the Erkenwald legends, see also Peterson, 35–38, and Morse, *St. Erkenwald*, 12–18. Morse also prints Caxton's version in an appendix, pp. 77–81.

6. See Whatley, "Heathens and Saints," and Morse, *St. Erkenwald*, 19–31, for opposing views on *St. Erkenwald*'s place in that debate. Both provide further bibliography.

7. Vincent Petronella points out a cluster of verbs like "chaunge" and its synonyms in "key positions" in the early part of the poem ("*St. Erkenwald*: Style as the Vehicle," 533–34).

8. See Longo, "The Vision of History in *St. Erkenwald.*" Longo is particularly interested in the poem's emphasis on the societal meaning of that confrontation.

9. Lines 93–104.

10. Hanning defines "historical imagination" as "the faculty which perceives the reality of the past" (*The Vision of History*, 2). In his argument, the term stands primarily for the ability to relate the past to the present, to bridge historical distance rather than to emphasize it. But it seems to me that the two faculties—recognizing the past as separate from one's own reality and recognizing it as relevant to one's present—are two sides of the same coin.

11. Peterson, 91 n. 52.

12. See chap. 1 at n. 132.

13. Gollancz, *St. Erkenwald*, xxvi–xxvii and lvi. Gollancz suggests, specifically, that the poem was composed in 1386, to commemorate the institution of several first-class feasts associated with St. Erkenwald at St. Paul's. Peterson rejects this suggestion as too conjectural, but does allow the possibility that the poem may have been composed for a specific occasion at St. Paul's.

14. See Longo, "The Vision of History in *St. Erkenwald*," 48.

15. Stierle, "Erfahrung und narrative Form," 97. See introduction at n. 21.

⤙ Works Cited ⤚

PRIMARY SOURCES

Manuscripts

Cambridge
  Corpus Christi College Ms. 26
Dublin
  Trinity College Ms. 177 (formerly Ms. E.i.40)
London
  BL Cotton Claudius E.iv
  BL Cotton Julius A.x
  BL Cotton Vespasian B.xx
  BL Harley 3776
Oxford
  Corpus Christi College Ms. F 134

Printed Sources

Abbo of Fleury. "Life of St. Edmund." [BHL 2392.] *Three Lives of English Saints*. Ed.
  Michael Winterbottom. Toronto: Pontifical Institute of Mediaeval Studies, 1972. 65–87.
Ailred of Rievaulx. "De sanctis Ecclesiae Haugustaldensis, et eorum miraculis libellus."
  [BHL 3747.] *The Priory of Hexham: Its Chroniclers, Endowments, and Annals*. Ed. James
  Raine, Jr. Vol. I. Surtees Society 44. Durham: Andrews, 1864. 173–203.
"Alia Acta SS Albani, Amphibali et sociorum. . . ." [BHL 213.] *AASS*, June 22, Junii Tomus
  Quintus. 129–38.
Ambrose, St. "Epistola XXII." *PL* 16, cols. 1019–26.
Augustine, St. *De Civitate Dei*. Aurelii Augustini Opera XIV. Corpus Christianorum
  Series Latina 47–48. Turnhout: Brepols, 1955.
———. *Sermones*. Sancti Aurelii Augustini Opera Omnia 5. *PL* 38.
Bede. *A History of the English Church and People*. Trans. and intro. Leo Shirley-Price. Rev.
  R. E. Latham. Harmondsworth: Penguin, 1968.
Bede's Ecclesiastical History of the English People. Ed. and trans. Bertram Colgrave and
  R. A. B. Mynors. Oxford: Clarendon, 1978.
Bede. *De temporum ratione*. *PL* 90, 294–578.
Bernard of Clairvaux. "Apologia ad Guillelmum Abbatem." *PL* 182:895–918.

Bouton, Jean de la Croix, and Jean Baptiste Van Damme. *Les plus anciens textes de Cîteaux*. Cîteaux—Commentarii Cistercienses: Studia et Documenta 2. Achel: Abbaye Cistercienne, 1974.

Bovo of St. Bertin. "Bovonis Abbatis relatio de inventione et elevatione S. Bertini." [BHL 1296.] Ed. O. Holder-Egger. *MGH SS*, vol. XV.1. Hanover 1887. Reprint, Stuttgart: Heisemann and New York: Kraus, 1967. 524–34.

Chrétien de Troyes. *Erec et Enide*. Ed. Mario Roques. Les Romans de Chrétien de Troyes, I; Les Classiques Français du Moyen Age. Paris: Honoré Champion, 1952.

The Chronicle of Battle Abbey. Ed. and trans. Eleanor Searle. Oxford: Clarendon, 1980.

Chronicon Abbatiae de Evesham ad annum 1418. Ed. William Dunn Macray. Rolls Series 29. London: Longmans, 1863.

Chronicon Abbatiae Rameseiensis. Ed. W. Dunn Macray. Rolls Series 83. London: Longmans, 1886.

Chronicon Monasterii de Abingdon. Ed. Joseph Stevenson. Rolls Series 2. 2 vols. London: Longmans, 1858.

"Corporis Sancti Fidelis Comensis Martyris anno circiter 964 inventio et prima translatio, auctore coaevo." [BHL 2925.] *Analecta Bollandiana* 9 (1890): 354–59.

Denis Piramus. *La Vie Seint Edmund le Rei*. Ed. Hilding Kjellman. Gothenburg: Elanders, 1935.

Dominic of Evesham. "Vita S. Ecgwini episcopi et confessoris." [BHL 2433.] Ed. Michael Lapidge. *Analecta Bollandiana* 96 (1978): 65–104.

Eadmer. "Epistola Eadmeri ad Glastonienses: Quale sit quod Glastonienses asserunt se corpus beati Dunstani habere." *Memorials of Saint Dunstan, Archbishop of Canterbury*. Ed. William Stubbs. Rolls Series 63. London 1871. Reprint, n.p.: Kraus, 1965. 412–22.

———. *Historia Novorum in Anglia*. Ed. Martin Rule. Rolls Series 81. London: Longmans, 1884.

———. "De reliquiis sancti Audoeni et quorundam aliorum sanctorum quae Cantuariae in aecclesia Domini Salvatoris habentur." [BHL 758.] Ed. A. Wilmaert. *Revue des sciences religieuses* 15 (1935): 362–70.

Fouke Le Fitz Waryn. Ed. E. J. Hathaway, P. T. Ricketts, C. A. Robson, and A. D. Wilshere. Anglo-Norman Text Society 26–28. Oxford: Blackwell, 1975.

"The Foundation of Kirkstall Abbey." Ed. and trans. E. K. Clark. *Miscellanea* 2. Thoresby Society Publications 4. Leeds: Thoresby Society, 1893. 169–208.

Fowler, J. T. *The Coucher Book of Selby*. Vol. 1. The Yorkshire Archaeological and Topographical Association Record Series 10. Durham: Yorkshire Archaeological Society, 1890.

Gaimar, Geffrei. *L'Estoire des Engleis*. Ed. Alexander Bell. Anglo-Norman Texts XIV–XVI. Oxford: Blackwell, 1960.

Geoffrey of Monmouth. *The Historia Regum Britanniae of Geoffrey of Monmouth*. Ed. Acton Griscom. London: Longmans, 1929.

———. *The History of the Kings of Britain*. Trans. Lewis Thorpe. Harmondsworth: Penguin, 1983.

Gerald of Wales. *The History and Topography of Ireland*. Trans. John J. O'Meara. Harmondsworth: Penguin, 1982.

―――. *Itinerarium Kambriae et Descriptio Kambriae*. In *Giraldi Kambrensis Opera*.
Vol. 6. Ed. James F. Dimock. Rolls Series 21.6. London: Longmans, 1868.

―――. *The Journey through Wales and The Description of Wales*. Trans. Lewis Thorpe.
Harmondsworth: Penguin, 1978.

[Gervase of Canterbury.] *The Historical Works of Gervase of Canterbury*. Ed. William
Stubbs. 2 vols. Rolls Series 73. London 1879–80. Reprint, n.p.: Kraus, 1965.

Gildas. *The Ruin of Britain and Other Works*. Ed. and trans. Michael Winterbottom.
History from the Sources: Arthurian Period Sources 7. Gen. ed. John Morris. London:
Phillimore, 1978.

[Goscelin of St. Bertin.] "Historia translationis S. Augustini Episcopi Anglorum Apostoli,
aliorumque sanctorum qui in ipsius monasterio Cantuariensi quiescebant." [BHL 781.]
PL 155, cols. 13–46.

―――. "Libellus contra inanes s. uirginis Mildrethae usurpatores" [BHL 5962] and
"Vita sanctorum Aethelredi et Aethelberti martirum et ss. uirginum Miltrudis et
Edburgis" [BHL 2644ab]. Marvin Colker, "A Hagiographic Polemic." *Mediaeval Studies*
39 (1977): 60–108.

―――. "Vita S. Yvonis." [BHL 4621.] *Acta Sanctorum*, June 10, Junii Tomus Secundus.
Paris and Rome: Victor Palmé, 1867. 284–89. Also in *PL* 155, cols. 81–90.

Henry of Huntingdon. *The History of the English*. Ed. Thomas Arnold. Rolls Series 74.
London: Longmans, 1879.

"Historia inventionis et miraculorum Sancti Gilduini." [BHL 3545.] *Analecta Bollandiana*
1 (1882): 149–77.

"Historia Selebiensis Monasterii, quod fundatum est in Anglia. . . ." [BHL 3464.] Ed.
J. T. Fowler. *The Coucher Book of Selby*. Vol. 1. The Yorkshire Archaeological and
Topographical Association Record Series 10. Durham: Yorkshire Archaeological
Society, 1890. 1–54.

Hugh of St. Victor. "De Tribus Maximis Circumstantiis Gestorum." Ed. and intro.
William M. Green [only the prologue is edited]. *Speculum* 18 (1943): 484–93.

"De Inventione Capitis S. Margaretae Virginis et Martyris in coenobio Gemblacensi
facta." [BHL 5312.] *Analecta Bollandiana* 6 (1887): 303–4.

"Inventio reliquiarum Sancti Eligii facta anno 1183 et a teste coaevo descripta." [BHL
2480.] *Analecta Bollandiana* 9 (1890): 421–36.

Jocelin of Brakelond. *Chronica Jocelini de Brakelonda de rebus gestis Samsonis Abbatis
Monasterii Sancti Edmundi. The Chronicle of Jocelin of Brakelond concerning the acts of
Samson, Abbot of the Monastery of St. Edmund*. Ed. and trans. H. E. Butler. Nelson
Medieval Texts. London: Nelson, 1957.

[John of Salisbury. Policraticus.] *Ioannis Saresberiensis episcopi Carnotensis Policratici sive
De Nugis curialium et vestigiis philosophorum libri VIII*. Ed. Clemes C. I. Webb. 2 vols.
London and Oxford, 1909. Reprint, Frankfurt: Minerva, 1965.

Laȝamon. *Brut*. Ed. G. L. Brook and R. F. Leslie. 2 vols. E.E.T.S. o.s. 250, 277. London:
Oxford University Press, 1963, 1978.

―――. *Layamon's Brut: A History of the Britons*. Trans. Donald G. Bzdyl. Binghamton:
Center for Medieval and Early Renaissance Studies, 1989.

Lehmann-Brockhaus, Otto. *Lateinische Schriftquellen zur Kunst in England, Wales und*

Schottland vom Jahre 901 bis zum Jahre 1307. 5 vols. Veröffentlichungen des
Zentralinstituts für Kunstgeschichte in München 1. Munich: Prestelverlag, 1955–60.

———. *Schriftquellen zur Kunstgeschichte des 11. und 12. Jahrhunderts für Deutschland,
Lothringen und Italien.* 2 vols. Berlin: Deutscher Verein für Kunstwissenschaft, 1938.

Liber Eliensis. Ed. E. O. Blake. Camden, Third Series 92. London: Royal Historical
Society, 1962.

Liebermann, Felix, ed. *Die Heiligen Englands. Angelsächsisch und lateinisch.* Hanover:
Hahnsche Buchhandlung, 1889.

The Life of King Edward Who Rests at Westminster. [BHL 2421.] Ed. and trans. Frank
Barlow. 2d ed. Oxford Medieval Texts. Oxford: Clarendon, 1992.

Marie de France. *Les Lais de Marie de France.* Ed. Jean Rychner. Classiques français du
moyen âge 93. Paris: Honoré Champion, 1983.

———. *The Lais of Marie de France.* Trans. Robert Hanning and Joan Ferrante. Durham,
N.C.: Labyrinth, 1982.

Matthew Paris. *Chronica Majora.* Ed. Henry R. Luard. 7 vols. Rolls Series 57. London:
Longmans, 1872–84. Reprint, n.p.: Kraus, 1964.

———. *Gesta Abbatum Monasterii Sancti Albani.* "Sectio prima" of Thomas
Walsingham's *Gesta Abbatum Sancti Albani.* Ed. Henry Thomas Riley. Vol. 1. Rolls
Series 28.4. London: Longmans, 1867. Reprint, n.p.: Kraus, 1965. 1–324.

———. *Illustrations to the Life of St. Alban in Trinity College Dublin ms. E.i.40.*
Reproduced in Collotype Facsimile. Ed. W. R. L. Lowe and F. Jacobs, with a
description of the illustrations by M. R. James. Oxford: Clarendon, 1924.

———. *Matthaei Paris Vitae Duorum Offarum.* . . . Ed. W. Wats. London, 1639.

———. *La Vie de Seint Auban.* Ed. Arthur Robert Harden. Anglo-Norman Texts 19.
Oxford: Blackwell, 1968.

Memorials of St. Edmunds Abbey. Ed. Thomas Arnold. Vol. 1. Rolls Series 96. London
1890. Reprint, n.p.: Kraus, 1965.

Michel, Francisque, ed. *Chroniques Anglo-Normandes.* Vol. 2. Rouen: Frère, 1939.

Mortet, Victor. *Recueil de textes relatifs à l'histoire de l'architecture et à la condition des
architectes en France, au moyen âge, XIe–XIIe siècles.* Paris: Picard, 1911.

Mortet, Victor, and Paul Deschamps. *Recueil de textes relatifs à l'histoire de l'architecture
et à la condition des architectes en France, au moyen âge, XIIe–XIIIe siècles.* Paris:
Picard, 1929.

Narratio de fundatione Fontanis monasterii in comitatu Eboracensi. In *Memorials of the
Abbey of St. Mary of Fountains.* Ed. John Richard Walbran. Surtees 42. Durham:
Andrews, 1863. 1–129.

Nennii Historia Britonum. Ed. Joseph Stevenson. London: English Historical Society,
1938.

Nigellus Wireker. *Speculum Stultorum.* Ed. John H. Mozley and Robert R. Raymo.
Berkeley: University of California Press, 1960.

Orderic Vitalis. *The Ecclesiastical History of Orderic Vitalis.* Ed. and trans. Marjorie
Chibnall. 6 vols. Oxford Medieval Texts. Oxford: Clarendon, 1968–80.

Pauli Orosii Historiarum Adversum Paganos Libri VII. Ed. Carl Zangemeister. 1882.
Reprint, New York: Johnson Reprint Corporation, 1966.

Peter of Blois. *The Later Letters of Peter of Blois*. Ed. Elizabeth Revell. Auctores Britannici
Medii Aevi XIII. Oxford: Oxford University Press, 1993.

———. "Epistola XIV: Ad sacellanos aulicos regis Anglorum." *PL* 207, cols. 42–51.

Raine, James, Jr., ed. *The Priory of Hexham: Its Chroniclers, Endowments, and Annals.*
Vol. I. Surtees Society 44. Durham: Andrews, 1864.

Ralph of Diceto. *Abbreviatio Chronicorum.* In *Radulfi de Diceto, Lundonensis Decani,*
Opera Historica. Ed. William Stubbs. Vol. 1. Rolls Series 68. London: Longmans, 1876.
Reprint, n.p.: Kraus, 1965. 3–263.

[Robert of Torigni.] *The Chronicle of Robert of Torigni.* In *Chronicles of the Reigns of*
Stephen, Henry II, and Richard I. Ed. Richard Howlett. Vol. 4. Rolls Series 82. London:
Eyre and Spottiswoode, 1889.

St. Erkenwald (Bishop of London 675–693). Ed. Sir Israel Gollancz. Select Early English
Poems 4. London: Oxford University Press, 1922.

St. Erkenwald. Ed. Ruth Morse. Cambridge: D. S. Brewer, 1975.

St. Erkenwald. Ed. Clifford Peterson. Philadelphia: University of Pennsylvania Press, 1977.

Sidney, Philip, Sir. *A Defence of Poetry.* Ed. J. A. van Dorsten. London: Oxford University
Press, 1966.

[Simeon of Durham.] *Symeonis monachi opera omnia.* Ed. Thomas Arnold. 2 vols. Rolls
Series 75. London 1882–85. Reprint, n.p.: Kraus, 1965.

Thomas [of Britain]. *Le Roman de Tristan par Thomas.* Ed. Joseph Bédier. 2 vols. Paris:
Firmin Didot, 1902–5.

Thomas of Monmouth. *The Life and Miracles of St. William of Norwich.* [BHL 8926.] Ed.
Augustus Jessopp and Montague Rhodes James. Cambridge: Cambridge University
Press, 1896.

Vanderlinden, S. "Revelatio Sancti Stephani." [BHL 7850–56.] *Revue des études byzantines*
4 (1946): 178–217. Also in *PL* 41, 805–18.

"Vie de S. Rumon; Vie, Invention et Miracles de S. Nectan." [BHL 7384m; 6050ac–ae.]
Ed. Paul Grosjean. *Analecta Bollandiana* 71 (1953): 359–414.

Vitae aliaeque historiae minores. Ed. L. de Heinemann, O. Holder-Egger, G. Waitz, and
W. Wattenbach. Monumenta Germaniae Historica Scriptorum Tomus XV [=MGH
SS XV]. 2 parts. Hanover 1887–88. Reprint, Stuttgart: Hiersemann, 1963.

"Vita et miracula S. Bege Virginis in Provincia Northanhimbrorum." [BHL 1080–81.]
The Register of the Priory of St. Bees. Ed. James Wilson. Surtees Society 126. Durham:
Andrews, 1915. 497–520.

"Vita Haroldi." *Chroniques Anglo-Normandes.* Ed. Francisque Michel. Vol. 2. Rouen:
Frère, 1836. 143–222.

"Vita, Inventio et Miracula Sanctae Enimiae." [BHL 2549–51.] Ed. C. Brunel. *Analecta*
Bollandiana 57 (1939): 237–98.

"Vita Oswini Regis Deirorum." [BHL 6382–84.] Ed. James Raine. *Miscellanea*
Biographica. Surtees Society 8. London: Nichols, 1838. 1–59.

"Vita Sancti Rumwoldi." [BHL 7385.] *Three Eleventh-Century Anglo-Latin Saints' Lives.*
Ed. and trans. Rosalind C. Love. Oxford Medieval Texts. Oxford: Clarendon, 1996.

Wace. *Le Roman de Brut.* Ed. Ivor Arnold. 2 vols. S.A.T.F. 93. Paris: Société des anciens
textes français, 1938–40.

Walter Map. *De Nugis Curialium: Courtiers' Trifles.* Ed. and trans. M. R. James. Rev.
C. N. L. Brooke and R. A. B. Mynors. Oxford Medieval Texts. Oxford: Clarendon, 1983.

The Waltham Chronicle: An Account of the Discovery of our Holy Cross at Montacute and its Conveyance to Waltham. Ed. and trans. Leslie Watkiss and Marjorie Chibnall. Oxford Medieval Texts. Oxford: Clarendon, 1994.

William of Malmesbury. [*De antiquitate Glastoniensis ecclesiae.*] *The Early History of Glastonbury: An Edition, Translation, and Study of William of Malmesbury's "De antiquitate Glastonie ecclesie."* By John Scott. Woodbridge: Boydell, 1981.

———. *Chronicle of the Kings of England.* Trans. J. A. Giles. London: Bohn, 1847. Reprint, New York: AMS, 1968.

———. *Gesta Pontificum Anglorum.* Ed. N. E. S. A. Hamilton. Rolls Series 52. London, 1870. Reprint, n.p.: Kraus, 1964.

———. *Gesta Regum Anglorum.* Ed. William Stubbs. 2 Vols. Rolls Series 90. London: Longmans, 1887.

William of Newburgh. *Historia Regum Anglicarum.* In *Chronicles of the Reigns of Stephen, Henry II, and Richard I.* Ed. Richard Howlett. 2 vols. Rolls Series 82.1-2. London 1884-85. Reprint, n.p.: Kraus, 1964.

———. *The History of English Affairs, Book I.* Ed. and trans. P. G. Walsh and M. J. Kennedy. Warminster, Wiltshire: Aris and Phillips, 1988.

Wolfram von Eschenbach. *Parzival.* Trans. A. T. Hatto. Penguin Classics 361. Harmondsworth: Penguin, 1980.

SECONDARY SOURCES

Abou-El-Haj, Barbara. "Bury St. Edmunds Abbey between 1070 and 1124: A History of Property, Privilege, and Monastic Art Production." *Art History* 6 (1983): 1-17.

———. *The Medieval Cult of Saints: Formations and Transformations.* Cambridge: Cambridge University Press, 1994.

Aigrain, R. *L'hagiographie: ses sources, ses méthodes, son histoire.* Paris: Bloud & Gay, 1953.

Alfonso, Isabel. "Cistercians and Feudalism." *Past and Present* 133 (November 1991): 3-30.

Anderson, Alan Ross. "St. Paul's Epistle to Titus." *The Paradox of the Liar.* Ed. Robert L. Martin. New Haven: Yale University Press, 1970. 1-11.

Anglo-Norman Dictionary. Ed. Louise W. Stone, William Rothwell, and T. B. W. Reid. London: Modern Humanities Research Association, 1983.

Ankersmit, F. R. "Reply to Professor Zagorin." *History and Theory* 29 (1990): 275-96.

Auerbach, Erich. *Mimesis: The Representation of Reality in Western Literature.* Trans. Willard R. Trask. Princeton: Princeton University Press, 1974.

Baker, L. G. D. "The Foundation of Fountains Abbey." *Northern History* 4 (1969): 28-43.

Bakhtin, Mikhail Mikhailovich. "Forms of Time and of the Chronotope in the Novel: Notes toward a Historical Poetics." *The Dialogic Imagination: Four Essays by M. M. Bakhtin.* Ed. Michael Holquist. Trans. Caryl Emerson and Michael Holquist. Austin: University of Texas Press, 1981. 84-258.

Baldwin, John W. *Masters, Princes and Merchants: The Social Views of Peter the Chanter and His Circle.* 2 vols. Princeton: Princeton University Press, 1970.

Bann, Stephen. *The Clothing of Clio: A Study of the Representation of History in Nineteenth-Century Britain and France*. Cambridge: Cambridge University Press, 1984.

Barlow, Frank. "The Effects of the Norman Conquest." *The Norman Conquest: Its Setting and Impact. A Book Commemorating the Ninth Centenary of the Battle of Hastings*. London: Battle and District Historical Society, 1966. 125-61.

Barnes, Guy D. *Kirkstall Abbey, 1147-1539: An Historical Study*. Publications of the Thoresby Society 58. Leeds: Thoresby Society, 1984.

Bartlett, Robert. *Gerald of Wales, 1146-1223*. Oxford: Clarendon, 1982.

Barwise, Jon, and John Etchemendy. *The Liar: An Essay on Truth and Circularity*. New York: Oxford University Press, 1987.

Bate, Keith. "La littérature latine d'imagination à la cour d'Henri II d'Angleterre." *Cahiers de civilisation médiévale (Xe–XIIe siècles)* 34 (1991): 3-26.

Bäuml, Franz H. "Varieties and Consequences of Medieval Literacy and Illiteracy." *Speculum* 55 (1980): 237-65.

Bennett, R. E. "Walter Map's *Sadius and Galo*." *Speculum* 16 (1941): 35-56.

Berman, Constance Hoffman. *Medieval Agriculture, the Southern French Countryside, and the Early Cistercians: A Study of Forty-Three Monasteries*. Transactions of the American Philosophical Society 76, pt. 5. Philadelphia: American Philosophical Society, 1986.

Bethell, Denis. "The Foundation of Fountains Abbey and the State of St. Mary's York in 1132." *Journal of Ecclesiastical History* 17 (1966): 11-27.

———. "The Making of a Twelfth-Century Relic Collection." *Studies in Church History* 8 (1972): 61-72.

———. "The Miracles of St. Ithamar." *Analecta Bollandiana* 89 (1971): 421-37.

Bezzola, Reto R. *Les origines et la formation de la littérature courtoise en occident (500-1200)*. Pt. II: *La société féodale et la transformation de la littérature de cour*. 2 vols. Paris: Champion, 1960.

Biddle, M., Mrs. H. T. Lambrick [*sic*], J. N. L. Myers. "The Early History of Abingdon, Berkshire, and Its Abbey." *Medieval Archaeology* 12 (1969): 26-69.

Blacker-Knight, Jean. "From *Historia* to *Estoire*: Literary Form and Social Function of the Twelfth-Century Old French Verse and Latin Prose Chronicle of the Anglo-Norman *Regnum*." Ph.D. diss., University of California, Berkeley, 1984.

Borst, Arno. "Weltgeschichten im Mittelalter?" *Geschichte—Ereignis und Erzählung*. Ed. Reinhart Koselleck and Wolf-Dieter Stempel. Poetik und Hermeneutik 5. Munich: Fink, 1973. 452-56.

Brall, Helmut. " 'Diz vliegende Bîspel': Zu Programmatik und kommunikativer Funktion des *Parzival*prologs." *Euphorion* 77 (1983): 1-39.

Brandin, Louis. "Nouvelles recherches sur *Fouke Fitz Warin*." *Romania* 55 (1929): 17-44.

Breisach, Ernst, ed. *Classical Rhetoric and Medieval Historiography*. Studies in Medieval Culture 9. Kalamazoo: Medieval Institute, 1985.

———. *Historiography: Ancient, Medieval, and Modern*. Chicago: University of Chicago Press, 1983.

Brett, Martin. *The English Church under Henry I*. London: Oxford University Press, 1975.

Briggs, Katherine M., ed. *A Dictionary of British Folk-Tales in the English Language*. 4 vols. Bloomington: Indiana University Press, 1970-71.

Brooke, Christopher N. L. "The Archbishops of St. David's, Llandaff and Caerleon-on-Usk." *Studies in the Early British Church*. Ed. Nora K. Chadwick. Cambridge: Cambridge University Press, 1958. 201–42. Reprinted (revised) in *The Church and the Border in the Central Middle Ages*. By Brooke. Ed. D. N. Dumville and C. N. L. Brooke. Woodbridge: Boydell, 1986. 16–49.

———. "The Archdeacon and the Norman Conquest." *Tradition and Change: Essays in Honour of Marjorie Chibnall*. Ed. Diana Greenway, Christopher Holdsworth, and Jane Sayers. Cambridge: Cambridge University Press, 1985. 1–19.

———. "Geoffrey of Monmouth as a Historian." *Church and Government in the Middle Ages*. Ed. Christopher Brooke et al. Cambridge: Cambridge University Press, 1976. 77–91. Reprinted in *The Church and the Border in the Central Middle Ages*. By Brooke. Ed. D. N. Dumville and C. N. L. Brooke. Woodbridge: Boydell, 1986. 95–106.

Brown, Peter. *The Cult of the Saints: Its Rise and Function in Latin Christianity*. Chicago: University of Chicago Press, 1981.

Bruckner, Matilda Tomaryn. *Shaping Romance: Interpretation, Truth, and Closure in Twelfth-Century French Fictions*. Philadelphia: University of Pennsylvania Press, 1993.

Butor, Michel. "Travel and Writing." Trans. John Powers and K. Lisker. *Mosaic* 8 (1974–75): 1–16.

Bynum, Caroline Walker. "Did the Twelfth Century Discover the Individual?" *Jesus as Mother: Studies in the Spirituality of the High Middle Ages*. By Bynum. Berkeley: University of California Press, 1982. 82–109.

———. "Material Continuity, Personal Survival, and the Resurrection of the Body: A Scholastic Discussion in Its Medieval and Modern Contexts." *History of Religions* 30 (1990): 51–85.

Campbell, James. "Some Twelfth-Century Views of the Anglo-Saxon Past." *Peritia* 3 (1984): 131–50.

Campbell, Mary B. *The Witness and the Other World: Exotic European Travel Writing, 400–1600*. Ithaca: Cornell University Press, 1988.

Canary, Robert H., and Henry Kozicki, eds. *The Writing of History: Literary Form and Historical Understanding*. Madison: University of Wisconsin Press, 1978.

Cheney, C. R. "Church Building in the Middle Ages." *Bulletin of the John Rylands Library* 34 (1951–52): 20–36.

Chenu, M.-D. "Theology and the New Awareness of History." *Nature, Man, and Society in the Twelfth Century: Essays on New Theological Perspectives in the Latin West*. Ed. and trans. Jerome Taylor and Lester K. Little. Chicago: University of Chicago Press, 1968. 162–201.

Chibnall, Marjorie. *The World of Orderic Vitalis*. Oxford: Clarendon, 1984.

Clanchy, M. T. *From Memory to Written Record: England 1066–1307*. 2d, rev. ed. Oxford: Blackwell, 1993.

———. "*Moderni* in Education and Government in England." *Speculum* 50 (1975): 671–88.

Clark, Cecily. "People and Languages in Post-Conquest Canterbury." *Journal of Medieval History* 2 (1976): 1–34.

Classen, Peter. "*Res Gestae*, Universal History, Apocalypse: Visions of Past and Future." *Renaissance and Renewal in the Twelfth Century*. Ed. Robert L. Benson, Giles

Constable, and Carol D. Lanham. Cambridge: Harvard University Press, 1982. 387–417.

Coleman, Janet. *Ancient and Medieval Memories: Studies in the Reconstruction of the Past.* Cambridge: Cambridge University Press, 1992.

Constable, Giles. "Forgery and Plagiarism in the Middle Ages." *Archiv für Diplomatik* 29 (1983): 1–41.

Cousin, Patrice. *Abbon de Fleury-sur-Loire: Un savant, un pasteur, un martyr à la fin du Xe siècle.* Paris: Lethilleux, 1954.

Crane, Susan. *Insular Romance: Politics, Faith, and Culture in Anglo-Norman and Middle English Literature.* Berkeley: University of California Press, 1986.

Crewe, Jonathan V. *Unredeemed Rhetoric: Thomas Nashe and the Scandal of Authorship.* Baltimore: Johns Hopkins University Press, 1982.

Curschmann, Michael. "Das Abenteuer des Erzählens: Über den Erzähler in Wolframs Parzival." *Deutsche Vierteljahrsschrift* 45 (1971): 627–67.

Dällenbach, Lucien. *The Mirror in the Text.* Trans. Jeremy Whiteley with Emma Hughes. Cambridge: Polity Press, 1989.

Danto, Arthur C. *Narration and Knowledge.* New York: Columbia University Press, 1985.

———. "Some Reflections on Literature and Life." *Funktionen des Fiktiven.* Ed. Dieter Henrich and Wolfgang Iser. Poetik und Hermeneutik 10. Munich: Fink, 1983. 529–34.

Dassman, Ernst. "Ambrosius und die Märtyrer." *Jahrbuch für Antike und Christentum* 18 (1975): 52–61.

Davies, R. R. *Conquest, Coexistence, and Change: Wales 1063–1415.* The History of Wales 2. Oxford: Clarendon, 1987.

———. *Domination and Conquest: The Experience of Ireland, Scotland and Wales 1100–1300.* Cambridge: Cambridge University Press, 1990.

Davies, Wendy. "*Liber Landavensis*: Its Construction and Credibility." *English Historical Review* 88 (1973): 335–51.

Delehaye, Hippolyte. *The Legends of the Saints.* Trans. Donald Attwater. New York: Fordham University Press, 1962.

———. "Loca Sanctorum." *Analecta Bollandiana* 48 (1930): 5–64.

Deluz, Christiane. "Indifférence au temps dans les récits de pèlerinage (du XIIe au XIVe siècle)?" *Annales de Bretagne et des pays de l'Ouest* 83 (1976): 303–13.

Demandt, Alexander. *Metaphern für Geschichte. Sprachbilder und Gleichnisse im historisch-politischen Denken.* Munich: Beck, 1978.

De Rijk, L. M. "Some Notes on the Medieval Tract De insolubilibus, with the Edition of a Tract Dating from the End of the Twelfth Century." *Vivarium* 4 (1966): 83–115.

Donoghue, Daniel. "Laȝamon's Ambivalence." *Speculum* 65 (1990): 537–63.

Dougherty, Carol. "When Rain Falls from the Clear Blue Sky: Riddles and Colonization Oracles." *Classical Antiquity* 11 (1992): 28–44.

Draper, Peter. "Bishop Northwold and the Cult of Saint Etheldreda." *Medieval Art and Architecture at Ely Cathedral.* Leeds: The British Archaeological Association, 1979. 8–27.

Dronke, Peter. "Peter of Blois and Poetry at the Court of Henry II." *Mediaeval Studies* 28 (1976): 185–235.

Dronkin, R. A. *The Cistercians: Studies in the Geography of Medieval England and Wales.* Studies and Texts 38. Toronto: Pontifical Institute of Mediaeval Studies, 1978.

Ebenbauer, Alfred. "Das Dilemma mit der Wahrheit: Gedanken zum 'historisierenden

Roman' des 13. Jahrhunderts." *Geschichtsbewußtsein in der deutschen Literatur des Mittelalters.* Ed. Christoph Gerhardt, Nigel Palmer, and Burghart Wachinger. Tübingen: Niemeyer, 1985. 52–71.

Edwards, A. J. M. "An Early Twelfth Century Account of the Translation of St. Milburga of Much Wenlock." *Transactions of the Shropshire Archaeological Society* 57 (1961–64): 134–47.

Fälschungen im Mittelalter: Internationaler Kongreß der Monumenta Germaniae Historica, München 16.–19. September 1986. 5 vols. Monumenta Germaniae Historica Schriften 33. Hanover: Hahnsche Buchhandlung, 1988.

Finberg, H. P. R. "St Mildburg's Testament." *The Early Charters of the West Midlands.* Studies in Early English History 2. Leicester: Leicester University Press, 1961. 197–216.

Finucane, Ronald C. *Miracles and Pilgrims: Popular Beliefs in Medieval England.* London: Dent, 1977.

Fleischman, Suzanne. "On the Representation of History and Fiction in the Middle Ages." *History and Theory* 22 (1983): 278–310.

Flint, Valerie I. J. "The *Historia Regum Britanniae* of Geoffrey of Monmouth: Parody and Its Purpose." *Speculum* 54 (1979): 447–68.

Foreville, Raymonde. "Canterbury et la canonisation des saints au XIIe siècle." *Tradition and Change: Essays in Honour of Marjorie Chibnall.* Ed. Diana Greenway, Christopher Holdsworth, and Jane Sayers. Cambridge: Cambridge University Press, 1985. 63–75.

Francis, E. A. "The Background to 'Fulk FitzWarin.'" *Studies in Medieval French Presented to Alfred Ewert.* Oxford: Clarendon, 1961. 322–27.

Freeman, Edward A. *The History of the Norman Conquest of England, Its Causes and Its Results.* 2d ed. Vol. 3. Oxford: Clarendon, 1875.

Fuhrmann, Horst. "Die Fälschungen im Mittelalter." *Historische Zeitschrift* 197 (1963): 529–601. (Includes responses by Karl Bosl, Hans Patze, and August Nitschke, as well as a final summation by Fuhrmann.)

Fuhrmann, Manfred. "Die Fiktion im römischen Recht." *Funktionen des Fiktiven.* Ed. Dieter Henrich and Wolfgang Iser. Poetik und Hermeneutik 10. Munich: Fink, 1983. 413–15.

Gagov, Giuseppe. "Il culto delle reliquie nell'antichità riflesso nei due termini 'patrocinia' e 'pignora.'" *Miscellanea Francescana* 58 (1958): 485–512.

Galbraith, V. H. "Historical Research in Medieval England." The Creighton Lecture in History, 1949. London: University of London, Athlone Press, 1951.

———. "Roger Wendover and Matthew Paris." David Murray Lecture II. Glasgow University Publications, 1944. Reprinted in *Kings and Chroniclers: Essays in English Medieval History.* By Galbraith. London: Hambledon, 1982. X5–X48.

Gale, Richard M. "The Fictive Use of Language." *Philosophy* 46 (1971): 324–40.

Geary, Patrick J. *Furta Sacra: Thefts of Relics in the Central Middle Ages.* Rev. ed. Princeton: Princeton University Press, 1990.

Genet, Jean-Philippe. "Cartulaires, registres et histoire: L'exemple anglais." *Le métier d'historien au moyen âge: Études sur l'historiographie médiévale.* Ed. Bernard Guenée. Publications de la Sorbonne: Études, 13. Paris: Sorbonne, 1977. 95–129.

Gillingham, John. "The Context and Purposes of Geoffrey of Monmouth's *History of the Kings of Britain.*" *Anglo-Norman Studies* 13 (1991): 99–119.

Ginsberg, Warren. *The Cast of Character: The Representation of Personality in Ancient and Medieval Literature*. Toronto: University of Toronto Press, 1983.

Ginzburg, Carlo. "Veranschaulichung und Zitat: Die Wahrheit der Geschichte." *Der Historiker als Menschenfresser: Über den Beruf des Geschichtsschreibers*. Berlin: Wagenbach, 1990. 85–102. (This is the translation of a revised version of "Ekphrasis and Quotation," *Tijdschrift voor filosofie* 50 [1988]: 3–19.)

Goetz, Hans-Werner. "Von der *res gesta* zur *narratio rerum gestarum*: Anmerkungen zu Methoden und Hilfswissenschaften des mittelalterlichen Geschichtsschreibers." *Revue Belge de philologie et d'histoire* 67 (1989): 695–713.

Goody, Jack, and Ian Watt. "The Consequences of Literacy." *Literature in Traditional Societies*. Ed. Jack Goody. Cambridge: Cambridge University Press, 1968. 27–68.

Gordini, Gian Domenico. "Stefano, protomartire, santo." *Bibliotheca Sanctorum*. Vol. 11. Roma: Città Nuova, 1968. Cols. 1376–90.

Graf, Arturo. "La leggenda di un pontefice (Silvestro II)." *Miti, leggende e superstizioni del Medio Evo*. Vol. 2. 1893. New York: Burt Franklin, 1971. 3–75.

———. *Roma nella memoria e nelle immaginazioni del medio evo*. Turin: Chiantore, 1923.

Gransden, Antonia. "Baldwin, Abbot of Bury St. Edmunds, 1065–1097." *Proceedings of the Battle Conference on Anglo-Norman Studies* 4 (1981): 65–76.

———. "Bede's Reputation as an Historian in Medieval England." *Journal of Ecclesiastical History* 32 (1981): 397–425.

———. "The Growth of the Glastonbury Tradition and Legends in the Twelfth Century." *Journal of Ecclesiastical History* 27 (1976): 337–58.

———. *Historical Writing in England c. 550 to c. 1307*. Ithaca: Cornell University Press, 1974.

———. "The Legends and Traditions Concerning the Origins of the Abbey of Bury St Edmunds." *English Historical Review* 100 (1985): 1–24.

———. "Realistic Observation in Twelfth-Century England." *Speculum* 46 (1972): 29–51.

Grosjean, Paul. "De Codice Hagiographico Gothano." *Analecta Bollandiana* 58 (1940): 90–103 and 177–204.

Guenée, Bernard. *Histoire et culture historique dans l'occident médiéval*. Paris: Aubier-Montagne, 1980.

———. "L'historien par les mots." *Le métier d'historien au moyen âge: Études sur l'historiographie médiévale*. Ed. Bernard Guenée. Paris: Publications de la Sorbonne, 1977. 1–17.

———. "Temps de l'histoire et temps de la mémoire au moyen âge." *Annuaire-Bulletin de la société de l'histoire de France* (1976–77): 25–35.

Gumbrecht, Hans Ulrich. " 'Das in vergangenen Zeiten Gewesene so gut erzählen, als ob es in der eigenen Welt wäre': Versuch zur Anthropologie der Geschichtsschreibung." *Formen der Geschichtsschreibung*. Ed. Reinhart Koselleck, Heinrich Lutz, and Jörn Rüsen. Beiträge zur Historik 4. Munich: Deutscher Taschenbuchverlag, 1982. 480–513.

———. "Wie fiktional war der höfische Roman?" *Funktionen des Fiktiven*. Ed. Dieter Henrich and Wolfgang Iser. Poetik und Hermeneutik 10. Munich: Fink, 1983. 433–40.

Guth, Klaus. *Guibert von Nogent und die hochmittelalterliche Kritik an der Reliquien-verehrung*. Studien und Mitteilungen zur Geschichte des Benediktiner-Ordens und seiner Zweige, Supplement 21. Augsburg: Kommissionsverlag Winfried-Werk, 1970.

Haidu, Peter. "Repetition: Modern Reflections on Medieval Aesthetics." *Modern Language Notes* 92 (1977): 875–87.

Halbwachs, Maurice. *La topographie légendaire des évangiles en Terre Sainte: Étude de mémoire collective.* Paris 1941. Reprint, Paris: Presses Universitaires de France, 1971.

Handwörterbuch des deutschen Aberglaubens. Ed. Hanns Bächtold-Stäubli and Eduard Hoffmann-Krayer. 10 vols. Berlin 1927–42. Reprint, Berlin: De Gruyter, 1987.

Hanning, Robert W. *The Individual in Twelfth-Century Romance.* New Haven and London: Yale University Press, 1977.

————. "Poetic Emblems in Medieval Narrative Texts." *Vernacular Poetics in the Middle Ages.* Ed. Lois Ebin. Studies in Medieval Culture 16. Kalamazoo: Medieval Institute, 1984. 1–31.

————. *The Vision of History in Early Britain.* New York: Columbia University Press, 1966.

Haskins, Charles Homer. *The Renaissance of the Twelfth Century.* Cambridge, Mass., 1927. Reprint, Cleveland: Meridian Press, 1963.

Haug, Walter. *Literaturtheorie im deutschen Mittelalter von den Anfängen bis zum Ende des 13. Jahrhunderts: Eine Einführung.* Darmstadt: Wissenschaftliche Buchgesellschaft, 1985.

————. "Die Symbolstruktur des höfischen Epos und ihre Auflösung in Wolframs 'Parzival.'" *Deutsche Vierteljahrsschrift* 45 (1971): 668–705.

Head, Thomas. *Hagiography and the Cult of the Saints: The Diocese of Orléans, 800–1200.* Cambridge: Cambridge University Press, 1990.

Heffernan, Thomas J. *Sacred Biography: Saints and Their Biographers in the Middle Ages.* New York: Oxford University Press, 1988.

Heinzelmann, Martin. *Translationsberichte und andere Quellen des Reliquienkultes.* Typologie des sources du moyen âge occidental 33. Gen. ed. L. Genicot. Turnhout, Belgium: Brepols, 1979.

Heinzle, Joachim. "Die Entdeckung der Fiktionalität: Zu Walter Haugs 'Literaturtheorie im deutschen Mittelalter.'" *Beiträge zur Geschichte der deutschen Sprache und Literatur* 112 (1990): 55–80.

Henrich, Dieter, and Wolfgang Iser, eds. *Funktionen des Fiktiven.* Poetik und Hermeneutik 10. Munich: Fink, 1983.

Herrmann-Mascard, Nicole. *Les reliques des saints: Formation coutumière d'un droit.* Paris: Klincksieck, 1975.

Hill, Bennett D. *English Cistercian Monasteries and Their Patrons in the Twelfth Century.* Urbana: University of Illinois Press, 1968.

Hinton, James. "Walter Map's *De Nugis Curialium*: Its Plan and Composition." *Publications of the Modern Language Association* 32 (1917): 81–132.

Holzfurtner, Ludwig. *Gründung und Gründungsüberlieferung. Quellenkritische Studien zur Gründungsgeschichte der bayerischen Klöster der Agilolfingerzeit und ihrer hochmittelalterlichen Überlieferung.* Münchener Historische Studien, Abteilung Bayerische Geschichte, 11. Kallmünz: Michael Lassleben, 1984.

Hughes, Kathleen. "British Museum Ms. Cotton Vespasian A.XIV ('Vitae Sanctorum Wallensium'): Its Purpose and Provenance." *Studies in the Early British Church.* Ed. Nora K. Chadwick. Cambridge: Cambridge University Press, 1958. 183–200.

Hutcheon, Linda. *A Theory of Parody: The Teachings of Twentieth-Century Art Forms.* New York: Methuen, 1985.

Jacob, Christian. "The Greek Traveler's Areas of Knowledge: Myths and Other Discourses in Pausanias' *Description of Greece.*" *Yale French Studies* 59 (1980): 65–80.

Jaeger, C. Stephen. *Medieval Humanism in Gottfried von Strassburg's "Tristan und Isolde."* Heidelberg: Winter, 1977.

―――. *The Origins of Courtliness: Civilizing Trends and the Formation of Courtly Ideals, 939–1210.* Philadelphia: University of Pennsylvania Press, 1989.

James, M. R. "The Drawings of Matthew Paris." *Walpole Society Journal* 14 (1925–26): 1–26.

James, J. W. "The Book of Llandav: The Church and See of Llandav and Their Critics." *Journal of the Historical Society of the Church in Wales* 9 (1959): 5–22.

Jauss, Hans Robert. "The Alterity and Modernity of Medieval Literature." Trans. Timothy Bahti. *New Literary History* 10 (1979): 181–227.

―――. "Zur historischen Genese der Scheidung von Fiktion und Realität." *Funktionen des Fiktiven.* Ed. Dieter Henrich and Wolfgang Iser. Poetik und Hermeneutik 10. Munich: Fink, 1983. 423–31. Reprinted in English in *Question and Answer: Forms of Dialogic Understanding.* By Jauss. Ed. and trans. Michael Hays. Minneapolis: University of Minnesota Press, 1989. 4–10.

Johnson, Leslie P. "Lähelin and the Grail Horses." *Modern Language Review* 63 (1968): 612–17.

Jones, Thomas. "The Black Book of Carmarthen 'Stanzas of the Graves.'" *Proceedings of the British Academy* 53 (1967): 97–137.

Kastner, Jörg. *Historiae fundationum monasteriorum: Frühformen monastischer Institutionsgeschichtsschreibung im Mittelalter.* Münchener Beiträge zur Mediävistik und Renaissanceforschung 18. Munich: Arbeo-Gesellschaft, 1974.

Ker, N. R. *English Manuscripts in the Century after the Norman Conquest.* Oxford: Clarendon, 1960.

Knapp, Fritz Peter. "Historische Wahrheit und poetische Lüge: Die Gattungen weltlicher Epik und ihre theoretische Rechtfertigung im Mittelalter." *Deutsche Vierteljahrsschrift* 54 (1980): 581–635.

Knowles, David. *The Monastic Order in England.* 2d ed. Cambridge: University Press, 1966.

Kocka, Jürgen, and Thomas Nipperdey, eds. *Theorie und Erzählung in der Geschichte.* Munich: Deutscher Taschenbuchverlag, 1979.

Köhn, Rolf. "'Militia curialis': Kritik am geistlichen Hofdienst." *Soziale Ordnungen im Selbstverständnis des Mittelalters.* Ed. Albert Zimmermann. Vol. 1. Miscellanea Mediaevalia 12/1. Berlin and New York: De Gruyter, 1979. 227–57.

Kolodny, Annette. *The Lay of the Land: Metaphor as Experience and History in American Life and Letters.* Chapel Hill: University of North Carolina Press, 1975.

Koselleck, Reinhart. *Futures Past: On the Semantics of Historical Time.* Trans. Keith Tribe. Cambridge, Mass.: MIT Press, 1985.

Koselleck, Reinhart, Heinrich Lutz, and Jörn Rüsen, eds. *Formen der Geschichtsschreibung.* Beiträge zur Historik 4. Munich: Deutscher Taschenbuchverlag, 1982.

Koselleck, Reinhart, and Wolf-Dieter Stempel, eds. *Geschichte—Ereignis und Erzählung.* Poetik und Hermeneutik 5. Munich: Fink, 1973.

Langmuir, Gavin I. "Thomas of Monmouth: Detector of Ritual Murder." *Speculum* 59 (1984): 820–46.

Lapidge, Michael. "The Medieval Hagiography of St. Ecgwine." *Vale of Evesham Historical Society* 6 (1977): 77–93.

Lapidge, Michael, and Michael Winterbottom. Introduction to *The Life of St. Æthelwold,* by Wulfstan of Winchester. Oxford: Clarendon, 1991.

Lausberg, Heinrich. *Handbuch der literarischen Rhetorik.* 2 vols. Munich: Hueber, 1960.

Leckie, R. William, Jr. *The Passage of Dominion: Geoffrey of Monmouth and the Periodization of Insular History in the Twelfth Century.* Toronto: University of Toronto Press, 1981.

Leclercq, H. "Reliques et reliquiares." *Dictionnaire d'archéologie chrétienne et de liturgie.* Vol. 14.2. 1948. Cols. 2294–358.

———. "Translations." *Dictionnaire d'archéologie chrétienne et de liturgie.* Vol. 15.2. 1953. Cols. 2695–99.

Lecouteux, Claude. *Mélusine et le chevalier au cygne.* Paris: Payot, 1982.

Legge, M. Dominica. *Anglo-Norman and Its Backgrounds.* Oxford: Clarendon, 1963.

Le Goff, Jacques. "Melusina: Mother and Pioneer." Trans. Arthur Goldhammer. *Time, Work, and Culture in the Middle Ages.* Chicago: University of Chicago Press, 1980. 205–22.

Lekai, Louis J. *The Cistercians: Ideals and Reality.* Kent, Ohio: Kent State University Press, 1977.

Le Saux, Françoise H. M. *Laʒamon's Brut: The Poem and Its Sources.* Cambridge: D. S. Brewer, 1989.

Lettinck, Nico. *Geschiedbeschouwing en beleving van de eigen tijd in de eerste helft van de twaalfde eeuw.* Amsterdam: Verloren, 1983.

Levison, Wilhelm. "St. Alban and St. Albans." *Antiquity* 15 (1941): 337–59.

Lewis, Suzanne. *The Art of Matthew Paris in the "Chronica Majora."* Berkeley: University of California Press, 1987.

Lifshitz, Felice. "The 'Exodus of Holy Bodies' Reconsidered: The Translation of the Relics of St. Gildard of Rouen to Soissons." *Analecta Bollandiana* 110 (1992): 329–40.

Longo, John. "The Vision of History in *St. Erkenwald.*" In *Geardagum: Essays on Old English Language and Literature* 8 (1987): 35–51.

Lundt, Bea. *Melusine und Merlin im Mittelalter: Entwürfe und Modelle weiblicher Existenz im Beziehungsdiskurs der Geschlechter.* Munich: Fink, 1991.

McCormick, Peter J. *Fictions, Philosophies, and the Problem of Poetics.* Ithaca: Cornell University Press, 1988.

McCrank, Lawrence J. "The Cistercians of Poblet as Medieval Frontiersmen: An Historiographic Essay and Case Study." *Estudios en homenaje a Don Claudio Sanchez Albornoz en sus 90 años.* Vol. 2. Cuadernos de Historia de España: Anexos. Buenos Aires: Istituto de Historia de España, 1983. 313–60.

McCulloch, Florence. "Saints Alban and Amphibalus in the Works of Matthew Paris: Dublin, Trinity College Ms. 177." *Speculum* 56 (1981): 761–85.

McLeod, W. "Alban and Amphibal: Some Extant Lives and a Lost Life." *Mediaeval Studies* 42 (1980): 407–28.

Marichal, Robert. "Naissance du roman." *Entretiens sur la renaissance du 12e siècle.* Ed. Maurice de Gandillac and Edouard Jeauneau. Decades du centre culturel international de Cerisy-la-Salle, nouvelle série 9. Paris: Mouton, 1968. 449–92.

Martin, Josef. "Die Revelatio S. Stephani und Verwandtes." *Historisches Jahrbuch* 77 (1957): 419–33.

Melville, Gert. "Wozu Geschichte schreiben? Stellung und Funktion der Historie im Mittelalter." *Formen der Geschichtsschreibung.* Ed. Reinhart Koselleck, Heinrich Lutz, and Jörn Rüsen. Beiträge zur Historik 4. Munich: Deutscher Taschenbuchverlag, 1982. 86–146.

Menefee, Samuel Pyeatt. "Circling as an Entrance to the Otherworld." *Folklore* 96 (1985): 3–10.

Meyer, Wilhelm. "Die Legende des h. Albanus des Protomartyr Angliae in Texten vor Beda." *Abhandlungen der königlichen Gesellschaft der Wissenschaften zu Göttingen, philol.-hist. Klasse,* neue Folge 8 (1904): 3–81.

Millinger, Susan. "Humility and Power: Anglo-Saxon Nuns in Anglo-Norman Hagiography." *Medieval Religious Women.* Vol. 1, *Distant Echoes.* Ed. John A. Nichols and Lillian Thomas Shank. Cistercian Studies Series 71. Kalamazoo: Cistercian Publications, 1984. 115–29.

Mink, Louis O. "Narrative Form as a Cognitive Instrument." *The Writing of History: Literary Form and Historical Understanding.* Ed. Robert H. Canary and Henry Kozicki. Madison: University of Wisconsin Press, 1978. 129–49.

Moos, Peter von. *Geschichte als Topik: Das rhetorische Exemplum von der Antike zur Neuzeit und die "historiae" im "Policraticus" Johanns von Salisbury.* Hildesheim: Georg Olms, 1988.

———. "*Poeta* und *Historicus* im Mittelalter: Zum Mimesis-Problem am Beispiel einiger Urteile über Lucan." *Beiträge zur Geschichte der deutschen Sprache und Literatur* 98 (1976): 93–130.

Morse, Ruth. *Truth and Convention in the Middle Ages: Rhetoric, Representation, and Reality.* Cambridge: Cambridge University Press, 1991.

Mostert, Marco. *The Political Theory of Abbo of Fleury: A Study of the Ideas about Society and Law of the Tenth-Century Monastic Reform Movement.* Hilversum: Verloren, 1987.

———. "Le séjour d'Abbon de Fleury à Ramsey." *Bibliothèque de l'École des Chartes* 144 (1986): 199–208.

Musset, Lucien. "Les contacts entre l'église normande et l'église d'Angleterre de 911 à 1066." *Les mutations socio-culturelles au tournant des XIe–XIIe siècles: Études anselmiennes (IVe session).* Ed. Raymonde Foreville. Spicilegium Beccense 2. Colloques internationaux du centre national de la recherche scientifique. Paris: Editions du CNRS, 1984. 67–84.

———. "La formation d'un milieu social original: Les chapelains normands du duc-roi au XIe et au début du XIIe siècle." *Aspects de la société et de l'économie dans la Normandie médiévale (Xe–XIIIe siècles).* Ed. Lucien Musset, Jean-Michel Bouvris, and Véronique Gazeau. Cahiers des Annales de Normandie 22. Caen: Centre d'Etudes Normandes de l'Université de Caen, 1988. 91–114.

Nelson, William. *Fact or Fiction: The Dilemma of the Renaissance Storyteller.* Cambridge: Harvard University Press, 1973.

Nichols, Stephen G., Jr. "Fission and Fusion: Mediations of Power in Medieval History and Literature." *Yale French Studies* 70 (1986): 21–41.

————. "The New Medievalism: Tradition and Discontinuity in Medieval Culture." *The New Medievalism.* Ed. Marina S. Brownlee, Kevin Brownlee, and Stephen G. Nichols. Parallax. Baltimore: Johns Hopkins University Press, 1991. 1–26.

————. *Romanesque Signs: Early Medieval Narrative and Iconography.* New Haven: Yale University Press, 1983.

Nykrog, Per. "The Rise of Literary Fiction." *Renaissance and Renewal in the Twelfth Century.* Ed. Robert L. Benson, Giles Constable, and Carol D. Lanham. Cambridge: Harvard University Press, 1982. 593–612.

O'Gorman, Edmundo. *The Invention of America.* Bloomington: Indiana University Press, 1961.

Oldoni, Massimo. " 'A fantasia dicitur fantasma.' Gerberto e la sua storia, II." *Studi Medievali,* 3d ser., 3.21 (1980): 493–622, and 3.24 (1983): 167–245.

————. "Gerberto e la sua storia." *Studi Medievali,* 3d ser., 18 (1977): 629–704.

————. "*Imago e fantasma*: L'incantesimo storiografico di Gerberto." *Gerberto: scienza, storia e mito: Atti del Gerberti Symposium (Bobbio 25–27 luglio 1983).* Ed. Michele Tosi. Bobbio: Archivi Storici Bobiensi, 1985. 755–61.

Ollier, Marie-Louise. "Utopie et roman arthurien." *Cahiers de civilisation médiévale, Xe–XIIe siècle* 27 (1984): 223–32.

Otter, Monika. "*Gaainable Tere*: Symbolic Appropriation of Space and Time in Geoffrey of Monmouth and Vernacular Historical Writing." *Discovering New Worlds: Essays on Medieval Exploration and Imagination.* Ed. Scott D. Westrem. New York: Garland, 1991. 157–77.

————. "New Werke: St. Erkenwald, St. Albans, and the Medieval Sense of the Past." *Journal of Medieval and Renaissance Studies* 24 (1994): 387–414.

Pähler, Heinrich. *Strukturuntersuchungen zur Historia Regum Britanniae des Geoffrey of Monmouth.* Ph.D. diss., University of Bonn, 1958.

P[aris], G[aston]. "Review of *Vie de Seint Auban*, ed. Robert Atkinson, 1876." *Romania* 5 (1876): 384–89.

Partner, Nancy F. "History without Empiricism/Truth without Facts." *Transformations in Personhood and Culture after Theory: The Languages of History, Aesthetics, and Ethics.* Ed. Christie McDonald and Gary Wihl. University Park: Pennsylvania State University Press, 1994. 1–12.

————. "Making Up Lost Time: Writing on the Writing of History." *Speculum* 61 (1986): 90–117.

————. "The New Cornificius: Medieval History and the Artifice of Words." *Classical Rhetoric and Medieval Historiography.* Ed. Ernst Breisach. Kalamazoo: Medieval Institute, 1985. 5–59.

————. "Notes on the Margins: Editors, Editions, and Sliding Definitions." *The Politics of Editing Medieval Texts.* Ed. Roberta Frank. New York: AMS Press, 1993. 1–18.

————. *Serious Entertainments: The Writing of History in Twelfth-Century England.* Chicago: University of Chicago Press, 1977.

Patterson, Lee. *Negotiating the Past: The Historical Understanding of Medieval Literature.* Madison: University of Wisconsin Press, 1987.

Patze, Hans. "Klostergründung und Klosterchronik." *Blätter für deutsche Landesgeschichte* 113 (1977): 89–121.

Perret, Michèle. "L'invraisemblable vérité: Témoignage fantastique dans deux romans des 14e et 15e siècles." *Europe: Revue littéraire mensuelle* 654 (October 1983): 25–35.

Petronella, Vincent. "*St. Erkenwald*: Style as the Vehicle for Meaning." *Journal of English and Germanic Philology* 66 (1967): 532–40.

Platt, Colin. *The Abbeys and Priories of Medieval England.* London: Secker & Warburg, 1984.

Powicke, F. M. "Gerald of Wales." *The Christian Life in the Middle Ages and Other Essays.* Oxford: Clarendon, 1935.

Ransford, Rosalind, ed. *The Early Charters of the Augustinian Canons of Waltham Abbey, Essex, 1062–1230.* Woodbridge: Boydell, 1989.

Ray, Roger. "Bede's *Vera Lex Historiae.*" *Speculum* 55 (1980): 1–21.

Renaissance and Renewal in the Twelfth Century. Ed. Robert L. Benson, Giles Constable, and Carol D. Lanham. Cambridge: Harvard University Press, 1982.

Ribard, Jacques. "Espace romanesque et symbolisme dans la littérature arthurienne du XIIe siècle." *Espaces romanesques.* Ed. Michel Crouzet. Paris: Presses Universitaires de France, 1982. 73–82.

Richards, Mary P. "The Medieval Hagiography of St. Neot." *Analecta Bollandiana* 99 (1981): 259–78.

Richter, Michael. "Gerald of Wales: A Reassessment on the 750th Anniversary of His Death." *Traditio* 29 (1973): 379–90.

———. *Giraldus Cambrensis: The Growth of the Welsh Nation.* 2d ed. Aberystwyth: The National Library of Wales, 1976.

Ricoeur, Paul. "The Hermeneutical Function of Distanciation." *Hermeneutics and the Human Sciences: Essays on Language, Action, and Interpretation.* Ed. and trans. John B. Thompson. Cambridge: Cambridge University Press, 1981. 131–44.

———. *Interpretation Theory: Discourse and the Surplus of Meaning.* Fort Worth: Texas Christian University Press, 1976.

———. *The Rule of Metaphor: Multidisciplinary Studies of the Creation of Meaning in Language.* Trans. Robert Czerny with Kathleen McLaughlin and John Costello, S.J. Toronto: University of Toronto Press, 1977.

Ridyard, S. J. "*Condigna Veneratio*: Post-Conquest Attitudes to the Saints of the Anglo-Saxons." *Anglo-Norman Studies IX: Proceedings of the Battle Conference 1986.* Ed. R. Allen Brown. 179–206.

Riffaterre, Michael. *Fictional Truth.* Baltimore: Johns Hopkins University Press, 1990.

Rigg, A. G. *A History of Anglo-Latin Literature 1066–1422.* Cambridge: Cambridge University Press, 1992.

Roberts, Brynley F. "Geoffrey of Monmouth and Welsh Historical Tradition." *Nottingham Mediaeval Studies* 20 (1976): 29–40.

Rollason, D. W. "Lists of Saints' Resting Places in Anglo-Saxon England." *Anglo-Saxon England* 7 (1978): 61–93.

————. *The Mildrith Legend: A Study in Early Medieval Hagiography in England.* Studies in the Early History of Britain. Leicester: Leicester University Press, 1982.

Rollo, David. "Gerald of Wales's *Topographia Hibernica*: Sex and the Irish Nation." Forthcoming in *Institutionalizing Sex and Gender in the Middle Ages.* Ed. Kathryn Gravdal. Special issue of *Romanic Review.*

————. *Specious Histories and Politic Fictions: Ethnicity, Counterfeit, and Romance in Twelfth-Century England.* Forthcoming.

————. "William of Malmesbury: Literacy and Necromancy." Unpublished paper, Dartmouth College.

Rüstow, Alexander. *Der Lügner: Theorie, Geschichte und Auflösung.* Leipzig 1910. Reprint, New York: Garland, 1987.

Saenger, Paul. "Silent Reading: Its Impact on Late Medieval Script and Society." *Viator* 13 (1982): 367–414.

Salter, H. E. "Geoffrey of Monmouth and Oxford." *English Historical Review* 43 (1919): 382–85.

Sayers, Jane E. "Papal Privileges for St. Albans Abbey and Its Dependencies." *The Study of Medieval Records: Essays in Honour of Kathleen Major.* Ed. D. A. Bullough and R. L. Storey. Oxford: Clarendon, 1971. 57–65.

Schapiro, Meyer. "On the Aesthetic Attitude in Romanesque Art." *Art and Thought: Issued in Honor of Dr. Ananda K. Coomaraswamy.* Ed. K. Bharatha Iyer. London: Luzac, 1947. 130–50. Reprinted in *Romanesque Art.* New York: Braziller, 1977. 1–27.

Schenck, David P. "Vues sur le temps et l'espace chez Chrétien de Troyes." *Oeuvres et Critiques* 5 (1980–81): 111–17.

Schirmer, Walter. *Die frühen Darstellungen des Arthurstoffes.* Cologne: Westdeutscher Verlag, 1958.

Schmidt, Paul Gerhard. "*Veritas naufragatur*: Das Leben und die Taten König Harolds von England nach 1066." *Fälschungen im Mittelalter: Internationaler Kongreß der Monumenta Germaniae Historica, München 16.–19. September 1986.* Hanover: Hahnsche Buchhandlung, 1988. 1:189–204.

Schmitt, Jean-Claude. "Temps, folklore et politique au XIIe siècle. A propos de deux recits de Walter Map: *De Nugis Curialium* I.9 and IV.13." *Le temps chrétien de la fin de l'Antiquite au Moyen Age—IIIe-XIIIe s.* Ed. Jean-Marie Leroux. Colloques internationaux du CNRS No 604. Paris: Editions du CNRS, 1984. 489–515.

Schrade, Hubert. *Die Vita des heiligen Liudger und ihre Bilder.* Münster: Aschendorff, 1960.

Schreiner, Klaus. "'Discrimen veri ac falsi': Ansätze und Formen der Kritik in der Heiligen- und Reliquienverehrung des Mittelalters." *Archiv für Kulturgeschichte* 48 (1965): 1–53.

————. "Zum Wahrheitsverständnis im Heiligen- und Reliquienwesen des Mittelalters." *Saeculum* 17 (1966): 131–69.

Schweikle, Günther. "Stiure und lere: Zum Parzival Wolframs von Eschenbach." *Zeitschrift für deutsches Altertum* 106 (1977): 183–99.

Searle, John. "The Logical Status of Fictional Discourse." *New Literary History* 6 (1974–75). Reprinted in *Expression and Meaning: Studies in the Theory of Speech Acts.* By Searle. Cambridge: Cambridge University Press, 1979. 58–75.

Seibt, Ferdinand. "Über den Plan der Schrift *De Nugis Curialium* des Magisters Map." *Archiv für Kulturgeschichte* 37 (1955): 183–203.

Shepherd, G. T. "The Emancipation of Story in the Twelfth Century." *Medieval Narrative: A Symposium*. Ed. Hans Bekker-Nielsen et al. Odense: Odense University Press, 1979. 44–57.

Short, Ian. "Gaimar's Epilogue and Geoffrey of Monmouth's *Liber vetustissimus*." *Speculum* 69 (1994): 323–43.

Sigal, P. A. "Histoire et hagiographie: Les *Miracula* aux XIe et XIIe siècle." *Annales de Bretagne et des pays de l'Ouest* 87 (1980): 237–57.

———. "Les voyages de reliques aux onzième et douzième siècles." *Voyage, quête, pèlerinage dans la littérature et la civilisation médiévales*. Sénéfiance: Cahiers du CUERMA 2. Aix-en-Provence: Editions CUERMA, 1976. 73–104.

Southern, Richard. "Aspects of the European Tradition of Historical Writing: 1. The Classical Tradition from Einhard to Geoffrey of Monmouth." *Transactions of the Royal Historical Society*, 5th ser., 20 (1970): 173–96.

———. "Aspects of the European Tradition of Historical Writing: 2. Hugh of St. Victor and the Idea of Historical Development." *Transactions of the Royal Historical Society*, 5th ser., 21 (1971): 159–79.

———. "Aspects of the European Tradition of Historical Writing: 3. History as Prophecy." *Transactions of the Royal Historical Society*, 5th ser., 22 (1972): 159–80.

———. "Aspects of the European Tradition of Historical Writing: 4. The Sense of the Past." *Transactions of the Royal Historical Society*, 5th ser., 23 (1973): 243–63.

———. "The Place of England in the Twelfth-Century Renaissance." *History*, n.s., 45 (1960): 201–16.

Spade, Paul Vincent. "The Origins of the Medieval *Insolubilia*-Literature." *Franciscan Studies* 33 (1973). Reprinted in *Lies, Language and Logic in the Late Middle Ages*. By Spade. Collected Studies Series 272. London: Variorum Reprints, 1988. 2.292–2.309.

Spiegel, Gabrielle M. "Genealogy: Form and Function in Medieval Historical Narrative." *History and Theory* 22 (1983): 43–53.

———. *Romancing the Past: The Rise of Vernacular Prose Historiography in Thirteenth-Century France*. Berkeley: University of California Press, 1993.

Stanley, E. G. "Laʒamon's Antiquarian Sentiments." *Medium Aevum* 38 (1969): 23–37.

Stenton, F. M. *The Early History of the Abbey of Abingdon*. University College, Reading Studies in Local History. Reading: University College, 1913.

Stierle, Karlheinz. "Erfahrung und narrative Form: Bemerkungen zu ihrem Zusammenhang in Fiktion und Historiographie." *Theorie und Erzählung in der Geschichte*. Ed. Jürgen Kocka and Thomas Nipperdey. Munich: Deutscher Taschenbuchverlag, 1979. 85–119.

Stock, Brian. *The Implications of Literacy*. Princeton: Princeton University Press, 1983.

———. *Listening for the Text: On the Uses of the Past*. Baltimore: Johns Hopkins University Press, 1990.

Stollberg, Gunnar. *Die soziale Stellung der intellektuellen Oberschicht im England des 12. Jahrhunderts*. Historische Studien 427. Lübeck: Matthiesen, 1973.

Tallis, Raymond. " 'As If There Could Be Such Things as True Stories.' " *The Cambridge Quarterly* 15 (1986): 95–106.

Tatlock, J. S. P. *The Legendary History of Britain: Geoffrey of Monmouth's "Historia Regum Britanniae" and Its Early Vernacular Versions.* Berkeley: University of California Press, 1950.

————. "St. Amphibalus." *University of California Publications in English* 4 (1934): 249–70.

Thomson, Rodney. *Manuscripts from St Albans Abbey 1066–1235.* 2 vols. Woodbridge, Suffolk: D. S. Brewer, 1985.

————. "Two Twelfth Century Poems on the 'Regnum-Sacerdotium' Problem in England." *Revue Bénédictine* 83 (1973): 312–25.

————. *William of Malmesbury.* Woodbridge, Suffolk: Boydell, 1987.

Thorpe, Lewis. "Walter Map and Gerald of Wales." *Medium Aevum* 47 (1978): 6–21.

Tobler-Lommatzsch Altfranzösisches Wörterbuch. Edited from Alfred Tobler's papers by Erhard Lommatzsch. Wiesbaden: Steiner [Vols. 1–2 Berlin: Weidmannsche Buchhandlung], 1925– .

Töpfer, Bernhard. "Reliquienkult und Pilgerbewegung zur Zeit der Klosterreform im burgundisch-aquitanischen Gebiet." *Vom Mittelalter zur Neuzeit: Zum 65. Geburtstag von Heinrich Sproemberg.* Ed. Hellmut Kretzschmar. Berlin: Rütten und Loening, 1956. 420–39.

Townsend, David. "Anglo-Latin Hagiography and the Norman Transition." *Exemplaria* 3 (1991): 385–433.

Trimpi, Wesley. "The Quality of Fiction." *Traditio* 30 (1974): 1–118.

Turner, Ralph V. "Changing Perceptions of the New Administrative Class in Anglo-Norman and Angevin England: The *Curiales* and Their Conservative Critics." *Journal of British Studies* 29 (1990): 93–117.

————. *Men Raised from the Dust: Administrative Service and Upward Mobility in Angevin England.* Philadelphia: University of Pennsylvania Press, 1988.

————. "The *Miles Literatus* in Twelfth- and Thirteenth-Century England: How Rare a Phenomenon?" *American Historical Review* 83 (1978): 929–45.

Ullmann, Walter. "On the Influence of Geoffrey of Monmouth in English History." *Speculum Historiale: Festschrift für Johannes Spörl.* Ed. C. Bauer et al. Munich: Karl Alber, 1966. Reprinted in *The Church and the Law in the Earlier Middle Ages: Selected Essays.* By Ullmann. London: Variorum Reprints, 1975. XIII257–XIII276.

van Houts, Elizabeth M. C. "Historiography and Hagiography at Saint-Wandrille: The 'Inventio et Miracula Sancti Vulfranni.' " *Anglo-Norman Studies* 12 (1990): 233–51.

Vance, Eugene. *From Topic to Tale: Logic and Narrativity in the Middle Ages.* Minneapolis: University of Minnesota Press, 1987.

Vaughan, Richard. *Matthew Paris.* 2d ed. Cambridge: Cambridge University Press, 1979.

————. "The Past in the Middle Ages." *Journal of Medieval History* 12 (1986): 1–14.

Vermette, Rosalie. "Terrae Incantatae: The Symbolic Geography of Twelfth-Century Arthurian Romance." *Geography and Literature: A Meeting of the Disciplines.* Ed. William E. Malony and Paul Simpson-Housley. Syracuse: Syracuse University Press, 1987. 145–60.

Vinaver, Eugene. *The Rise of Romance.* Oxford: Oxford University Press, 1971.

Walker, David. "Cultural Survival in an Age of Conquest." *Welsh Society and Nationhood:*

Historical Essays Presented to Glanmor Williams. Ed. R. R. Davies et al. Cardiff: University of Wales Press, 1984. 35–50.

Ward, Benedicta. *Miracles and the Medieval Mind: Theory, Record and Event 1000–1215.* Rev. ed. Philadelphia: University of Pennsylvania Press, 1987.

Ward, John O. "Some Principles of Rhetorical Historiography in the 12th Century." *Classical Rhetoric and Medieval Historiography.* Ed. Ernst Breisach. Studies in Medieval Culture 9. Kalamazoo: Medieval Institute, 1985. 103–65.

Warning, Rainer. "Formen narrativer Identitätskonstitution im höfischen Roman." *Le roman jusqu'à la fin du XIIIe siècle. Tome I (partie historique).* Ed. Jean Frappier and Reinhold R. Grimm. Grundriss der romanischen Literaturen des Mittelalters. Ser. ed. Hans Robert Jauss and Erich Köhler. Vol. 4. Heidelberg: Carl Winter Universitätsverlag, 1978. 25–59.

———. "Staged Discourse: Remarks on the Pragmatics of Fiction." *Dispositio* 5.13–14 (1981): 35–54.

Waswo, Richard. "The History That Literature Makes." *New Literary History* 19 (1988): 541–64.

Weimar, Klaus. "Der Text, den (Literar-) Historiker schreiben." *Geschichte als Literatur: Formen und Grenzen der Repräsentation.* Ed. Hartmut Eggert, Ulrich Profitlich, and Klaus R. Scharpe. Stuttgart: Metzler, 1990. 29–39.

Wenzel, Siegfried. "St. Erkenwald and the Uncorrupted Body." *Notes and Queries,* n.s., 226 (1981): 13–14.

Wetzel, Andreas. "Reconstructing Carthage: Archaeology and the Historical Novel." *Mosaic* 21 (1989): 13–23.

Whatley, Gordon. "Heathens and Saints: *St. Erkenwald* in Its Legendary Context." *Speculum* 61 (1986) 330–63.

White, Hayden. *Metahistory: The Historical Imagination in Nineteenth-Century Europe.* Baltimore: Johns Hopkins University Press, 1973.

———. "The Value of Narrativity in the Representation of Reality." *Critical Inquiry* 7 (1980–81): 5–27.

Wilhelm, Friedrich. "Ueber fabulistische Quellenangaben." *Beiträge zur Geschichte der deutschen Sprache und Literatur* 33 (1908): 286–339.

Williams, David H. *The Welsh Cistercians.* Vol. 1. Calden Island, Tenby: Cyhoeddiadau Sistersiaidd, 1984.

Wilson, David M. *The Bayeux Tapestry.* New York: Knopf, 1985.

Wormald, Francis. "Some Illustrated Manuscripts of the Lives of the Saints." *Bulletin of the John Rylands Library* 34 (1952–53): 248–67.

Zagorin, Perez. "Historiography and Postmodernism: Reconsiderations." *History and Theory* 29 (1990): 263–74.

Zink, Michel. "Une mutation de la conscience littéraire: Le langage romanesque à travers des exemples français du XIIe siècle." *Cahiers de civilisation médiévale* 24 (1981): 3–27.

⊁ Index ⊱

Abbo of Fleury, 29, 31, 83, 167 (n. 53)

Abingdon, 23, 41–42, 54, 81–82

Abundance, 65–66, 68. See also *Descriptio Britanniae*; Foundation legends; *Gaainable tere*

Access. See Historian

Æthelthryth, Saint, 31–32, 34–35

Affectus. See *Gaainable tere*: and affectus

Ailred of Rievaulx, 33

Alban, Saint, 23, 24–26, 46–47, 49–50, 177 (n. 130)

Allegory, 131, 139, 195 (n. 32). See also Reference

Amphibalus, Saint, 24, 45–46

Ancestral romance, 87, 88, 185 (n. 121). See also *Fouke le Fitz Waryn*

Antiquarianism, 3, 81, 90, 176 (n. 121), 183 (n. 86)

Apparitions. See Marvels

Appropriation, 61, 73–75, 82–83, 88, 89, 101, 121, 149. See also *Gaainable tere*

Aptus. See *Gaainable tere*

Archaeology. See *Inventio*

Archdeacons, 3, 125

Argumentum. See Fiction

Auerbach, Erich, 3, 93, 131, 133, 195 (n. 32)

Augustine, Saint, 27, 105–6, 117–18

Authentication, 36, 38–39, 55. See also Landmarks

Author: absence of, 6, 15, 92; fictionality of, 6, 15, 92, 127, 155; "birth" of, 15; authority of, 92, 94, 110, 121, 124–25, 130, 154–55; stand-ins for, 101, 108–9, 129, 155. See also Historian; Narrator; Textuality

Authorial guidance. See Guide, unreliable

Authority, 140, 194 (n. 8), 196 (n. 39). See also Author; Nichols, Stephen; Walter Map

Bakhtin, Mikhail, 4, 131–32

Baldwin (archbishop of Canterbury), 130, 145–46, 148, 150, 197 (nn. 57, 61)

Battle Abbey, 42–43, 61

Bäuml, Franz, 15–16, 17, 95, 139–40, 155

Bede: *De temporum ratione*, 2, 27; *Historia Ecclesiastica*, 23, 31, 41, 180

Bertin, Saint, 42

Body, saint's: as corporate body, 34; wholeness, 34, 35, 53. See also Relics; names of individual saints

Book of Llandaff, 79–80, 182 (n. 72)

Bovo of St. Bertin, 42

Brown, Peter, 42, 43, 45

Brut. See Laȝamon

Brutus (character), 71, 73–75, 89–90, 148

Bury St. Edmunds, 23, 34–35. See also Denis Piramus; Jocelin of Brakelond

Caerleon-on-Usk, 78, 151

Canonization, 37

Canterbury: St. Augustine's Abbey, 22, 23, 33–34; Christ Church, 22, 23, 34

Caradoc of Llancarfan, 76–77, 81

Cartularies, 3, 22

Charlemagne, *inventio* of, 175–76 (n. 113), 178 (n. 143)

Chrétien de Troyes, 3, 8, 16, 18, 91, 195 (n. 36)

Chronotope, 4, 8, 9, 69

Circularity, 109, 111. *See also* Liar, Cretan

Cistercians, 61–64, 149, 181 (n. 51). *See also* Gerald of Wales; Walter Map

Colonialism, 59, 181 (n. 51). See also *Gaainable tere*

Conjointure, 16, 113. *See also* Chrétien de Troyes; Haug, Walter

Connections, multiple. *See* Textuality

Conquest, 59–60, 75–76, 84–86, 132; of Wales, 60, 78–79, 131, 148–49; metaphorical, 80, 82, 85–86, 89–90, 149. See also *Gaainable tere*; Norman Conquest

Consensus, 5, 94

Continuity, 22, 29, 31, 33, 34, 54, 61, 158

Contract. *See* Fiction

Court, royal: clerics at, 125–27, 193 (n. 123). *See also* Walter Map

Crusade, 131, 140, 148, 150

Cuthbert, Saint, 34

Curiales. See Court, royal

Dällenbach, Lucien, 52, 101, 167 (n. 52)

Danish incursions. *See* Viking raids

Denis Piramus, 41, 59, 83, 84–87, 148, 167 (n. 53)

Descriptio Britanniae, 71–73, 84. See also *Gaainable tere*

Digressions, 98, 103. See also *Series temporum*

Distance, historical, sense of, 43–51

Doubt, 93, 102, 103, 110–11

Durham, 34

Eadmer, 23, 80

Eavesdropping, 124, 196 (n. 51)

Edmund, Saint, 31, 34, 35. *See also* Abbo of Fleury; Denis Piramus; Galfridus de Fontibus; Jocelin of Brakelond

Elevatio. See Relics

Elidyr (character), 105, 144, 146, 155

Ely, 23, 31–33, 34–35

Emplotment, 11, 97

Enimia, Saint, 53

Ethnic groups, in post-Conquest Britain, 22–23, 75–79. *See also* Geoffrey of Monmouth: and Wales; Gerald of Wales: political commentary; Normans; Welsh-English relations

Etymology, 30, 54, 144, 147. *See also* Welsh language

Event, as historiographical unit, 11

Evidence, 40–41, 44, 56. *See also* Eyewitness; Testimony

Exodus, 61

Exordium Parvum, 61–62

Expansionism, 67–69

Eyewitness, 10, 44–45. *See also* Evidence; Testimony

Fabula. See History: medieval notions of; Lying; *Narrationum genera*

Fairies. *See* Marvels; Underground worlds

Fall of Britain, 75

Fiction: as contract, 7, 8, 160; as nonserious assertion, 7, 12, 165 (n. 19); and lying, 7, 16, 95, 97, 128, 165 (n. 23); as bracketing of truth claims, 7, 135; as role play, 12, 16; and metaphor, 12–17; as withdrawal of referential function, 15, 17, 52, 95; as pseudo-reality, 15, 95; as play, 80, 166 (n. 23); and *argumentum*, 165 (n. 23). *See also* Bäuml, Franz; Fictionality; Gale, Richard M.; Haidu, Peter; Latin; Parody; Ricoeur, Paul; Romance; Searle, John; Secularity; Vernacular

Fictionality, 6–18, 128, 140, 155; medieval understandings of, 6, 82, 95; pragmatic definition of, 7, 12; and textuality, 6–7, 10, 15–16, 140; as emancipation from Latin, 16–17, 195 (n. 36); and the court, 127. *See also* Fiction; Textuality

Fleury, 29

Folcart of St. Bertin, 22

Forgery, 56, 57, 79, 173 (n. 73)

Fouke le Fitz Waryn, 84, 87–89. *See also* Ancestral romance

Foundation legends, 21, 30, 60, 61–66, 67, 82

Furta sacra, 37, 42

Gaainable tere (topos): defined, 59; and Denis Piramus, 59, 84–87; and colonialist rhetoric, 59–60, 74–75, 84–85; compared to *inventio*, 59–61; and referentiality, 60–61, 71, 75, 84; and foundation legends, 60–66, 82; and *affectus*, 66, 74, 89–90; and Walter Map, 66–69, 121; as metaphor, 69, 71, 84; and Geoffrey of Monmouth, 69, 71–75; land seen as *aptus*, 72, 73, 74, 87; as legitimization, 74–79, 84–86, 88; and Laȝamon, 89–90, 92; and underground worlds, 101; and Gerald of Wales, 132, 148–49, 152, 197 (n. 63). *See also* Appropriation; Conquest; Foundation legends; Search

Gaimar, 77

Gale, Richard M., 12, 165 (n. 19)

Galfridus de Fontibus, 83, 167 (n. 53)

Gaps, chronological, 80–81, 83, 96, 97

Genealogy, 87, 89

Geoffrey of Monmouth, 3, 18, 27, 138, 148, 161, 196 (n. 42); on Saint Amphibalus, 45, 46; source fiction, 46, 47, 51, 81, 82, 83; *Historia Regum Britanniae*, 69–84; politics of, 75–79, 181–82 (n. 58); and Wales, 76–78, 181 (n. 57); critics of, 78, 81; and imaginative historiography, 79, 81–82, 83–84, 87–89; as parody, 79–80; referentiality of, 79–80; as source, 81–82, 83–84, 87–88, 89–90, 183–84 (n. 91); and William of Newburgh, 95–97; career, 125, 126; and Gerald of Wales, 152–54. *See also* Caradoc of Llancarfan; Conquest; Denis Piramus; Ethnic groups; *Fouke le Fitz Waryn*; *Gaainable tere*; Gaimar; Gaps, chronological; Hanning, Robert; Henry of Huntington; Laȝamon; Merlin; Meilyr the Welshman; Prophecy; Stanzas of the Graves; Topography; Wace; William of Malmesbury

Geography. *See* Reference: spatial

Gerald of Wales, 3, 18, 161; *Itinerarium Kambriae*, 95, 105, 130–55; career, 125, 146; on knowledge, 130, 140; on interpretation, 130, 140, 142, 152; underground worlds, 130, 142, 144–47; political commentary, 131, 138, 145–46; *Topographia Hibernica*, 133; *Descriptio Kambriae*, 133, 138, 149, 152; on revenge, 136–37, 138; and Walter Map, 140, 193. *See also* Baldwin; Conquest: of Wales; Crusade; *Gaainable tere*; Geoffrey of Monmouth; Hostages; Itinerary format; Journey metaphor; Merlin; Meilyr the Welshman; Nichols, Stephen; Parataxis; Polyphony; Prognostication; Prophecy; Quicksand; Reader; Wales; Welsh-English relations

Gerbert of Aurillac (Pope Silvester II), 98–102, 108–9, 110–11, 147, 186–87 (n. 18), 187 (n. 29), 189–90 (n. 60), 191 (n. 103). *See also* Ingenuity; Magic; Oldoni, Massimo; Treasure; Underground worlds; Walter Map; William of Malmesbury

Germain, Saint. *See* Selby

Gervase of Canterbury, 34

Gildas, 71, 72

Glastonbury, 22–23

Gold, 144, 151. *See also* Treasure; Underground worlds

Goscelin of St. Bertin, 22, 23, 29, 42, 160; *Vita S. Yvonis*, 29–30, 42, 53–54; *Historia translationis S. Augustini*, 33–34, 41. See also *Revelatio Sancti Stephani*

Gregory of Tours, 93, 173 (n. 74)

Guide, unreliable, 132, 142, 147, 153, 155. *See also* Gerald of Wales; Rhydderch the Liar

Hagiography, and history, 3, 40, 79, 167 (n. 53)

Haidu, Peter, 17, 52, 79, 95, 139–40

Hanning, Robert, 75–76, 79–80, 153, 199 (n. 10). *See also* Geoffrey of Monmouth; Merlin; Poetic emblem

Harold, 38, 174 (nn. 82, 83). *See also* Battle
Abbey; *Vita Haroldi*; Waltham
Haug, Walter, 18, 195 (n. 36)
Henry II (king of England), 119–20, 126,
137, 138, 139, 145, 194 (n. 9)
Henry of Huntingdon, 71, 77–78
Hexham, 23, 33
Historia Britonum, 71
Historian: as mediator between past and
present, 50–51, 56; as mediator between
oral and written traditions, 51, 83,
90–92; access to past, 51, 101, 108, 110,
129, 130, 147; as prophet, 53; rescuing
almost-lost traditions, 56, 82; self-aware,
80–81, 92, 127–28; as conqueror, 81, 82,
121, 123; ownership of historical subject,
81, 90; animating inert past, 101, 108–9;
as magician, 107–9. *See also* Author;
Meilyr the Welshman; Merlin; names of
individual historians
Historical distance, sense of, 43–51
Historical imagination, 158, 199 (n. 10)
History: medieval notions of, 5, 9–10, 40,
80–81, 94, 96–97, 107–8, 178 (n. 143);
and moral instruction, 5, 115; and fiction, 6, 128; referentiality of, 6–7, 127–28;
and narrative, 10–11, 107–8; and underground worlds, 101–2. *See also* Gaps,
chronological; Historian; Linearity;
Narrationum genera; Reference; *Res
gesta*; *Series temporum*; Textuality; Walter Map
Holy Lance, *inventio* of, 49
Horizontal. *See* Reference: horizontal and
vertical
Hostages, 135–36
Hugh of St. Victor, 4

Ingenuity, 98, 101, 109, 129, 187–88 (n. 29).
See also Gerbert of Aurillac
Insolubilia, 111. *See also* Liar, Cretan
Interlacing, 139, 195 (n. 32)
In utramque partem, 138, 195 (n. 31)
Inventio: of saints, 21–47 passim, 104;
defined, 21, 28–29; illustrated by Mat-

thew Paris, 24–26; manuscript contexts,
30, 172 (n. 49); as symbolic story, 30–31;
as foundation stories, 30–31, 42; as textual model, 31, 38–39, 42–43, 56, 61; and
truth, 36, 37–41, 56; referentiality of,
35–36, 40–41, 54, 56–57; setting in time
and space, 41–43; of books, 51, 53, 55, 82;
and archaeology, 52–53, 54–55, 158; as
revelation, 53–54; compared to *gaainable
tere*, 59–61; and *St. Erkenwald*, 157–60;
iconography of, 170 (n. 27). *See also*
Charlemagne; Goscelin of St. Bertin;
Holy Lance; Matthew Paris; Relics; William of St. Albans; names of individual
saints
Inventio Crucis, 26–27, 81
Irony, 11, 15, 80, 92, 125–26
Isidore of Seville, 9, 10
Itinerary format, 130, 132–33, 134, 137,
194 (n. 15). *See also* Gerald of Wales;
Journey metaphor; Landmarks; Landscape; Reference: horizontal and vertical; Reference: spatial; Space; Textuality;
Topography

Jocelin of Brakelond, 23, 34, 45
Journey metaphor, 132, 148, 150, 196 (n. 57),
197 (n. 58). *See also* Gerald of Wales;
Itinerary format

Kirkstall Abbey, 62–64, 82

Landmarks, 47, 48, 49–50, 177 (n. 129)
Landscape, 50; as "substratum," 60–61, 70
Latin: and fictionality, 16–17, 19, 140, 161;
and *auctoritas*, 17, 95, 135. *See also*
Vernacular
Laȝamon, 81, 84, 89–92
Legitimization. See *Gaainable tere*
Liar, Cretan, 111, 124–25, 128, 153, 190
(n. 64). *See also* Gerald of Wales; Ger-
bert of Aurillac; *Insolubilia*; Lying;
Meilyr the Welshman; Rhydderch the
Liar; Self-reference; Walter Map
Libellus, 170 (n. 24)

Liber Eliensis, 23, 29, 31–32, 34–35. *See also*
    Æthelthryth; Cartularies; Ely
Life of King Edward, 40
Lindisfarne, 34
Linearity, 80, 96–97
Literacy: and fiction, 15; and history, 51, 96,
    110. *See also* Orality
Literariness, 5, 12, 17, 52
Llandaff, 78. *See also Book of Llandaff*
Local history, 2–3, 22, 23–24, 30
Lying, 40, 41, 80, 124, 128, 152–53, 155, 165
    (n. 23), 192 (n. 107). *See also* Fiction;
    Liar, Cretan

Magic, 99–102, 105–7
Marie de France, 8, 18, 191 (n. 103)
Marvels: as intrusions into everyday
    reality, 94, 107, 123, 128; in William of
    Malmesbury, 98, 107–8; in William of
    Newburgh, 102–7, 128; Augustine on,
    105–6; in Walter Map, 121–23, 128
Matthew Paris, 23, 24–26, 82; *Chronica
    Majora*, 24, 49–50, 177 (nn. 129, 130);
    Gesta Abbatum Sancti Albani, 24, 55,
    56; as artist, 24–26; *Vie de Seint Auban*,
    24–26; autograph manuscript (Ms.
    Trinity College Dublin 177), 24–26, 170
    (n. 24), 172 (n. 49); "Cum Danorum
    Rabies," 37; *Vitae Duorum Offarum*, 167
    (n. 53)
Meilyr the Welshman (character), 152–54.
    See also Gerald of Wales; Liar, Cretan;
    Merlin; Prophecy
Melusine, 89, 191–92 (n. 104)
Merlin, 70–71, 75, 152, 153. *See also* Geoffrey
    of Monmouth; Meilyr the Welshman;
    Prophecy
Metaphor, 3–4, 12–14, 52, 60, 80, 82, 152.
    See also Conquest; Fiction; *Gaainable
    tere*; *Inventio*; Reference; Ricoeur,
    Paul
Milburga, Saint, 40, 44, 54, 175 (n. 101)
Mining, 150
Mink, Louis O., 11, 180 (n. 12)
Miracles. See *Inventio*; Marvels; Relics

Mise-en-abyme, 5, 110. *See also* Dällenbach,
    Lucien; Poetic emblem; Self-reference
Monasteries: as centers of historical writ-
    ing, 2–3; in-house historiography of, 3,
    4, 22, 23–24, 32–35, 65–66; and *inven-
    tiones*, 21, 30–31; "embodied" in their
    saints, 34–35. *See also* Cistercians; Foun-
    dation legends; names of individual
    monasteries
Moos, Peter von, 166 (n. 23)
Much Wenlock. *See* Milburga, Saint

Narrationum genera, 165 (n. 23)
Narrative and history, 10–11
Narrator, 16–17. *See also* Author; Persona
Nennius. See *Historia Britonum*
Nichols, Stephen, 131, 140, 145, 176 (n. 113),
    178 (n. 143), 195–96 (n. 39)
Norman Conquest, 22, 29, 87, 171–72
    (n. 44)
Normans, 76, 77; attitudes toward English
    saints, 22–23. *See also* Ethnic groups
Novi homines. See Court, royal: clerics at
Numinosity, 44, 177 (n. 130)

Odo of Ostia, 40–41, 44
Offa (king of Mercia), 24, 26, 41, 56
Oldoni, Massimo, 101, 109, 110, 123, 186–91
    passim
Oracle. *See* Prophecy
Orality, 51, 90–91, 147. *See also* Literacy
Orderic Vitalis, 3, 164 (n. 6)
Origin: legends, 31, 60, 61, 89; of text, 52,
    147; of marvels, 123
Orosius, 27, 71
Oswin, Saint, 172 (nn. 44, 49)
Other worlds, 93, 95, 97, 109–10. See also
    Series temporum; Underground worlds;
    William of Newburgh
Overdetermination, 14, 134

Paradox. *See* Liar, Cretan
Parataxis, 131, 134, 155, 193 (n. 5). *See also*
    Itinerary format; Reference; Textuality
Parody, 17, 66–67, 79, 128, 153. *See also*

Geoffrey of Monmouth; Haidu, Peter; Hanning, Robert; Walter Map

Partner, Nancy F., 103, 193 (n. 5), 195 (n. 32)

Past, sense of, 158; as place, 110, 127–28. *See also* Historical imagination

Patria, 74–75

Persona, 126–27. *See also* Author: stand-ins for; Historian: self-aware; Narrator

Place names, 42, 55, 69–70

Platonism, Christian, 36, 40, 57

Poetic emblem, 5, 51, 159. *See also* Hanning, Robert; Mise-en-abyme

Politics. *See* Geoffrey of Monmouth: politics of; Gerald of Wales: political commentary

Polyphony, 6, 131–32, 140, 193–94 (n. 8), 196 (n. 39). *See also* Bakhtin, Mikhail; Nichols, Stephen

Praesentia. *See* Relics

Prognostication, 138, 141

Proliferation, 67–69. *See also* Expansionism; Walter Map: on religious orders

Promised Land, 61, 65

Prophecy, 70, 75; Diana oracle, 73, 74, 82, 179 (n. 14); Eagle of Shaftesbury, 81, 183 (n. 88); Gerbert, 109; Walter Map on, 153; prescient eagles, 196 (n. 42). *See also* Meilyr the Welshman; Merlin; Prognostication

Quicksand, 143–44, 145, 147–48, 150, 154

Ralph of Diceto, 164 (n. 6)

Ramsey, 23, 29–30

Reader, role of, 130, 135, 140, 147–48, 195 (n. 36)

Reference: metaphoric, 4, 6, 13–14, 159–60; horizontal and vertical, 5, 18, 131, 133, 134, 139, 155, 195 (n. 36); literal, 6; allegorical, 6, 16, 18, 36, 41, 54, 57; modes of, 6, 18, 19, 60, 75; spatial, 7–9, 13–14, 50, 69, 160; internal and external, 8; of texts, 11; split, 12–13, 14; primary and secondary, 12–14; 52. *See also* Referentiality; Ricoeur, Paul; Stierle, Karlheinz; Self-reference

Referentiality, 9, 48, 79–80, 93, 94, 128, 155, 159–60; undercut, 70, 110, 127–28. *See also* Fiction; *Inventio*; Reference; Truth claim

Relevance criteria, 11, 79

Relic cult, as closed system, 36, 39

Relics: *translatio*, 21, 29, 31–32, 33–34; and continuity, 31–34; as metonymies, 34, 35; as *pignora*, 36–37, 44; and truth, 36–37, 173 (n. 73); *elevatio*, 37; lists of, 43, 175 (n. 106)~; *praesentia*, 43, 44, 87; partial, 177–78 (n. 139). *See also* Brown, Peter; Canonization; *Furta sacra*; *Inventio*; *Revelatio Sancti Stephani*; names of individual saints

Res gesta, 9–10, 108

Revelatio Sancti Stephani, 27–30, 32, 39, 43–44, 45, 53–54, 175 (n. 101)

Rhydderch the Liar (character), 138, 143, 153, 155. *See also* Gerald of Wales; Guide, unreliable; Liar, Cretan

Ricoeur, Paul, 12–14, 15

Ridyard, Susan, 22

Roger Wendover, 24, 49

Romance, 15, 16, 87–89. *See also* Ancestral romance; Fiction; Vernacular

Round Table, 90–92

St. Albans, 23–24, 31, 41, 42, 45–51. *See also* Alban, Saint; Amphibalus, Saint; Matthew Paris; William of St. Albans

St. David's, 78, 143

St. Erkenwald, 157–60

St. Omer, 29, 42

Search, 29, 31, 86–87, 90. See also *Gaainable tere*: and *affectus*

Searle, John, 7, 8

"Secgan." *See* Relics: lists of

Secularity, 95, 115–16, 126, 140

Selby, 64–66, 82, 90

Self-reference, 14, 17, 50, 52, 57, 69, 88, 128, 132, 141, 160. *See also* Fiction; *Insolubilia*; Liar, Cretan; Literariness; Reference; Textuality

Series temporum, 80–81, 96–97, 103, 109–10. *See also* Digressions

Sidney, Sir Philip, 165 (n. 23)

Source fiction, 46, 47, 51, 52, 183 (n. 90). *See also* Geoffrey of Monmouth; *Inventio:* of books; William of St. Albans

Space, 3; as metaphor for time, 41; superseding time, 43. *See also* Chronotope; Itinerary format; Reference: spatial

Stanzas of the Graves, 175 (n. 106), 180 (n. 34)

Stephen, Saint. See *Revelatio Sancti Stephani*

Stierle, Karlheinz, 7, 11, 160

Stock, Brian, 10, 62, 175–76 (n. 113)

Testimony, 98, 102–3, 108

Textuality: and literariness, 5; of history, 5, 9–10, 92, 93–94, 128; and author, 6, 15, 92; and fictionality, 10–12, 14, 15–16; and *inventiones*, 41; and self-reference, 52; and parataxis, 131, 155; and multiple connections, 132, 134, 137–38, 139–40; and the reader, 140.

Theft, 124, 129, 196 (n. 51). *See also* Treasure

Thomas of Monmouth, 29, 38–39, 41, 45

Topography, 2, 8, 69, 148

Translatio. See Relics: *translatio*

Transparency, of historical narrative, 5, 97

Travelogue. *See* Itinerary format

Treasure, 88, 99–100, 101, 142. *See also* Gold; Theft; Underground worlds

Truth, 128, 144–45; referential, 5; allegorical, 5, 54; auctorial comments on, 40, 102, 105–8, 110, 122, 145, 147, 189–90 (n. 60). *See also* Fiction; *Inventio;* Lying; Reference; Relics; Truth claims

Truth claims, 7, 9, 11, 41, 56, 57, 79, 92, 155. *See also* Fiction; Reference; Truth

Tynemouth, 171–72 (n. 44), 172 (n. 49)

Underground worlds, 5, 129, 130, 146, 151; in William of Malmesbury, 98–102; in William of Newburgh, 103–7; in Gerald of Wales, 130, 142, 144–47. See also *Fouke*

le Fitz Waryn; Gaainable tere; Gerbert of Aurillac; Gold; Treasure

Universal history, 2–3, 163–64 (n. 5)

University, 126

Vampires, 103. *See also* Marvels

Vernacular: and fiction, 14, 16–17, 95, 140, 161; emancipation from Latin, 16–17, 95; historiography, 83–84, 88–92; and literacy, 90–92. *See also* Latin; Romance; Welsh language

Verulamium (Roman town), 45, 46–47, 55

Viking raids, 32, 33, 34, 53, 86, 171 (n. 44), 178 (n. 140)

Vinaver, Eugene, 195 (n. 32)

Virgil, 64, 73, 75

Vita Haroldi, 174 (n. 83)

Wace, 77, 81, 89

Wales, 78–79; as dangerous terrain, 135, 145–46, 196 (n. 51). *See also* Conquest; Geoffrey of Monmouth; Gerald of Wales; Walter Map; Welsh-English relations

Walter Map, 18, 93, 94, 105, 111–25, 140, 153, 161; on history, 9–10; on Cistercians, 66–69; on religious orders, 67–68, 115–16; and epistemology, 93, 118–19, 123; and the Cretan Liar, 111, 124–25; and *modernitas*, 112, 123, 125, 128; and authority, 112–14, 120–21, 123, 124–25; *De Nugis Curialium*, 112–25; on the royal court, 113, 114, 117–18, 119–20; mock-scholasticism, 114, 117; as self-aware narrator, 113–25 passim; and "hell," 114, 118; secularity, 116; skepticism, 119–23; and Wales, 124; career, 126; and Gerbert of Aurillac, 191 (n. 103). *See also* Expansionism; Gerald of Wales; Marvels; Oldoni, Massimo

Waltham, 23, 38, 42

Welsh-English relations, 134–35, 137, 138, 145–46, 148–49. *See also* Baldwin; Conquest: of Wales; Ethnic groups; Gerald of Wales

Welsh language, 144, 146. *See also* Etymology

White, Hayden, 11, 165 (n. 17)

William the Conqueror, 42–43, 61, 64, 87

William of Malmesbury, 77, 80–81, 94, 147; *Gesta Pontificum* 3, 23; and Glastonbury, 22–23; *Gesta Regum*, 23, 96–97, 97–102, 107–8, 109–10, 111; historical method, 97–98; and Gerbert of Aurillac, 98–102. *See also* Digressions; Historian; Linearity; Marvels; Oldoni, Massimo; Underground worlds

William of Newburgh, 78, 94, 107, 108–9, 147, 160–61; and Geoffrey of Monmouth, 95–97. *See also* Marvels; Underground worlds

William of Norwich, Saint. *See* Thomas of Monmouth

William of St. Albans, 24, 45–51, 82, 159, 160, 170 (n. 23), 176 (n. 119)

Witnesses. *See* Testimony

Wolfram von Eschenbach, 18, 194 (n. 15), 195 (n. 36), 197 (n. 81)

Yvo, Saint. *See* Goscelin of St. Bertin